DAVID RIEFF

SIMON & SCHUSTER

New York   London   Toronto   Sydney   Singapore

A
BED
FOR THE
NIGHT

HUMANITARIANISM
IN CRISIS

SIMON & SCHUSTER
Rockefeller Center
1230 Avenue of the Americas
New York, NY 10020

For information about special discounts for bulk purchases,
please contact Simon & Schuster Special Sales:
1-800-456-6798 or business@simonandschuster.com

Designed by Lisa Chovnick
Manufactured in the United States of America

10 9 8 7 6 5 4 3 2 1

Library of Congress Cataloging-in-Publication Data
Rieff, David.
    A bed for the night : humanitarianism in crisis / David Rieff.
        p. cm.
    Includes bibliographical references and index.
    1. War relief.   2. International relief.   3. International agencies.
    4. Humanitarianism.   I. Title.
    HV639.R543 2002
    361.2'6—dc21   2002029432
    ISBN 0-684-80977-X

The author and publisher gratefully acknowledge permission
to reprint material from the following work:

"A Bed for the Night" in
Bertolt Brecht, Werke. Große kommentierte Berliner und Frankfurter Ausgabe.
30 Bände, Hg. Werner Hecht, Jan Knopf u.a.
© Frankfurt am Main Suhrkamp Verlag 1988–2000.

This book is for Alice Mayhew

Contents

Every document of civilization is also a document of barbarism.

—Walter Benjamin

A BED FOR THE NIGHT

I hear that in New York
At the corner of 26th Street and Broadway
A man stands every evening during the winter months
And gets beds for the homeless there
By appealing to passers-by.

It won't change the world
It won't improve relations among men
It will not shorten the age of exploitation
But a few men have a bed for the night
For a night the wind is kept from them
The snow meant for them falls on the roadway.

Don't put down the book on reading this, man.

A few people have a bed for the night
For a night the wind is kept from them
The snow meant for them falls on the roadway
But it won't change the world
It won't improve relations among men
It will not shorten the age of exploitation.

— Bertolt Brecht
Translated by George Rapp

A BED FOR THE NIGHT

THIS BOOK WAS BEGUN IN 1995 IN SARAJEVO, while the siege was still going on and the snipers were working as diligently as ever, blowing people's heads and limbs off in the streets of the Bosnian capital. It was concluded in the fall of 2001, as the ruins of the World Trade Center continued to smolder, and as New Yorkers, of whom I am one, but of course not only New Yorkers, dazedly mourned their dead and wondered about their future. In other words, it is a book begun in despair and completed . . . well, in whatever state of mind that lies beyond despair.

I make no apologies for this. It should go without saying, but probably doesn't in an era that no longer can distinguish between cynicism and pessimism, that I hope this book will make some small contribution to awakening conscience about the wars, famines, and refugee crises that are its theme, and not make people more cynical or more resigned. But I will not deny that I see little if any empirical basis for optimism. When I titled an earlier book on Bosnia *Slaughterhouse*, I don't think I knew how apt a description it was of such a wide swath of the world. An eighteenth-century French aphorist said that one would have to swallow a live toad at breakfast to be sure of not encountering something more disgusting in the course of the day. Looking back, I often think that is what I have been doing over the course of the past decade—deliberately gulping down one live toad after another. To put it less histrionically, between the time I first set foot in northern Bosnia in the late summer of 1992, and followed far braver colleagues like Ed Vulliamy and Roy Gutman into the Serb concentration camps of the Bosanska Krajina, and the night I lingered near the bottom of the six-story mound of rubble that had been the World Trade Center, watching as dust that included pulverized human beings as well as pulverized steel covered my boots, I have, at what cost I do not yet know and for reasons I doubt I will ever fully understand, done my best to rub my own nose in the horror of the world.

My itineraries have been those of the wars and what we rather antiseptically and misleadingly call the humanitarian emergencies that scar our times. I have not seen all of them, by any means, and I have done far less, not to mention risked far less, both physically and psychologically, than many of my colleagues in this peculiar amalgam of voyeurism and witness that we all practice. I was not even present at a number of the most terrible of these catastrophes, though I discuss some of their implications in this book. I was not in East Timor, or Kurdistan, or Chechnya. But I have seen more than my share. I do not say this proudly, as I claim neither to be particularly intrepid nor to have any great fondness for those journalist-cowboys and the danger freaks who are. Before I left for Bosnia for the first time, the great historian of Africa, Basil Davidson, who spent World War II as a British Special Operations executive officer fighting with Tito's Partisans, warned me, "You don't learn anything from the bang-bang."

He was almost certainly exaggerating for effect. But after a decade of this work, I am aware of how skewed my sense of things became at times. In war, you experience all sorts of horrible things, and, to be strictly honest, some marvelous things as well, above all in the personal generosity of strangers that comes as close to fulfilling the Christian notion of grace as anything this vertebral nonbeliever has ever encountered. But learn anything worth communicating? Only if seeing people die, in your arms, at your feet, by your side, within your sight, while all the while there is absolutely nothing you can do to save them or rescue them, constitutes learning. And it does not. It's just death and suffering in all their infinite variety, clogging one's nostrils and taking over one's brain until one doesn't know whether to dream of justice or flight, or simply of being somewhere else, where there is silence when you crave it, noise only when you need it, light, heat, comfortable beds, and cold glasses of good white wine.

I do not know if I have learned enough in the past decade to justify the life I have lived. I have watched, even when I didn't want to watch. I have written in defense of causes I knew to be hopeless. Of course, at times I have given in to hopelessness when, if only for the sake of the victims, perhaps I should have soldiered on. Who hasn't? The moral test of being an onlooker at other people's tragedies is one that few of us are likely to pass reliably. Only in the Balkan wars, where, uniquely in my experience of such conflicts, I believed that it was not just possible but imperative to take sides, was I confident enough about my political opinions to move from being a writer to being an activist. And even then, as is the case with all writers who are too skeptical by temperament, or perhaps too pessimistic to be comfortable in the activist's motley, there was no moment when I was not also a voyeur.

If I have a bad conscience about that, and choose to lay those particular cards on the table at the very outset of this book, almost inviting the reader to be on his or her guard, it is because, like everyone else who has covered the Bosnias, Rwandas, and Afghanistans of this world, I richly deserve to have one. In Sarajevo during the siege, they called the photojournalists who would congregate at particularly dangerous corners, where the Serb snipers in the hills operated to deadliest effect, "angels of death." But just because a writer does not have to point his or her notebook in the face of someone who has just been wounded, as a photographer must point a lens, does not make the moral ambiguity (and this is putting it charitably) any less disturbing. The caricatural journalist, the one who arrives in some zone of atrocity pointing a microphone and asking, "Anyone here been raped and speak English?" may indeed never have existed outside the fouler fancies of Evelyn Waugh. But what of the Western journalist, photographer, or writer for whom, willingly or unwillingly, the dead of the World Trade Center carry more emotional and symbolic weight than the dead of Kigali, Aceh, or Kabul? We may all reject this logic of the double standard emotionally, but if we really are being honest, that includes all of us.

That is why I can only hope that what follows will represent some moral repayment for what otherwise could seem like a long and aimless ramble through the landscapes of modern atrocity by someone who always had the privilege of coming and going as he pleased, no matter how much he tried to make the sufferings of strangers his concern. There will, in any case, be no more of that. The shoe is on the other foot now. Less than forty blocks from where I have lived for most of my adult life, there is a smoking ruin in which the burned corpses of thousands of my fellow citizens lie entombed. It may seem like the most dreadful moral obtuseness, but it is only now that I am able even to come close to properly apprehending the degree of moral license we journalists and photographers from this small, rich corner of the planet have been taking all along as we ventured on our safaris to the wars of the poor world.

What I knew only intellectually, I now know in my nostrils and on my skin. Doubtless it is well past time that lesson registered. And yet, if we are to be honest with ourselves, surely one of the most troubling consequences of the World Trade Center attack is that it reinforced the same moral hierarchy among victims of the world's horrors. If anything, the fact that the death toll on September 11, 2001, was truly atrocious has only reinforced what had already been in place for so long—the difference, even when speaking of the dead, between the West and the rest. In saying this, I am not suggesting Americans should have been more concerned about strangers than about themselves. Quite the contrary. That there could be so many deaths of people from "our" world, where death by political violence, let alone death on such a massive scale, had been almost inconceivable. It is hardly surprising that Americans looked to themselves, or cared more about their own losses than they had cared about those in parts of the world that are remote from their experience. Why should they have been expected to behave with some ahuman self-abnegation or to have transcended the natural and primeval claims of human attachment? After all, it has never been my experience that people in Somalia inquired after the fate of people in Bosnia, or people in Angola worried about people in Nagorno-Karabakh. Wounds breed self-absorption; that is simply human.

And it was not just human but appropriate that what Americans thought about in the wake of the attacks was how to respond to them—politically, militarily, and in terms of the measures needed to protect the country from future attacks. I do not share the view that one cannot fight fire with fire, as an antiwar demonstrator in London put it in October 2001. To the contrary, I think that violence is the only responsible answer to the Osama bin Ladens of this world. But this is not a book about terrorism and state power; it is a book about the dilemmas of humanitarian action. And in the context of humanitarianism, the deaths of September 11, 2001, must of necessity have a very different resonance and moral significance.

I mean absolutely no disrespect to the victims, who included two acquaintances of mine, when I insist that their deaths registered on us in a way that deaths in the poor world, no matter how lamentable we find them, do not. With regard to the former, we are psychologically and politically unreconciled. With regard to the latter, we have had a tendency to regard them almost as a natural calamity, as regrettable but no more avoidable than deaths from an earthquake or a typhoon. In the aftermath of the World Trade Center attack, this double standard was evident. There was the story of *individuals* who had died in the Twin Towers and then there was another story—a humanitarian story—of undifferentiated victims in Afghanistan who were on the move, in grave danger, and needed to be helped. As described, these Afghans remained abstractions, as perhaps strangers always do, even though it is now possible to watch their sufferings in real time on television.

We have been changed in so many ways by the catastrophe of September 11, 2001. But while I would love to believe that these deaths will change what we do when we go out into what we have been pleased to call "the field"—that strangely distancing, Boy-Scoutish term, much beloved of journalists and aid workers, for what are, in reality, other people's countries, tragedies, destinies—or how we will feel when we return home, I don't believe it for a minute. On one level, it is true that the distance between home and field was shrunk that fine September morning when that beautiful, shining Boeing airliner banked in the brilliant New York sky, then came level with the horizon before flying with such amazing, terrifying velocity into the North Tower of the World Trade Center. As it hit, it blew up more than a building. The world we had known was dissolved in that fireball.

But the truth must not be made the first casualty of the catastrophe. Not just in America, but in many other parts of the world as well, people felt those thousands of deaths more acutely than any of the many atrocities of the previous decade. The eight thousand men and boys killed by Serb forces at Srebrenica, the eight hundred thousand believed to have died in the Rwandan genocide of 1994, the tens of thousands who died in the refugee emergency that followed, and the more than one hundred thousand killed by Rwandan Tutsi forces in 1996, the capstone year of the crisis—the sad truth is that their deaths exerted none of the fascination over the world that September 11, 2001, did. Not everyone sympathized, of course. But even the way so many of the sympathizers of Osama bin Laden throughout the poor world reveled in what happened on September 11 was testimony to the fundamental inequality between the emotional charge of a disaster in New York and a disaster in Kabul.

I am not saying this to score some cheap moral point. Any adult who does not understand that the world is an unjust place, *even* in its treatment of catastrophe, is a fool or a dreamer. And there are good moral reasons, not to mention instinctual ones that are probably hardwired into us, for why we usually care more about the fate of neighbors and fellow citizens than that of strangers. It may not be politically correct or morally reassuring to say this, but surely it is to be expected, because we are human beings and not altruism machines, that we empathize more readily with people who more closely resemble us and are near than with people who have very different customs, or are of a different color or a different confession and are far away. This may not be true for a small minority of people who can genuinely claim to be cosmopolitan in the best and truest sense of the word—people for whom flag, or tribe, or race, or religion really no longer are essential for their sense of self, and, indeed, may seem to them like atavisms that stand in the way of their self-realization. But for most people, the emotion-laden abstraction that is a national flag and the sustaining integument that is family and neighborhood are not so easily superseded.

Human rights activists, United Nations officials, and humanitarian aid workers tend to pretend as if things were otherwise. Think of the loose talk in diplomatic circles about "the international community." At the UN General Assembly, it has become part of the rhetorical boilerplate for almost every resolution to include phrases like "the international community condemns" this or "the international community welcomes" that. The recommendations of the 1997 Carnegie Commission report *Preventing Deadly Conflict,* which was a kind of apotheosis of the thinking of the Western international establishment on these issues, was encrusted with phrases like "the international community must champion the norm of responsible leadership" and "the international community must expand efforts to educate publics everywhere that preventing deadly conflict is both necessary and possible." Or listen to the appeal by Kofi Annan, the UN secretary-general, who, in a speech to the General Assembly in 1999, insisted, "From Sierra Leone to the Sudan to Angola to the Balkans to Cambodia and to Afghanistan, there are a great number of peoples who need more than just words of sympathy from the international community."

What decent person would disagree? But what thinking person can take seriously the idea that there is any such thing as the international community? Where are the shared values uniting the United States and China, Denmark and Indonesia, Japan and Angola, that make such talk anything more than an exercise in self-flattering rhetoric? Of course, there is an international order, dominated by the United States, and there are international institutions, like the United Nations, the World Trade Organization, and the World Bank. But the reality is that the international community is a myth and a way to conceal the bad news about the present in septic sheets of piety about the future. This should be clear to anyone who considers the question of force. As Sir Brian Urquhart, one of the key figures of the first four decades of the UN's existence, once put it, "If there is a world community, then who is the sheriff?" Does anyone imagine that the United States will act in the altruistic way such a mandate implies? And if not the United States, then who? The Russians? The Chinese? The reality is that the moment one taps on the idea of the international community it falls apart like a child's broken toy.

Despite the dreams of those who founded the UN, figures such as Gladwyn Jebb and Eleanor Roosevelt, there is no world consensus on most matters of importance. One has only to look at the kind of bribing and horse-trading the Bush administration had to engage in just to get acquiescence for American plans to go after the Taliban, Osama bin Laden and his followers, and the other terrorist networks. The international institutions—first and foremost, the UN itself—and international treaty regimes that exist are not the expression of community but of power. But just because these institutions exist does not mean any moral consensus exists, and, at least barring the institution of serious enforcement mechanisms, it seems unlikely that these regimes will ever have much force. I am haunted by the fact that the leaders of Rwanda who plotted the greatest genocide since Hitler's extermination of Jews and Gypsies were in many cases the same men who had been in power when their country signed the Convention on Genocide, which is certainly one of the great documents of civilization in our time.

But when the moment arrived to become a beast, those Rwandan members in good standing of "the international community" became very good beasts indeed. They were no more dissuaded by some shard of international law than a drug addict in the inner city is dissuaded from committing a robbery or breaking into a house by national laws. Indeed, if anything, the gap between what Jurgen Habermas has called facts and norms has grown alarmingly as international lawyers extend their reach and institute new legal regimes. This is not to say such efforts should not be undertaken, nor that, when occasionally they have an effect—as with the trial of Slobodan Milosevic before the ad hoc International Criminal Tribunal for the Former Yugoslavia in The Hague—such an outcome is not to be welcomed. But there will be no judicialization of the world, for the simple reason that there is no international community to uphold such a transformation.

Where is the evidence, apart from the creation of new legal norms and the assertion and reassertion of the idea that the human rights culture is beginning to have a real impact on wars and famines and failed states, for the claims of the optimists who speak, like Michael Ignatieff, of "a revolution of moral concern"? Is there not in fact more evidence to support the opposite conclusion, at least at the moment? Here is Ignatieff, writing in 1997, on why there was no reason to despair. "For every society like Afghanistan mired in ethnic conflict," he wrote, "there is a South Africa making its arduous journey back from the abyss. As soon as the world pronounces some part of the world beyond hope—Central Africa, for example—leaders appear who seem capable of forging the strong and legitimate states these regions need if they are to lift themselves out of the pit of war. For every failed intervention like Somalia there is an Angola, where some hope remains that a durable peace can be brokered. Just when the world appears to be letting war criminals off the hook, some are brought to justice and the cycle of impunity is broken."

This is the kind of rhetoric that gives hope a bad name. Every sunny statement in the paragraph is open to question. South Africa is being destroyed from within by AIDS and crime, and there is no reason to be hopeful except because one doesn't want be dispiriting. And yet surely the experience of intellectuals who defended Communism throughout the twentieth century should make us wary of that approach. Toward the end of his life, Jean-Paul Sartre stunned an interviewer by admitting he'd known about the Gulag. Why hadn't he said anything? the interviewer asked. And the great philosopher replied: "So as not to demoralize the French working class."

Some of the same spirit seems to inform many human rights activists. Sartre did not want the truth he was privy to about the horrors of Communism as it actually existed to stand in the way of the radiant future of justice and peace he believed the Communist ideals still had the potential to bring into being. Obviously, human rights activists are not the modern-day equivalent of Communist fellow travelers. But too often, they choose to ignore any bad news that goes against their repeated assertion that the "revolution of moral concern" is well under way.

Michael Ignatieff has been to Angola. He must know how little hope there is, at least if he means hope for the people, as I understand him to, not some new political settlement that slightly rejiggers the division of spoils among conflicting elites. And as for the notion that Central Africa provides a model for anything, the mind rebels. Leaders like Paul Kagame in Rwanda and the late and unlamented Laurent-Desiré Kabila in Congo did seem promising for a moment in the mid-1990s, and many of us, including myself, were far too taken in by them. But they have proven to be classic African "big men," active participants in the continued criminalization of the state from one end of the continent to the other, and ruthless in their pursuit of power. According to a recent International Rescue Committee survey of mortality rates in eastern Congo, the last three years—the period of the first general war in Africa since decolonization—have led to some two and a half million deaths. Almost all the deaths were civilian, and almost all of them were attributed not to combat but to the destruction of the medical and agricultural infrastructures on which these people depended for their survival. This is the accomplishment of these leaders Ignatieff insisted were bringing legitimacy to the region.

That Ignatieff continues to hope against hope, to borrow the phrase of the great heroine of Russian dissidence, Nadezhda Mandelstam, may do his heart credit, but such optimism too often leads to misunderstanding. He is right to insist that the moral imagination of the West "has been transformed since 1945." Where he goes wrong is in believing, against most (though, in fairness, not all) of the evidence, that this shared human rights culture offers the way out of the horror that he knows so well. He preaches against disillusion, but the truth is, anyone who is not disillusioned has not heard the bad news. As Africa collapses before our eyes, strangled by debt, AIDS, and bad government, by bandits and apparatchiks, and weakened by a brain drain the likes of which has rarely been seen in human history, is optimism really the only legitimate moral stance? It consoles, to be sure. We may feel that with each norm established we move slowly toward more palpable commitments. And it is indeed a marvelous narrative. The problem, alas, is that there is no reason to think it's true.

Let me put it more starkly. Not only should our consciences not be clear, but because they are grounded in such a mistaken premise, the solutions and, worse, the confidence of human rights activists like Ignatieff and of UN officials from Secretary-General Annan on down constitute an offer of false hope to people who are desperately in need of rescue. "Keep hope alive," Kofi Annan has insisted time and time again. But when people in Bosnia or Rwanda or Angola see a blue UN flag or a white-painted armored personnel carrier, those people believe "the international community" has intervened, and that they will be protected. They give themselves permission to hope, but only because they are being encouraged to do so. But we saw time and time again in the 1990s how often they were wrong to do so. We have seen that such hopes—in the UN, in "the international community"—were misguided, at times even suicidal. UN officials like to announce how many lives their humanitarian efforts have saved all over the world. And they are right to do so. But their presence has also cost lives by raising in people who might have succeeded in fleeing and saving themselves the false confidence that they would be protected. I have talked to scores of people in Rwanda, and not only in Rwanda, who lost their families because of such a waste of hope.

The point is not to bash the United Nations. Most people at the UN Secretariat today are well aware of the moral hazards of peace-keeping operations and are anything but content about the prospect of engaging in new ones except those "classic" operations that involve separating forces whose governments have already concluded a truce, as in Ethiopia-Eritrea in 2001. Rather, it is to ask whether it is wise to insist that the moral universalism championed by human rights activists is making enough headway in the world to make it safer for the victims of contemporary atrocities. Or whether, despite widely hailed new norms of international law, above all the supposed end of the inviolability of state sovereignty, populations in danger today have no more reason to count on being rescued than the populations of Auschwitz or the Warsaw Ghetto did in 1943?

This may seem an unfair exaggeration. To compare what is going on today to what occurred during the Shoah has something practically impious about it. And yet it is thought that two out of five children in the eastern Congo have died in the past three years. Even if such figures are wildly exaggerated—which they may be, since even

the best mortality figures for such calamities are based on comparatively small demographic samples—do we not need to look skeptically on our own cherished moral assumptions, above all as they
concern the reach of the human rights revolution and the reality of
the international community? How much longer will it be before
people are prepared to consider with an open mind, no matter how
demoralizing it may be, what, if anything, our good intentions, our
new legal norms, and our faith in the binding nature of this new
ethic of moral concern have accomplished in societies like the
Congo that, whatever the precise death toll, are unquestionably in
agony? How many more genocides will it take to shake the advocates' faith in their revolution of global concern?

There is a real question about whether we are analyzing what is
going on in the poor world or extrapolating from what these new
norms, above all the discourse of rights, have accomplished for the
rich world. In this well-intended but mistaken account, the victims
of a Rwandan genocide are sometimes equated with the victims of
racial discrimination in the United States or anti-immigrant xeno-
phobia in Europe. But while legal rights can go a long way toward
securing and improving the situation of immigrants or racial minorities in the West, they are unlikely to help the victims of a genocide. Nor does the language of oppressor and oppressed, already a
simplification when applied to Western societies, seem of much use
in describing the reality of a Rwanda or a Kosovo, where today's oppressor is all too commonly tomorrow's victim. To say this is not to
criticize the use of rights language in the West. Undeniably, that language has been good for us. We in the West have done the moral
thing *and* helped ourselves weather the storm of mass immigration
from the poor world by institutionalizing rights-based ideas about
tolerance and diversity.

But in so many countries, there have been false dawns. While the best minds in the liberal West have focused on new rights and new international norms, struggled to create international tribunals and urged an end to impunity for tyrants and warlords, a 2002 World Bank study has shown that the income gap between the rich and poor worlds has been widening steadily. And yet we are told that enormous progress has been made. Reality is elsewhere. Even in many of the countries, particularly in Africa, that have done all the things the neoliberal consensus demanded of them, and opened up their societies to free press debate and rights-based governance, the specter of AIDS promises to stop development in its tracks. I am sorry, but while I would like to believe the narrative of a Michael Ignatieff or of an organization like Human Rights Watch, I do not see how it is possible to say that in sub-Saharan Africa and in most of the Islamic world there is no reason for disillusion. Rather, it seems to me that too often the basis for their optimism is not an improvement in people's lives but an improvement in human rights norms. And to me it remains not just an open question, but a question that desperately needs to be asked, what this has actually accomplished for people in need of justice, or aid, or mercy, or bread, and whether it has actually kept a single jackboot out of a single human face.

It may seem both wrong and counterproductive to even ask such a question in the moment when the human rights movement has purportedly made so much progress, and when, in the words of a recent Canadian government–sponsored study, "The protection of human security—including concern for human rights, but broader than that in its scope—has become an increasingly important element in international law and international relations." Is one not giving aid and comfort to the ethnic fascists like Slobodan Milosevic, the racist skinheads, and the Islamic fascists like Osama bin Laden? Does one not risk becoming part of the problem rather than part of the solution? I can only reply that one does the poor and the oppressed no favor by misrepresenting reality, or by confidently offering up prescriptions for ills for which the sad truth is that there may be no cure. To the contrary, one consoles oneself without succoring them, and, if one is not careful, one does indeed begin to traffic in false hope.

The cruelty of the world is so overwhelming, and hope—real hope—so hard to come by. That is what I have learned in the past ten years. In dozens of cities in the poor world, I have listened to officials of the United Nations Development Programme (UNDP) or to human rights advocates making a case for the end of impunity, or the beginning of grassroots activism, or—especially fatuously in places where people have no electricity and live on a dollar a day—the promise of information technology. "In a global world," a UNDP official once told me, "there are global values, above all human rights." Had we not been speaking in Monrovia, Liberia, the ultimate failed state, and one of the cruelest places on earth, I might have taken him more seriously. And this was years before September 11, 2001, when the promise of globalization as an engine of prosperity rather than mayhem suddenly looked far more doubtful.

Let me say also that if the optimists are right, and I am wrong, I will be overjoyed. Michael Edwards, one of the most intelligent writers on aid and development, states in a recent book that "a world that manages its affairs to mutual benefit is well within our reach." He insists that if we can only learn to cooperate intelligently, we should be able to attain it, since we have "the resources, the technology, the ideas and the wealth," and all that is missing is "the will and imagination." And he adds that the moral obligation to help others escape from the constraints and limitations should be manifest to any decent person who thinks about the issue seriously. (As a veteran of eighteen years of development work with the British group Oxfam, he could, with justice, have put the matter far more harshly.) I agree to the extent that the world could be this way and certainly should be this way. Nonetheless, I cannot share Edwards's optimism, for it is grounded in the idea that, as he puts it, "in an increasingly interdependent world, no one has a future unless we learn to work together."

There I am not so sure. It is of course true that we are connected in many ways we never were before—by the global economy, by the Internet and television, and by mass migration. If nothing else, what the attacks of September 11 brought home in the United States, a country where the passions of the rest of the world seem, for all the talk of our living in a global village, far away and abstract, was that there is no shelter from the chaos of the Middle East, or Afghanistan, or sub-Saharan Africa. America may not be obsessed with the rest of the world, but the rest of the world is obsessed with America. But chaos is not the same thing as interdependence. Nor is it clear that those, like the *New York Times* columnist Thomas Friedman, who have claimed that the triumph of American-style globalization was both inevitable and to be welcomed, have bet on quite the sure thing they thought they had. Again, history is not a set of buzzwords. We may talk about the global village, but has the fact that ordinary Africans have grown poorer over the past ten years really been of any concern to ordinary Western Europeans or North Americans who have grown so much richer during the same period? I wish it had been, but I doubt it, and I am skeptical of a blueprint for political action based on the idea that somehow there will be such a radical shift in consciousness in the West that people here will pressure their own officials to do something for the poor.

An inchoate idea about witness, in the Quaker sense of the term, was what set me on my journeys to all those ground zeros. But the truth remains the ultimate obligation for any writer, no matter how much he or she may regret the political or social consequences of telling it. Of course, truth and justice are often on the same side, but sometimes they are in contradiction. Even some human rights activists admit that basic rights of the type Edwards and Ignatieff call for need a legally administered cosmopolitan society. In other words, for the Universal Declaration of Human Rights and all those other marvelous creations of civilization to mean anything, an international community—whether one envisages this as a UN that can enforce its resolutions, or as some other form of global governance—really has to take shape. And I see no prospect of that whatsoever.

Is that cynicism? I don't think so. I think it is reality, no matter how much we might wish things were otherwise. La Rochefoucauld says somewhere that no man can stare for long at death or the sun. But if there is anything to what I am saying, and if I have not simply been cauterized by my experience and my anguish, then is it not time to face up to the possibility that things will go on over the course of the next twenty years much as they have since the end of the Cold War, or even get worse? Of course, there will be a plethora of reports produced by commissions of eminent persons suggesting how things might be ordered differently. The Canadian government-sponsored study that I quoted earlier, "The Responsibility to Protect," is a recent example of the genre. But there is absolutely no reason to expect any other fate for such reports than that they will be ignored by the great powers whose consent and support is needed to set in motion the reforms that almost everyone agrees the international system desperately needs.

One has only to look at the UN's self-examination in the aftermath of the peacekeeping disasters in Bosnia and Rwanda in the mid-1990s to see this process in operation. That peacekeeping had failed miserably on those occasions was clear to everyone who was paying attention, whether they were within the UN system or outside it, supporters of the UN or critics of the institution. To his credit, Secretary-General Annan asked Lakdar Brahimi, the former Algerian foreign minister and one of the most brilliant diplomats of his generation, to write a report on how peacekeeping could be reformed. The report was serious, careful, and, to anyone who knew anything about peacekeeping, eminently commonsensical. Hailed upon its release, the Brahimi report engendered a series of working conferences held all over the world. Finally, it was said, both the UN and the major powers were going to get serious about peacekeeping. But privately, UN officials conceded there was no chance at all that such reforms would be permitted. They would simply have involved powerful states giving over too much power to the UN and that was—that is—unimaginable in any useful time frame.

Is that the way the world should be? Obviously it isn't. But bear with me and assume not only that this is the way the world is, but that this is the way it will continue to be. If I am right, and the future we face is as bad as or worse than the present, then how is one to serve those in need—the refugees, the war victims, the raped women, the people without shelter—from Afghanistan to the Congo? In other words, what is to be done if Ignatieff's "revolution of moral concern" fails, or never really takes hold to begin with, and my account of a world of moral desolation is closer to the mark? It was that question that brought me to humanitarianism. The defining point for me was when I heard an official of the International Committee of the Red Cross (ICRC), who had served in the worst places in northern Bosnia, say that his job was "to bring a measure of humanity, always insufficient, into situations that should not exist."

The ICRC is the oldest of the humanitarian organizations. It is the richest and the best organized, and its mandate is the clearest. By international treaty it is the custodian of the laws of war. It is also committed to an austere and sometimes morally troubling conception of neutrality that, during World War II, allowed its senior leadership to decide not to make public what it knew—and it knew a lot—about the Nazi concentration camps. The anti-Semitism of upper-class Swiss society from which the ICRC leadership mostly came (and still comes) doubtless played a role. But the rationale for the decision, which was that to go public would imperil all the other activities in which the organization was engaged in Nazi Europe, was the same one used almost twenty-five years later by ICRC officials during the Biafran war. Then, too, they refused to compromise their neutrality and go public, despite reports that the Nigerian federal government was attempting a kind of genocide by starvation of the Biafran rebels in the southeastern part of the country.

I am not sure which side of the debate on the ICRC's stance in Biafra I would have taken, since it is by no means as clear as it seemed at the time that the Nigerian authorities were guilty of creating a famine. But knowledge of the ICRC's shameful conduct in Nazi-occupied Europe had always made me skeptical of the organization. (The ICRC itself now grudgingly admits it should have behaved differently during World War II.) And yet I remember that when I heard the words of that ICRC delegate, with his simultaneous expression of an ironclad determination to act and his seeming acceptance of the fact that these "situations that should not exist" were unlikely to stop existing anytime soon, I thought that my doubts were misplaced, and that these people, these humanitarians, were the real heroes of the refugee emergencies and genocidal wars of "ethnic cleansing." I still think so today, although few of my friends within the humanitarian world, including the ICRC, would subscribe to the stark and resigned credo that attracted me in the first place.

For an American writer, the humanitarians were interesting in part because they came from Western Europe, Canada, and the

United States and seemed, whether willingly or unwillingly, to have become the rich world's designated consciences in all these landscapes of disaster. By humanitarian organizations, I do not simply mean the ICRC. I mean relief groups, most of which are private voluntary organizations like Médecins Sans Frontières (MSF), Oxfam, or the International Rescue Committee, and UN organizations such as the Office of the United Nations High Commissioner for Refugees (UNHCR), the World Health Organization (WHO), and the United Nations Children's Fund (UNICEF). Their specific mandates vary, but their basic remit is to bring aid—whether medical aid, food, shelter, sanitation, or psychosocial services—to suffering populations after a natural disaster like the Mexico City earthquake of 1985 or a calamity of human design like the siege of Sarajevo. These are the groups that try, often at great risk, to be present on the ground, whether the emergency is of enormous concern to the states where they raise their funds or get government grants, like Kosovo in 1999 or Afghanistan in 2001, or whether the emergency, like the one ongoing in Liberia throughout the 1990s, is of no serious interest at all to any outside power.

It is important to state at the outset that however noble the humanitarian enterprise is, and however extraordinary it is, when one thinks about it, for groups to arise that are committed solely to caring about strangers, humanitarianism is by definition an emblem of failure, not success. The disaster has already happened; the famine has started; the cholera is raging; or the refugees are already on the move. Nor is it clear that humanitarians will succeed in working effectively even in the context of the crisis. In Rwanda, in 1994, more than a million refugees crossed a border in twenty-four hours. As H. Roy Williams, who was vice president for overseas programs for the International Rescue Committee at the time, and intimately involved in the crisis, put it, "We have been overwhelmed by the magnitude of the problems and the rapidity with which they develop." Williams was speaking in the mid-1990s. By 2001, after Somalia, Bosnia, Rwanda, Kosovo, and Afghanistan, no humanitarian relief worker needed to be told such a thing. It had become a truism of relief work. As Sadako Ogata, the former UN high commissioner for refugees, put it, "There are no humanitarian solutions to humanitarian problems."

The recognition of this has caused many humanitarian groups to look for something else to do besides giving relief. They are trying to incorporate human rights analyses into their programs, training their people in the laws of war, and generally coming to view their own enterprise as part of a larger process of "peace-building," to use the currently fashionable term, and social reconstruction. Not for them the stony resignation of the ICRC. And on both a human and a moral level, this is not only understandable, it must almost seem like an imperative—as the only responsible way to do one's job. Otherwise, most relief workers eventually come to feel that they have been wasting their time. Once, in the mid-1990s in northern Afghanistan, I met an Italian UN official who took me to the local hospital, which had just been raided by the forces of the Uzbek warlord Abdul Rashid Dostam. "This will be the third time I've rebuilt this place," the aid worker told me. "I can't see doing it a fourth time."

His experience was not atypical. The aid worker's life is a constant effort to get supplies or services to those who need them, trying all the while as best he or she can—often with mixed and sometimes with bitter and unintended results—to, as the doctors say, do no harm, while attempting to mitigate horrors most people in their home countries are at best dimly aware of. Perhaps there was once, but today there is nothing innocent or unself-conscious about these efforts. Of course, it is impossible to really do no harm, unless one is a Jain, and, following strictly the tenets of that religion, sweeps the streets to save the lives of insects as one walks along. And aid workers can do great harm, however inadvertently, so they are absolutely right to worry, despite all the undeniable good they do. Are they serving as logisticians or medics for some warlord's war effort (as they probably are in southern Sudan)? Are they creating a culture of dependency among their beneficiaries? And are they being used politically, by virtue of the way government donors and UN agencies give them funds and direct them toward certain places while making it difficult for them to go to others? As one senior UN official in eastern Congo put it to me, "Some of us think we're part of the problem, not part of the solution, and that at best we're becoming a containment system for the rich world, its operational arm in the regions of the world where there are no big economic interests or strategic concerns."

The increased collaboration between humanitarians and rich donor governments would probably have occurred whether or not these political considerations had been so important. Aid is vastly expensive, and is growing more so every year. And the logistical hurdles are staggering, and can only be resolved, assuming there is a pressing need and a relief agency must react quickly, with a great deal of money. But while the biggest humanitarian agencies have annual budgets in the hundreds of millions, most, with the notable exception of Médecins Sans Frontières, are constrained in their actions and increasingly dependent on donors, the largest of which is an arm of the European Union, the European Commission Humanitarian Aid Office (ECHO).

These sums do sound like a lot, but when you compare them to the budgets of corporations, let alone governments, or when you realize that there are more than twenty million refugees on the move, the sums of money—and the reproach by some critics of aid that humanitarianism has been corrupted and rendered harmful in many cases by the fact that it has itself become a business—seem pathetic and the reproaches rather beside the point.

It is also true that in terms of reputation, the past ten years have been extraordinarily successful ones for humanitarian groups. Their public support has broadened to an astonishing degree; they have received—not that they themselves like to admit it—Niagaras of adulatory media attention; and, increasingly, Western governments have placed humanitarian issues at the center of policy decisions from which they were almost wholly absent before the 1980s. One can question all these elements of the story, and concede that each has its complications and its moral undertow, but the fact remains that humanitarianism as an ideal has achieved an authority and reach that would have been inconceivable even twenty years ago.

And yet humanitarianism is also generally agreed to be in crisis. All of its historic certainties—the neutrality so prized by the ICRC, the notion that aid should be fundamentally apolitical and should have no other agenda than service and solidarity—are being questioned by aid workers themselves, as well as by outside critics. Giving aid has proved to be a more ambiguous act than aid workers ever imagined. "We have lost our innocence about the impacts of aid," writes Mary B. Anderson, probably the most influential American thinker on the subject of how to deliver relief with as few negative effects as possible. "We know that aid provided in conflict settings can feed into and exacerbate the conflicts that cause the suffering it is meant to alleviate. And we know that aid too often does nothing to alter—and very often reinforces—the fundamental circumstances that produced the needs it temporarily meets."

What aid workers have learned painfully is that while politics and political analyses matter desperately to them, moral fables matter more to the general public. We who are citizens of rich countries, and who are unlikely ever to face the prospect of being killed, or dispossessed, or made into a refugee, may need to tell ourselves fairy tales about those who have suffered such fates in order to sympathize with them. They are victims; that should go without saying. But too often we need to think of them as *innocent* victims. And many of them are not. Only children are innocent. The adults who cross a border, or get caught in a crossfire, or risk starving to death as a war intensifies, have political opinions and often have themselves taken part in killing. This became starkly evident in the case of the Rwandan Hutu refugees who fled their country after the genocide in 1994. Many of them had participated willingly in the slaughter of the Tutsis. In the camps, at least in the beginning, they said so openly. Which made them killers, but did not mean that as they sat in those camps, with the cholera and dysentery raging, they were not victims as well. And what was true in eastern Congo in 1994 and 1995 has also been true to a greater or lesser extent in every humanitarian crisis of the past thirty years.

We do those who are in pain and in need no favor by infantilizing them, even though such infantilization obviously makes the moral choices that confront relief workers and their supporters in the West seem far easier than they really are. To accept people's humanity and respect their dignity as individuals should not entail spinning fairy tales about their innate innocence. Such a perspective is perfectly appropriate when the victims in question are children. But most people who suffer in the wake of wars or man-made famines are not children, and it is no use pretending otherwise.

The moral hazard should be obvious. Dr. Rony Brauman, former president of the French section of Médecins Sans Frontières, summed up this particular pathology well when he remarked that it could not be an accident that the one thing tyrants and aid workers have in common is their liking for being posed next to children. Of course, the United Nations Children's Fund and some private aid agencies, notably Save the Children, have the relief of children as their particular mandate. But the association in many aid workers' minds between the fundamental innocence of children and the fundamental innocence of *all* those they are pledged to help permeates the relief world far more deeply than the fitting sense of obligation toward the most vulnerable, above all children, felt by any decent relief worker.

Part of the reason is that it makes life much less complicated for relief workers in their dealings with the people they have come to help. Children are assumed to have no views; they are assumed, quite rightly, to have no responsibility for what is going on, either. Thus they are the perfect vessels for the sympathy of strangers. But every intelligent aid worker knows that while it may be the suffering of children that gets people to contribute back home, a humanitarianism that infantilizes its beneficiaries or holds itself aloof from the political consequences of its actions is increasingly becoming indefensible. That was why, in the 1990s, many of the most important mainline agencies, notably Oxfam, turned to what they called advocacy—that is, lobbying governments and the UN for funds, but also for political commitments and, as the decade progressed, military action.

Some relief workers thought that this provided a way out of the problem. But it was also an emblem of it. As Cornelio Sommaruga, former president of the ICRC, pointed out, "Politicians and governments have abused humanitarianism to disengage from their own responsibilities, and, in doing so, have provoked an enormous and grave confusion." It is to cope with this dereliction that humanitarian aid workers have increasingly accepted the idea that their work has to be political as well, abandoning the notion of humanitarianism-against-politics for the politics of humanitarianism. Perhaps this was inevitable. But can an ideal based on both universal values and unbending neutrality be politicized successfully? The price for such a transformation would seem to be very high—perhaps too high.

For at its core, humanitarianism remains the vocation of helping people when they most desperately need help, when they have lost or stand at risk of losing everything they have, including their lives. It is certainly possible that the more politicized view of aid will prevail. It is also possible that modern humanitarianism as it has existed over the past thirty years, since Médecins Sans Frontières was founded in 1971 by young French doctors who had rebelled at the ICRC's insistence on absolute public discretion even when faced with the worst atrocities, will cease to exist. It is easy to imagine a schism as radical as the one between MSF and the ICRC in which some groups will become absorbed with running programs that emphasize human rights at least as much as relief, while others—as happened in Kosovo in 1999—will in effect become subcontractors for national governments or for UN agencies.

Whatever happens, whether or not institutions are transformed and norms strengthened, even an optimist would have to agree that the need for humanitarian action will only increase in the coming decades. And the work itself will only get harder. Where twenty years ago humanitarians operated in the reasonable expectation that they would not themselves be attacked, today they are at times the favorite targets of fighters in the zones in which they operate. Killings are all too frequent; kidnapping and extortion are commonplace. But the challenge to humanitarianism goes far beyond the issue of security, or, for that matter, the moral dilemma of whether, while trying to do good, *and doing good,* relief also causes harm. The deepest challenge of all is how humanitarianism will survive its own supposed successes. Can the saving vision of human solidarity it offers in this cruel, fearful, and self-centered time be maintained, or does the current crisis in humanitarianism reflect the sad truth that our moral ambitions have been revealed as just that—ambitions, and little more?

Those ambitions are profound. All major religious traditions accept that suffering and death are simply part of life. The deep radicalism of humanitarian action is its belief that people are not made to suffer. To assume such a stance in a time of such widespread evil and pain is astonishing in and of itself. It allows hope in situations that appear hopeless. The question, of course, as the most original critic of aid, the British writer and human rights activist Alex de Waal, has remarked, is whether or not humanitarianism is a waste of hope. It is that question that first drew me to humanitarian aid workers—my own hope, as it were, that there was hope—and it is that question that I try to answer in this book.

Designated Consciences

CHAPTER I

The Humanitarian Paradox

YOU ARE THE PROSPEROUS citizen of a prosperous country. In practice, this means you are almost certainly a citizen of the United States, Canada, Japan, or one of the countries of the European Union. It also means that, in global terms, you belong to a minority group, at most no more than a tenth of the world's population, and probably a good deal less. Of course, it is a minority of privilege, not of oppression. You, or, to be more accurate, we (I belong to this group too), have the habit of spending at least part of your mornings reading a decent broadsheet newspaper and part of most evenings watching your national television news program. The particular newspaper or TV broadcast is not all that relevant to the scenario that I am trying to construct. After all, when viewed from the perspective of Central Africa, or the slums of Rio de Janeiro, or the jungles of the southern Philippines, or the mountains of Afghanistan, the differences between *The New York Times* and *Le Monde*, CNN and TV España, don't amount to very much. What counts is that your habit of reading a newspaper and, above all, of watching the news on television means that you voluntarily expose yourself on a regular basis to at least some of the most horrible things taking place in the world.

If there is a refugee crisis in Burundi, a famine in Somalia, or a war in the Balkans, the fact that you are a faithful consumer of the news will lead to your being confronted by at least some tiny corner of them. To be sure, that exposure is usually both fleeting and superficial. To anyone who knows a subject in any depth, television news, even at its best, seems like reality doled out with an eye-dropper for someone assumed to have the attention span of a gnat. Nowhere is this more true than in the coverage of humanitarian crises, in large measure because no other story that gets any airtime or major newspaper attention at all is so dependably unfamiliar. Somalia, Rwanda, Bosnia, Kosovo, East Timor, Afghanistan—these are places that capture the attention of mainstream, nonspecialist journalists only when a disaster is taking place.

That in itself is a recipe for distortion and misapprehension. The idea that we live in a "global village" was first popularized by the Canadian futurist Marshall McLuhan and then repeated ad nauseam during the great stock market bubble of the 1990s in the form of paeans to globalization and the new "wired" world. This cliché is true and false at the same time. It is true that we have unprecedented access to information thanks to television and the Internet. But it is false that this information necessarily means we understand what we are seeing in any usable way. You can know that there is a famine in southern Sudan. You can wish that it weren't happening, and hope that something will be done about it. But what do you understand about southern Sudan from the images of horror and want that you see on your television screen? Just that there is horror and want, nothing else. You are watching something take place in southern Sudan, but apart from the fact that the people are black, how do you distinguish what you are seeing from something going on in

Afghanistan, or East Timor, or Central America? There is horror, but no context, and therefore as much mystification as information results from this new way of accessing the world's tragedies.

The average international story on national television news in the United States lasts one minute and twenty seconds. On that basis alone, it appears almost inevitable that there will be misreporting, even if inadvertent, on the journalist's side and misunderstanding on the viewer's. In Europe, the rhythm is slightly less impatient and commercially driven, but even there such stories rarely clock in at more than three minutes. And what can one say in eighty or ninety seconds or in three minutes? Perhaps it is easier to predict what one cannot say. It is difficult to say something original; it is difficult to explain anything in depth; and it is difficult not to fall into the same clichés about humanitarian disasters that were employed during the last disaster, thus leaching the crisis one is covering of all its tragic specificity. You, the viewer, are not in Afghanistan, Cambodia, or Bosnia so much as you are in humanitarian-tragedy land—a world of wicked warlords, suffering and *innocent* victims, and noble aid workers. And whether you know why or not, you have the distinct impression that you have been there before.

It could hardly be otherwise. Given the way humanitarian emergencies are covered, what other impression can the viewer retain but the feeling that out there in the poor world there is a planet of sufferers? The television camera operator's stock-in-trade in a famine or a war is the close-up—the focus on the baby in the aid worker's arms, the child with flies lighting on her face, the vultures slyly approaching the rotting corpse of the dead militiaman. But the effect on the viewer is to encourage him or her to see this world in long shot. He or she becomes unable to differentiate one person in pain from another, much as someone standing on a high hill will have trouble making out the physiognomy of people in the valley below.

To point this out is not to blame either the media or the audience, let alone the aid workers, whose symbiotic relationship with the media is one of their greatest challenges. These crises *are* far away and difficult to understand, and human beings are not solidarity machines or professional carers, however much we might wish it otherwise. It is not even clear that if the media were given more time and resources, were permitted to be more deliberate and more serious, people could cope psychologically or morally with the reality of the poor world in all its horror, rage, and complexity. To sympathize in the way that the television images invite us all to do is not difficult. It is with the question of how that sympathy can be translated into action that the problems arise. Does having seen images of starving babies really allow people to come to any kind of informed view about whether there should be an airlift of food, or political engagement, or even a military intervention? And even assuming that the atrocious images of famine do provoke a military intervention, as was the case in Somalia in 1992, is it not inevitable that the public will be utterly unprepared for that intervention to have costs other than financial ones?

In Somalia, this battle of images was soon joined. First there were the images of the famine. As Philip Johnston, former president of the relief group CARE USA, put it in his memoir, *Somalia Diary,* "Television brought home the urgency of Somalia's tragedy, translating a faraway crisis into a story of human beings who were days, perhaps hours, away from death." As an example of this, he cited an ABC report in which the reporter described a young Somali girl who was "little more than a walking skeleton." As Johnston writes, the point of the story was clear: "As long as marauders kept food from reaching those who needed it most, relief workers would have nothing to offer the most vulnerable."

Johnston's own role in the humanitarian crisis in Somalia was extraordinarily important. Some aid workers believe that he was the driving force behind the militarization of the humanitarian aid effort in the country and the eventual decision by the U.S. government to send in military forces. At the time, he said that if necessary we would "have to fight the Somalis themselves" to make sure the aid got delivered. But what is noteworthy about Johnston's account is something that has become an integral part of the humanitarian repertory, even in crises where there is no question of military force being deployed. His account of the media's role in helping make the American public aware of the crisis is largely devoid of historical context, geographical specificity, and even any real personalization. There is a starving girl, unnamed; there are marauders, unidentified; and there are relief workers, also unspecified. When Johnston speaks approvingly of the media's ability to turn a faraway crisis into a story of human beings, it is hard not to feel that he means human beings in the generic sense. After all, there are no real individuals in the story—only victims, victimizers, and relief workers who want to help and urgently need the means, which for Johnston at the time meant military force to escort the relief convoys and fight the Somalis who preyed on them.

Johnston was successful in persuading the United Nations to take a more militarized approach to the crisis, and in getting the administration of George Bush senior to commit U.S. troops. And the result was almost inevitable: He who lives by the image, dies by the image. Because of the sympathy these images Johnston approved of had evoked, the American public supported the decision to intervene. Such sympathy may license actions that cost money; it never licenses actions that cost lives. The American public thought its troops were in Somalia on a humanitarian mission—that is, to do good, not to kill, and certainly not to get killed. And yet to the leading Somali warlord, Mohammed Farah Aidid, the U.S. troops were there to thwart his effort to seize power. From his perspective, their mission was political—that is, to attack him.

And attack they did. But while Aidid could never match the military power of the United States, his fighters in Mogadishu, the Somali capital, soon proved that they were more than a match for the Americans in resolve and determination. On October 3, 1993, they responded to the attempt of American elite forces to seize two of Aidid's lieutenants by shooting down two American helicopters, killing eighteen U.S. soldiers and wounding seventy-seven others. That evening, American television viewers were shocked to see jubilant Somalis dragging the naked bodies of two American helicopter pilots through the dust of Mogadishu. That image far outweighed the images of starving babies. Americans wanted no part of war; they had thought their troops were there to do good. As Johnston—still, it seems, uncomprehending—puts it in his book, "Sadly, in all of this, the plight of the Somali people became lost."

Aid workers like to say, in moments of crisis when they are trying to persuade the Western public to support action, that there are times when there is a moral imperative to act. They are not wrong. Where they err is in imagining that either Western governments or the Western public will be willing to sacrifice as well as sympathize in response to images of nameless victims and fables of innocent, apolitical civilians. (Was it really safe to assume that *none* of these starving people had any politics, or that it was impossible to be, simultaneously, an Aidid supporter *and* a victim of the famine in Somalia?) Somalia proved the error in this sort of thinking. President Bill Clinton's idealized account of the mission was that the United States "came to Somalia to rescue innocent people in a burning house." It begged the question of how many people it is acceptable to kill in order to be able to save the people in that burning house. But even taken at face value, it made sense only as long as there were no casualties, as Clinton himself would later demonstrate, first by claiming he had never been properly briefed about the military operation to seize Aidid and then by deciding in the aftermath of the debacle to negotiate with Aidid and withdraw U.S. forces.

And if the President of the United States was confused, how could the general public not be confused when the image of the American pilot being dragged through the streets of Mogadishu seemed to trump the images of the starving Somalis? Americans had been fed a benign fairy tale, and when malign reality intruded, public as well as political pressure to get their soldiers out of this unexpected danger as quickly as possible was only to be expected. And despite other humanitarian military interventions in Bosnia (after four years of war), in Kosovo, and in East Timor, the same confusions repeat themselves over and over again. Only when humanitarianism is melded with national interest, as has been the case for most Americans with regard to the war in Afghanistan, is there likely to be any tolerance for casualties. It is for this reason that humanitarians' reliance on the power of images, and on the utopian fantasy of a global village of moral concern, is such a trap. For in reality, few people have as yet become so committed or so conscience-stricken that they are willing to sacrifice their loved ones' lives or even much of their own material comfort to aid strangers. Those who believe themselves bound by these moral imperatives—and they are the best among us—tend, if they are not actively engaged already, to get up from their chairs, turn off their television sets, and go work for a relief agency or a charity.

But for all the talk of the "new" activism, and of the rise of what is rather misleadingly called civil society, such conscience-stricken people are still rare. They influence events more than in the past, but their influence is often overstated, by activists anyway. For the most part, the norm remains the same as it has been since we began to understand the limitations of the power of images. The viewer or the reader is hard pressed not to slot the sound bite from the reporter in, say, Afghanistan today into the continuum of sound bites from scenes that he or she has seen since Biafra in the 1960s; or Cambodia at the end of the 1970s; or Ethiopia in the 1980s, when the rock singer Bob Geldof's Live Aid project for the first time made celebrities of humanitarians; or Somalia, Bosnia, Rwanda, and Kosovo in the 1990s. These tragedies have not lost their power to shock, but they have become familiar, almost as if they were scripted, which in a sense they are, since the reporters who cover them, the aid workers themselves, and, perhaps, the Western public as well, have all been through these stories before. In the end, it is less a question of motives than of structures.

And of course to assume this level of concern in the first place is only relevant to those crises that are actually covered on television. In reality, most of the world's horrors never get any airtime at all. For every Rwanda that is covered, a dozen other unspeakable catastrophes never find their journalistic chroniclers, or, if they do, they get covered perhaps once or twice in the course of a year. From a political standpoint, this means that there will be no public pressure in the West for something to be done. And let us be clear: whether one supports humanitarian intervention or not, whether one believes that humanitarian action is best kept separate from state power or, realistically, must interact with it, the fact remains that only the West is rich enough and powerful enough to intervene in a far-off humanitarian catastrophe in a way that can make a major difference. Again, this is not to say that those few humanitarian interventions that have taken place—Somalia in 1992–1993, the Balkans between 1991 and 1999, Rwanda in the aftermath of the genocide in 1994, and East Timor in 1999—have been wholly disinterested. That is not the way great powers act, and it is confusing dream with reality to imagine otherwise.

Taken case by case, these interventions invariably reveal mixed motives and hidden agendas. The intervention in Somalia appears to have won the support of the then chairman of the Joint Chiefs of Staff, Colin Powell, in part because he bitterly opposed American intervention in Bosnia and understood that a humanitarian deployment in Somalia would make any U.S. move in the Balkans far less likely. The American decision to bomb the Bosnian Serbs in 1995 was due at least in part to the threat by the British and French to withdraw their UN peacekeeping forces—a move that would have obliged the United States, as their NATO partner, to deploy troops to cover their retreat. Even in Kosovo, which looks like the most altruistic of this wave of interventions—the British prime minister, Tony Blair, insisted at the time that NATO had intervened in defense of "its values, not its interests"—the reality was far more complicated. It is true that the plight of the Kosovars did engage the sympathies of the Western public. But NATO acted as much because, after Croatia and after Bosnia, it had decided, however belatedly, that it had had enough of Slobodan Milosevic and Serbian nationalism and was determined to stamp out this ethnic fascist rebellion in the European backlands once and for all, as it did out of any deep-seated sympathy for the Kosovars.

Of course, this was not the way the story was presented in the media. Instead, each of these crises involved a return to the script of largely apolitical moral concern. The poor suffering Ethiopians for whom Bob Geldof had raised money through Band Aid and Live Aid (and that led an otherwise uninformed Western public to believe that what was taking place was a natural disaster rather than mass deaths caused by the Ethiopian government's policy of forcible resettlement) were replaced by the starving Somalis. They were followed by the suffering, besieged Bosnians, who were replaced by the martyred Rwandans, who in turn gave way to Bosnia again when NATO broke the Serbs in 1995, then by the Kosovars, and then the Timorese. But then, if you are a discerning television news consumer, you already know that serial monogamy is the international journalist's stock-in-trade. To say this is hardly to underestimate the power of the press in affecting the response to humanitarian emergencies. To the contrary, during the 1990s the foreign disasters the press homed in on were precisely the ones where interventions did eventually take place—Somalia, Bosnia, Rwanda, Kosovo, and East Timor.

Philip Johnston's narrative of the cumulative effect that press coverage of the Somalia crisis had on building a constituency for action is emblematic. "In September [of 1992]," he wrote, "a trickle of television reports and newspaper stories had become a steady stream of news coverage. By October the number of stories became a wave of media attention that lifted Somalia to a new level of international awareness and concern." The media, he concluded, "helped the world community care about Somalia."

The same trajectory could be traced in terms of the media coverage of Bosnia, Rwanda, Kosovo, and East Timor. And given the fact that the other twenty-three crises and dozens more humanitarian emergencies went largely unattended, the truth of Johnston's words—for better and for worse—is surely undeniable. The former secretary-general of the United Nations, Boutros Boutros-Ghali, who bitterly resented the Western media's attacks on his role in the Balkans, once remarked that CNN functioned as if it were the sixteenth member of the UN Security Council. To be sure, he exaggerated. To cite only the most obvious example, for all its efforts, an

intensely partisan international press corps in Bosnia (I include myself) was unable to shame its governments into intervention to lift
the siege of Sarajevo.

But Boutros-Ghali was also correct. The fact that the media paid
attention to Bosnia—that reporters were obsessed with the story and
that editors back home allowed their obsession airtime and column
inches, month in and month out—kept the Bosnian story alive in
the minds of people in Western Europe and North America. It was
not enough, yet without it nothing else would have been possible.
Bosnia was a special case in the sense that it was a war in Europe,
where war was both easier for Europeans and Americans to identify
with and was seen as the ultimate man-bites-dog story, because war
was not supposed to happen in Europe in the 1990s. But a similar
dynamic operated in Somalia, Rwanda, and Kosovo. There, too, the
press's almost obsessional focus was what distinguished these particular fields of horror from all the other places undergoing similar
miseries at the same time. For while Somalia starved, so did Sudan;
while Sarajevo burned, so did Kabul. Only Rwanda, the third and last
great genocide of the twentieth century, after the Armenians in 1915
and the Jews and Gypsies between 1941 and 1945, can be said, in its
horrific way, not just to have been virtually a unique event in its time
but to have been understood as such. (One of the ironies of international law is that the death of a million Cambodians at the hands of
Pol Pot was not, strictly speaking, a genocide since it did not target a
particular religious or ethnic group.)

It is easy to discern the limitations of the way television imparts
information. And yet the fact that one can even be aware, in any ap-
proximation of real time, of the siege of Sarajevo, the Rwandan
genocide, or the refugee exodus from Afghanistan is not just a recent phenomenon but an amazingly powerful one. It is true that the

fantasy of knowledge awakening conscience is comparatively old. In 1899, Gustave Moynier, the first president of the Red Cross, wrote: "We now know what happens every day throughout the whole world . . . the descriptions given by daily journalists put, as it were, those in agony on fields of battle under the eyes of [newspaper] readers and their cries resonate in their ears . . ."

In fact, before the 1960s no one saw such images or read such descriptions until well after the event. Still, while Moynier, writing at the high-water mark of European optimism, could not have imagined that the twentieth century would become the era of total war, his para-McLuhanite intuition was nonetheless not wrong. It would just take another seventy-five years to realize it. The photographs of the Nazi concentration camp inmates after they had been liberated by Russian, American, or British forces are often cited as utterly transforming by people who saw them when they first appeared in newspapers or were shown in movie theaters. And yet these images were not disseminated until weeks after the Allied forces entered the camps. Only the camp inmates, the camp guards, and the Allied soldiers experienced the events in real time. You could not turn on your television set in May 1945, switch over to the BBC, and have a reporter say, "This is John Smith, BBC News, Auschwitz, liberated Poland," let alone watch the same reporter doing a "live" stand-up from the camp, one or two years earlier, while the Jews were being murdered by the millions.

I am not trying to be grotesque. But the point has to be made: The interconnectedness that we all now take for granted, the fact that it is possible for journalists to report live from the battlefield via videophone, or for those dying in the fire and smoke of the World Trade Center to call their loved ones on their cell phones to say good-bye, means that the basic terms of information have been transformed. Here is one example where the revolutionary nature of globalization is reality, not hype. Given the Nazi regime's obsession with secrecy and its bureaucratic efficiency, a reporter probably would not have been allowed into Auschwitz or the Warsaw Ghetto in 1942. But reporters did film and report from the killing fields of Rwanda in real time, just as they are likely to be able to do from every field of atrocity the future has in store for us. I do not believe that this means we care more now than we did in the past. But it does mean that the possibility of caring exists in a way that it did not before, if only because one is looking at events in real time rather than after it is too late to do anything about them. And it means that through that television, we, as representative First World citizens, can choose to expose ourselves to that world of suffering, injustice, violent death, want, and cruelty that is the lived reality for so many people on this planet.

It is to our credit, I think, that so many of us do not turn the page or flick the channel selector, however problematic both the quality of the coverage and the quality of our response to it. One does not have to have a simpleminded view of the press, or of the world for that matter, to see that this is an important advance. But how much of an advance? What does the message that there is a humanitarian imperative—that when people are suffering, even if they are strangers, it is our collective obligation as human beings to come to their aid—amount to in reality? I am not speaking here of the practical difficulties of mobilizing coalitions or lobbying to get governments to act, let alone the challenges of trying to deliver humanitarian aid properly in the field without making things worse, and being careful that humanitarianism does not come to serve as a fig leaf either for inaction or for other agendas. All those difficulties presuppose that we have understood what we have seen, and that this slice of human suffering to which we have been exposed gives us enough to go on to think and commit as well as to sympathize.

What do we actually see? It is one thing to be able to sit down, switch on the television, and be able to call up the world on demand—from golf to genocide in a half-hour news program—and quite another even to begin to come to terms with what we are seeing. The images are moving, yes, but usually they are also almost infinitely remote, like the spoken narratives of the reporters that accompany them. And unless they are repeated endlessly, as was the case in Bosnia, and Kosovo, and Afghanistan, they are almost impossible to take in. There you are in your living room, and wedged somewhere in among the politicians' squabbling, the car crash on the highway, the stock market report, and the sports is the news that a bunch of people in a place you've barely heard of are starving to death, or fleeing for their lives, or being shelled and sniped at. And unless it is your own country that is doing the shelling and the sniping, or perhaps offering the protection, or, as in the case of the United States in Afghanistan, a bit of both, how is it possible to remember and how is it possible to understand in any meaningful way?

Part of the problem is structural. Not only does television news have limited time at its disposal to air the stories that seem urgent, it has no time at all to present stories about humanitarian crises that might become urgent sometime in the future. Even in the best newspapers, such stories are usually buried somewhere in the inner pages. Journalists are engaged with the stories that have reached the boiling point. They rarely have the time to track Burma and Burundi, Angola and Afghanistan before they explode. So when something really atrocious takes place in such a country, something that even the most parochial news editor knows has to be covered, in effect the reporter must try in somewhere between ninety seconds and three minutes to give the entire history of the country, the reasons for the catastrophe, and the actual story he or she is covering to a viewer who is probably hearing all the names, places, and dates for the first time. What is surprising, when one thinks about it, is not that people understand so little but that they understand anything at all.

Critics of the press—indeed, critics of the West more generally—tend to forget this. It is as if they somehow imagine that the geography of central Bosnia, the hierarchies of Somali clans, the nature of ethnicity in colonial Rwanda, or the Christian-Muslim rivalries of the Indonesian archipelago, are elements of knowledge that are easily mastered. In the film *Sammy and Rosie Get Laid,* the angry young hero reproaches his immigrant father for not being more politically militant. "I'm a professional businessman," the weary parent replies, "not a professional Pakistani." By the same token, it is perfectly normal, and even obligatory, for someone like me who spends his life writing about the Rwandas, Bosnias, and Afghanistans to know the respective roles in their respective countries of Paul Kagame and Patrick Mazimpaka, Radovan Karadzic and Ratko Mladic, or Abdul Rashid Dostam and Burhanuddin Rabbani. Knowing who these people are makes it possible to understand what is happening in the countries and tragedies in question. But to name these names on television as if they were intelligible, or to listen to them as if one had the faintest idea of who they were? This would be a demonstration of the triumph of hope over experience if ever there was one. Because, like the father in that film, people are professional businessmen, or doctors, or laborers, or accountants, or housewives, not professional consumers of other people's tragedies.

Actually, despite the condescension that is often directed at them by people who are either professionally or affectively involved with wars and humanitarian emergencies, the television anchors and the newspaper editors do their best to communicate these almost incommunicable realities. Think again, if you can bear to, of Auschwitz. Let's suppose that my imaginary BBC reporter somehow could have gained entry and done a stand-up in front of one of the crematoria.

How could he have made it real to people sitting in San Francisco or Houston? And what would the anchor have done after the story was over? In all likelihood, he would have done what anchors do now, which is look solemn and go to an advertising break before returning to focus on some domestic news story.

You may say that the Holocaust is the exception and that television's business-as-usual would not have taken place. Perhaps you are right. But only if you admit that the criteria include not simply the horror of the event per se—does anyone think American audiences would have fixated on the Japanese slaughter in China in the 1930s, before the outbreak of World War II?—but the horror of an event *plus* the fact that for whatever reason it concerns you. Nazi concentration camps would have concerned British or American audiences in 1942 because Britain and the United States were at war with Germany. But World War II was not the main thing on people's minds in Argentina or in Mexico in 1942. And in Asia, which had been at war for a decade, the fate of European Jewry would have been a tangential concern, just as the fate of the hundreds of thousands of Chinese murdered by Japanese forces in Nanking in 1937 was of no great concern to the American or Western European public. "They had other things to worry about" may be the most terrifying utterance in the language.

Yes, confronted by the reality of an event as catastrophic and epochal as the Rwandan genocide, perhaps a more ethically delicate society would turn reading the morning paper or watching the evening news into something analogous to going to a funeral. And given the abundance of horror in the world, a more precise analogy would be going to funerals in the middle of an AIDS epidemic. As I write, there are twenty-seven major armed conflicts taking place in the world; 1.2 billion people are living on less than one dollar a day; 2.4 billion people have no access to basic sanitation; and 854 million adults, 543 million of them women, are illiterate. One of the most important things that has happened over the course of the past fifty years is that the world has increasingly become divided into three parts. There is the small, underpopulated commonwealth of peace and plenty that is North America, most of Europe, and Japan; there is the part made up of Latin America, the former Soviet Union, China, and India, in which wealth and poverty coexist and where the future is unclear; and finally, above all in sub-Saharan Africa and an area stretching from Algeria to Pakistan, there is a vast, teeming dystopia of war and want whose future no decent and properly informed person should be able to contemplate without sadness, outrage, and fear.

The images from that world are moving. Even in the distracted context of television news, they have not lost their power to affect us. Michael Ignatieff was correct when he wrote that television images of humanitarian disasters and wars have contributed to "the breaking down of the barriers of citizenship, religion, race, and geography that once divided our moral space into those we were responsible for and those who were beyond our ken." As recently as the 1930s, it was only missionaries intent on saving souls and Communists intent on fomenting revolution who acted on the basis of an ethos of universal solidarity. Today, such notions are universal, or at least receive lip service almost universally. It could hardly be otherwise in an era when almost no international figure, no matter how tyrannical—and indeed very few warlords of even the most unreconstructed kind—would today come out in opposition to the secular religion of human rights. And it is more than just the sincerity of dictators that is at issue. The essential problem of how far human sympathy and solidarity can be expanded is more pressing than ever before.

It is not just the voyeurism with regard to the sufferings of others that television engenders (and against which Ignatieff rightly warned) that makes the experience of watching horrors like the Rwandan genocide or the refugee emergency in Afghanistan on television a far less certain path to solidarity than the ideologues of the globalization of consciousness pretend. Rather, anyone who continues to hope that the world, for all its horrors, can be made a better place through Ignatieff's "revolution of moral concern" in the West must confront the following question: Is it even possible for people who live in comfort to care deeply enough for people who do not to act to alleviate those sufferings? For it is not enough to watch television, be moved, and in especially tragic instances—a Somalia, a Rwanda, an Afghanistan—translate that emotion into a contribution to a charity or a letter to a politician demanding that something be done. By definition, such caring, like the televised images that so often engender it, is too selective, too inconsistent, and too intermittent to do much good. The crisis ends; the news goes back to being almost exclusively about the local, the quotidian, and the banal; and when the next humanitarian emergency comes, it is as if it is the first one ever to occur.

Yes, of course we in the West who live in such privilege should care more. It is right to do so, and we all know that. It is not as if, for all our comforts, we have forgotten how to care. When the World Trade Center was destroyed, there was no question of treating the event as just another news story. Understandably, for days the television networks ran no advertisements and focused on the attack, on the victims, and on the consequences. In the United States, at least, to watch television *was* to attend a funeral. But even in the United States, some semblance of normalcy returned within a matter of weeks. The soap operas, the sporting events, the stock market reports all began running as they had before, just as the government had urged. Even for those obsessed with the war in Afghanistan, unsettled by the downturn in the economy, and terrified by anthrax, the assumption was that sooner or later everything would get back to normal. And this was usually understood to mean a few months, or, at worst, a year or two. What eloquent testimony such confidence, misplaced or not, provides as to how reduced, even in the aftermath of the worst terrorist atrocity in American history, the imagination of disaster had become in the West by 2001.

For no matter how shocking and terrible the destruction of the World Trade Center was, and despite the insistence of the Bush administration that the United States was at war, this was hardly war in the sense that our ancestors understood the word. For people who came of age in the first half of the twentieth century, war was not a single strike that extinguished three thousand lives on one's own side, followed by a military campaign in which it was assumed that a far lesser number of one's own soldiers would die. The loss of thousands of lives would have been seen as the predictable result of any substantial battle. And such a loss would have been seen as a relatively small one at that, if not by American then by Western European standards. Anyone doubting this has only to remember that almost a million German and French soldiers died in the battle of Verdun in 1916. And twenty million Russians died in World War II. As for the destruction of buildings, to our grandparents and great-grandparents, destruction was not the fall of two towers, however tragic, but the ruin of whole cities. Think of Coventry and Rotterdam, of London during the Blitz; and think of Dresden, where on one night, February 13, 1945, at least twenty-five thousand people were killed and virtually the entire city was leveled. Above all, think, if you can bear to, of Hiroshima and Nagasaki.

The miracle of our own time, a miracle that probably only the very old among us still fully appreciate, is that in Western Europe and North America such horrors appear to have become quite literally inconceivable. A person who lives in these countries inhabits the

one tiny corner of the planet where war, hunger, and fear as lived realities have become—or, as the generation that lived through World
War II leave us, are rapidly becoming—events one reads about in
books. In this sense, Immanuel Kant's dream of a world of states in
which perpetual peace reigned, while hardly the norm anywhere
else in the world, has become part of the political DNA of the West.
And so the gap widens between this Western world, in which the primacy of individual rights is taken for granted and in which peace is
assumed to be the natural state of things (even though anyone who
has read history knows that throughout all of it, war, not peace, has
been the human norm), and that huge part of the world in which
war is either an everyday reality or a looming threat.

It is this that makes the predicament of our emblematic television watcher, our Western everyman or everywoman, so complex.
Let us assume the best intentions. Not only is the crisis in question
difficult to understand, but the afflicted population is difficult to empathize with, as opposed to sympathize with—a more abstract and
less compelling reaction. To put it starkly, there is nothing about
them, except the brute fact of their humanity, with which those Europeans or North Americans who in fact want to connect can easily
connect. In other words, not only are we not in Kansas anymore, as
Dorothy says in *The Wizard of Oz,* but we are not even in Bosnia,
where the refugees were white Europeans. Instead, imagine that we
are talking about Congo or Afghanistan. Though activists sometimes claim otherwise, it is at most only tangentially a matter of
racism. In every sense, these tragedies simply take place at too great
a remove. From the unfamiliar countryside or urban landscape to
the unpronounceable names of the people, warlords and refugees
alike, there is nowhere except in the rarified world of moral concern
for the viewer to get his or her bearings.

And in any case, our television viewer is better than his or her prejudices. The sight of the starving babies in that refugee camp in eastern Congo or that column of refugees trying to flee from Afghanistan into Pakistan seems genuinely intolerable, particularly when our viewer contrasts their ordeal to his or her own comfort. And the sight may continue to resonate long after the television has been switched off. In this sense, the fleeting images and the over-simplified narrative that accompanied them have awakened a con-science.

It is no exaggeration to say that, over the course of the past thirty-five years, roughly since the Biafran crisis of 1967, this particular awakening of conscience, or solidarity, this "revolution of moral con-cern," has taken place in literally millions of homes all over the rich world and continues to take place.

That is the good news. But it also begs the question. For while our viewer's conscience may be alerted, what he or she has seen remains basically incomprehensibile. Where those who trumpet the revolu-tion of moral concern go wrong is in assuming that sympathy somehow can be turned into understanding. And the one thing someone who has seen images of a refugee camp or a city being shelled on television has not done is understand, except in the most simplistic sense of understanding, that fellow human beings are at risk or are being harmed. Reporters may try to impart such infor-mation, but how much can they do in a couple of minutes? In any case, what is compelling about the image is the suffering, not the history or the political context. Indeed, faced with a starving child or a pregnant woman forced from her home, it seems callous, almost inhuman, to bring up politics or try to contextualize the disaster by going on about the events that led up to it.

And yet failing to do so is fraught with moral risks. The first in-volves misplaced sympathy or, to put it another way, sympathy that distorts understanding. Imagine, for example, that in 1943 a film crew had gone to film both the German soldiers at Stalingrad and the Russian defenders of the city. Both groups suffered horribly. But while these sufferings were humanly identical, they were neither politically nor morally identical. Morally, Stalingrad was a zero-sum game, and the defeat of the Germans, even if it meant their atrocious suffering, was a moral imperative.

Understandably, many people today find analogies to World War II and the fight against Nazism morally invidious. They see them as too extreme, and as inapplicable to the murky complexities of today's wars, in which right and wrong are often impossible to determine and where frequently both sides are monstrous. But in fact, the refugee emergency in the aftermath of the Rwandan genocide of 1994 exposed much the same moral dilemma. Facing defeat by the forces of the Rwandan Patriotic Front, the people who committed the genocide—the old Rwandan army and the Interahamwe militia—fled into Congo (formerly Zaire) with their families. In all, they numbered almost two million, although of course probably no more than a few hundred thousand had killed. But then the average family size in Rwanda is eight people, so in all likelihood most heads of household among the fleeing refugees had committed mass murder.

The refugees suffered appallingly on their route of march out of Rwanda. Things only got worse once they crossed into eastern Congo and settled into vast refugee camps hastily set up by the Office of the United Nations High Commissioner for Refugees. The refugees were wracked by cholera and dysentery and a host of other infectious diseases. It was difficult to dig latrines in the hard, volcanic soil of the region, and there was little clean drinking water. Only the most heroic humanitarian effort, one that involved various UN agencies, private relief organizations, and the American and

French militaries, managed to blunt the epidemics. And still some thirty thousand died. In humanitarian terms, this initial effort was an impressive achievement in preventing an even greater catastrophe. (What happened later in the refugee camps was more problematic.) And yet in political terms and even in a moral context in which humanitarian relief is not viewed as an imperative that trumps all other imperatives, it is possible to portray things rather differently. In a way, what had happened is comparable to what might have taken place had two hundred thousand SS soldiers taken their families out of Nazi Europe as it fell to the Allies to somewhere they could hope to be sheltered from retribution.

Of course, no such place existed in 1945 except for the few lucky Nazis who made it to Argentina and Paraguay. But the principle of what befell the Rwandans who had committed genocide is exactly the same. Their humanitarian needs, which were entirely real, were generally what captured the attention of the Western media and, subsequently, of the Western governments that mounted the aid effort in eastern Congo. Here was where the distortion of the way humanitarian stories had been covered since Biafra in the late 1960s all but guaranteed that what was going on would be misunderstood. What Western journalists, Western news consumers, and Western governments saw were innocent victims. How could it have been otherwise? In the humanitarian story, at least the kind of story promoted by the Philip Johnstons of the aid world, victims are always innocent, always deserving of the world's sympathy, its moral concern, and beyond that, its protection, even if that means killing in the name of protection.

Reality is elsewhere. Victims can be victims and not be innocent. We know this in our daily lives. But somehow the canonical narrative of humanitarian relief, and of that putative "revolution of moral concern," occludes that fact when it comes to those in need of humanitarian aid. Hence the befuddlement. In 1991, we had expected the Somalis to welcome us. Our interests and theirs were complementary, or so we supposed: they were victims, we were bringing relief. And those Rwandan Hutus in 1994—they had such desperate needs. If ever there was a victim people, it was they. So how could so many of them have turned out to have been guilty of mass murder? And then what of those other Rwandans, the Tutsis? Their relatives were the ones who had been murdered by the hundreds of thousands during the genocide. By any reckoning, they were victims par excellence. But if this was the case, how could they have become killers in their turn in 1996?

And yet of course they did, and not only in Rwanda. In reality, such stories have repeated themselves over and over again throughout the annals of contemporary humanitarianism. The reason for this is simple: The history of contemporary humanitarianism is only one aspect of contemporary history. And history is never the fairy tale of innocent victims, oppressive gunmen, and caring outsiders that the humanitarian narrative so often presents. In private, humanitarian officials debate these issues passionately. In the aftermath of the cholera epidemic in eastern Congo, for example, UNHCR held a meeting about whether to exclude the killers from the camps. As one of those officials, Fabrizio Hochschild, a veteran of Sudan, Bosnia, and Kosovo, would recall later, "In a perfect world, we would have screened people. The International Tribunal would have been on hand, and there would have been proper security. But we were alone, and our alternative was looking after people." And, he added, "Even the guilty need to be fed."

What Hochschild expressed was the humanitarian creed at its purest. And yet few humanitarian officials in eastern Congo at the time would have risked expressing such harsh truths openly. Most hewed instead to their fables of innocent victims trapped in a war and refugee crisis they had had no responsibility for creating. The distortion was, and remains, entirely understandable as a strategy. (On this score, little has changed in the world of humanitarian action since the Rwandan genocide.) If humanitarians had told the truth about Rwanda, or Bosnia, or Afghanistan, if they had come out and said publicly to their donors and to the general public through the media that here were places where the victims were not just "innocent women and children," to use the handy old sexist phrase, but were often killers as well—the women too, especially in Rwanda—would the public still have cared? Was its moral concern, whether or not revolutionized by television and the Internet, that sophisticated? It was hardly likely. As Jean-François Vidal, a leading official of the French aid group Action Against Hunger, or Action Contre la Faim (ACF), once put it, "Only compassion sells. It is the basis of fundraising for humanitarian agencies. We can't seem to do without it."

In a sense, Vidal was being too hard on the aid agencies. For the reliance verging on dependency on these tales of blameless victims richly deserving of the help of aid workers and the money of the general public in the rich world was not simply a matter of money. It was a question of both morality and morale as well. Could the humanitarians themselves have carried on with what they were doing while really assimilating the somber sense of moral ambiguity that an accurate account of their effort in eastern Congo would have evoked? Perhaps the most sophisticated and the most insensitive among them could have pulled this off. But for many, probably even a majority, being constantly confronted by the fact that one was fighting to save the lives of murderers in all likelihood would have been too painful. They had not given up lives and jobs in the West to save the families of 1990s Central Africa's equivalent of the Nazi SS. Or had they?

Many writers have talked about the humanitarian trap. By this they usually mean the problem of aid prolonging wars, or giving great powers an excuse either for intervention or nonintervention. But the first and greatest humanitarian trap is this need to simplify, if not actually lie about, the way things are in the crisis zones, in order to make the story more morally and psychologically palatable— in short, to sugarcoat the horror of the world, which includes the horror of the cost of a good deed.

CHAPTER 2

The Hazards of Charity

W̲H̲A̲T̲ ̲W̲E̲ ̲N̲O̲W̲ ̲C̲A̲L̲L̲ humanitarianism, our ancestors called charity. The idea that it is a moral obligation of the more fortunate to assist the less fortunate and that those who are in need may legitimately expect help is one that is normative in all the major world religions. Call it altruism, call it pity, call it solidarity, call it compassion, but the impulse to help is so deeply rooted in human culture that, whether it is intrinsic or learned, it can rightly be described as one of the basic human emotions. Rousseau classed it among the "natural" feelings. Adam Smith, who defined compassion as "the emotion we feel for the misery of others," thought it "inherent." Historically, however, humanitarianism can be situated far less abstractly. The treatment of the sick, the insane, and wounded soldiers on the battlefield has been largely the work of religious orders. In the Western tradition, the concept of charity is part of that moral imperative Christians know as "service."

At first glance, no activity could seem more morally unimpeachable. But reality is more complicated. Even humanitarianism conforms in practice to the sere adage of Walter Benjamin's that I have used as an epigraph to this book. "Every document of civilization," he wrote, "is also a document of barbarism." The missionaries' dedication to succoring the sick, the wounded, and the poor, and, by the middle of the nineteenth century, their commitment to eradicating slavery in Africa, were also justification first for conquest and then for imperial domination. There were exceptions, of course. In the seventeenth century, the great Spanish missionary Bartolomé de Las Casas denounced the Spanish Crown's oppression of the native peoples of the Americas. In the eighteenth century, Jesuits in Paraguay actually instigated a revolt against the Spanish authorities. But the usual pattern was for the priest not only to arrive with the conqueror but also to give the conquest its moral warrant.

Before the middle of the nineteenth century, that warrant was principally the duty to propagate the Christian faith. Beginning in the 1870s, however, the European colonial enterprise was virtually reinvented. The roots of this transformation can be traced back to 1807, when Britain, much of whose wealth over the previous two centuries derived from slavery, abolished the slave trade (slavery itself was abolished only in 1833). The British then decided to move against the slave trade. In 1816, a naval squadron was deployed to patrol the West African coast and interdict the slavers' vessels. In one form or another, it would remain on station until the 1860s.

Significantly, this "humanitarian" project also involved a reinterpretation of international law. The British authorities insisted that they had the right to board and inspect any vessel, no matter what flag it flew. This represented one of the first assaults on the notion of the inviolability of state sovereignty that had been accepted by European nations since the middle of the seventeenth century. And the assault was explicitly undertaken in the name of a higher, humanitarian morality—a categorical imperative that, given the horror of slavery, trumped all other imperatives.

In the latter part of the nineteenth century, this new humanitarian colonialism had become the European norm. With a few notable exceptions, antislavery activists lent their considerable moral prestige to the imperial project. Obviously, for the architects of colonialism, this warrant was often nothing more than a pretext. When King Leopold II of Belgium was searching for a way to acquire a colony in Africa, he seized upon the issue of slavery in what is now the Democratic Republic of the Congo as a moral cover for demanding that he be granted *personal* ownership of what came to be called the Congo Independent State. But as his critical biographer Adam Hochschild has pointed out, Leopold was widely viewed in Europe as the "humanitarian" king, and was even elected honorary president of the Aborigines Protection Society, what we would now call a leading British human rights organization.

At the Conference of Berlin (1884–1885), in which the European powers agreed on the terms for dividing up Africa among themselves, Leopold won de facto approval for his private colony. His personal control was solidified at the Brussels Conference of 1889, ostensibly called by the Western powers to further the antislavery cause. Leopold promised the assembled delegates that, in return for permission to tax imports (the Berlin Conference had established the Congo Independent State as a free trade zone), and for other financial concessions, he would prosecute the war against the slavers. The reality for the peoples of the Congo basin was that Leopold's "humanitarian" project inaugurated the most horrific era in their history—a period in which possibly as many as ten million people died.

But for Europeans of the time, not only was there no moral incompatibility between the antislavery project and the imperial enterprise, but the latter was seen widely as the guarantor of the former. It was John Stuart Mill, that greatest of nineteenth-century liberals, who, as Adam Hochschild has pointed out, insisted in his book *On Liberty*: "Despotism is a legitimate mode of government in dealing with barbarians, providing the end be their improvement." This is comparable to contemporary justifications for establishing de facto protectorates in the aftermath of humanitarian interventions and maintaining them until the establishment or reestablishment of what today would be called the rule of law, good government, and human rights, and what, in the nineteenth century, was usually called civilization.

The African slavers of the 1870s who aroused the outrage of decent Europeans were mostly Muslim. To some extent, at least, this led to the European antislavery campaign's becoming a crusade in the literal as well as metaphorical sense of the term. On the occasion of his jubilee, Pope Leo XIII called upon the Christian world to launch this crusade to stop the horrors of slavery. His prestige did a great deal to provide a moral warrant for the "new imperialism." But even more commercially minded imperialists often emphasized the moral dimension of their enterprise. As Cecil Rhodes, a central figure in British colonialism in southern Africa, put it, "Colonialism is philanthropy plus five percent."

Such was the interconnectedness of the colonial enterprise with this missionary and, indeed, this Enlightenment vocation to do good that when, for example, the French colonialists spoke of their "civilizing mission," they were in no sense being disingenuous. If they viewed their campaigns as, in large measure, undertaken to relieve human suffering as much as if not more than to exploit the natural resources of their new colonies, they were in a position to justify their claims. From this perspective, which cannot be dismissed as simply a rationalization or a flag of convenience, colonialism was viewed not so much as an opportunity to make money but as a burden—"the white man's burden," as Rudyard Kipling described it in his famous poem exhorting the Americans to take up where the British imperial enterprise had left off.

What is striking about a good part of the poem is that, in fact, it is concerned with what we would now call humanitarian action. It describes colonial wars in something of the way today's proponents of humanitarian intervention often describe the missions they lobby for. Particularly striking is the similarity in the way the invocation of a higher moral norm led, in practice, to an alliance between activists intent on relieving suffering and great powers in the era of late-nineteenth-century imperialism, and to twentieth-century humanitarian interventionism. Was United Nations Secretary-General Kofi Annan so far from Leo XIII when he hailed "the developing international norm in favor of intervention to protect civilians from wholesale slaughter" as "testimony for a humanity that cares more, not less, for the suffering in its midst, and a humanity that will do more, not less, to end it"?

For all that divides them, dyed-in-the-wool imperialists and contemporary advocates of state humanitarianism share something of the same faith that a combination of high moral intent, military force, the imposition of good government, and benign tutelage (for Kipling's "lesser breeds beyond the law," read today's "failed states") could be a force for the betterment of humanity. Kipling wrote in tones that were both a good deal more pessimistic and infinitely more contemptuous of those in need of help than most contemporary relief workers, let alone Secretary-General Annan, would dream of adopting. But the great poet's sentiments are not so far removed from those of today's humanitarian intervenors as most would be comfortable acknowledging. The salient portion of the poem reads:

> Take up the White Man's Burden—
> The savage wars of peace—

Fill full the mouth of Famine
    And bid the sickness cease;
And when your goal is nearest
    The end for others sought,
Watch Sloth and Heathen Folly
    Bring all your hope to naught.

It is important to be extremely precise here. To say that in its Christian variant (and probably in its Muslim one as well) this kind of faith-based charity was both the accompaniment to and the hand-maiden of nineteenth-century European colonialism should not be taken as implying a defense of colonialism, or any wish to expunge from the historical record its terrible crimes. King Leopold's holocaust in the Congo; the German genocide of the Herero in what is now Namibia; British complicity in the famine in the Indian state of Bihar in 1943 in which more than a million died, and, arguably, in the Great Potato Famine in Ireland from 1845 to 1849—these are only a few *episodes* in the long-running tale of mass murder that was European colonialism in Africa, Asia, and Latin America, and even in Europe.

Nonetheless, it would be disrespectful to the truth to assert with confidence that the missionaries or, indeed, the colonial authorities they sometimes served and sometimes countered always failed to fulfill the humanitarian imperative they had set themselves, or that this imperative was pure pretext. The record is mixed. Abolitionism was a great cause, and it is by no means clear that it would have been successful without the ships of the Royal Navy or the guns of the French foreign legion. Nor was it simply rhetoric on the part of missionary leaders like Cardinal Charles Lavigerie, founder of the order of the White Fathers (Society of Missionaries of Africa) that long dominated the educational and medical structures of the Congo,

Rwanda, and Burundi, when he insisted that participating in the war against slavery was a Christian duty.

Even beyond the abolition of slavery, the "humanitarian" accomplishments of European colonialism were undeniable. Anyone doubting this has only to look at the career and accomplishments of the French colonial physician Eugene Jamot. Jamot was a military doctor in the French colonial forces in West Africa. All but single-handedly, he created a mobile medical unit that succeeded in mitigating for the first time the ravaging effects of a number of major tropical diseases, notably sleeping sickness. His most famous utterance was, "I will awaken Africa!" and to the end of his life he remained true to this apparently disinterested project. And Jamot, though he was a particularly romantic figure, a sort of T. E. Lawrence of tropical medicine, was anything but unique. The American military doctors who attempted to stamp out yellow fever in Panama are another example of the colonialist as successful humanitarian. Politically correct or not, it is simply a fact that one of the principal ways European colonialists saw themselves was as healers. In a letter, Marshal Lyautey, the French colonial governor of Morocco, boasted: "My doctor has undertaken . . . to systematically cure the diseases that for so long have corrupted this people."

For the missionaries themselves, at least for the most committed and serious among them, propagating the faith involved looking after and struggling to improve the material conditions in which those they sought to convert lived. This kind of unswerving vocation endured until well after the decolonization of Africa. One has only to think of the emblematic figure of Dr. Albert Schweitzer, playing his organ and tending the sick in his bush hospital in Lambaréné in French Equatorial Africa, who was treated as a secular saint in the West until his death in 1965. Schweitzer's self-abnegation and his devotion to his patients seemed to exemplify the humanitarian enterprise at its purest. In practical terms, all the elements of the contemporary humanitarian enterprise—tending to the sick, improving sanitation and housing, and upgrading education—were fundamental to the enterprise of European missionaries in Asia, Africa, the Middle East, and Latin America. So was the perception that the success of this humanitarian mission depended on securing the support of European public opinion, which Lavigerie called "the queen of the world today."

The necessity of securing public consent for the imperial enterprise is one of the fundamental differences between nineteenth-century imperialism and all the variants of conquest that had been undertaken previously. And again, the role of what was then called humanitarianism was essential in helping provide the justification European colonialist politicians needed to offer to their citizens (and, probably, to themselves as well) for the project of conquest. Speaking of the necessity of colonization, the French politician Jules Ferry insisted that "the superior races have a right [to subjugate others] because they have a duty as well. That duty is to civilize the inferior races." And that duty was largely construed, throughout the latter part of the nineteenth century until decolonization in the 1960s, as humanitarian and, more broadly, reforming in nature.

In reality, the nineteenth-century colonial picture is terribly muddled. Racist presuppositions coexisted in Europe, and later in the United States, with an emancipatory humanitarianism with which they could never entirely be reconciled. The great philosophers of the Enlightenment, from Condorcet to the framers of the American Constitution to Kant, were united in believing every human being (or at least every male) had individual and inalienable rights. Because of this, they imagined what the Abbé de Saint-Pierre and later Kant called an international community that, if it could be realized, would lead to a world of perpetual peace. But this idea of humanity, when it did not actually imply revolution, at least presupposed a commitment by the fortunate to improving the situation of the less fortunate and those in pain or in need. It was not exactly charity, in the traditional Christian and fatalistic sense, because Christian charity did not imply equalizing the condition of different people, only of alleviating the pain of those worst off. But in the Enlightenment conception, the task for human beings is to realize the human happiness of all. This is a fundamentally democratic moral vision, one that rejects the notion of the accidents of birth and station as fate. And it would eventually provide the moral and intellectual underpinnings of the contemporary humanitarian project.

From the beginning it was a project that was easily misused by governments as a pretext for their own political agendas. Repeatedly in the nineteenth century, from Greece in the 1820s, to the Crimea in the 1850s, to Lebanon in the 1860s, European powers used a humanitarian pretext to justify intervening militarily to support the Christian side in battles with either the Ottomans or local Muslim groups. The justification that there must be military intervention in some foreign country because innocents are suffering there did not begin with Somalia; it began with the Greek war of independence against the Turks, the cause that Lord Byron died for. In short, by the early nineteenth century the morality play of humanitarian intervention in which a victimized population must be rescued from the depredations of warlordism and tyranny was already well elaborated.

Such scenarios continued to rely for their moral force on the Enlightenment vision of a world that was constantly in the process of improvement, and in which no injustice was impossible to rectify, no technical problem impossible to solve, and no project of human betterment impossible to realize. The fact that this vision not only coexisted with colonialism but in many ways existed in a symbiotic relationship with it is only one of the many ironies that have accompanied the genesis of modern humanitarianism. Another, more alive today than many humanitarians like to admit, is an extrapolation from the reality that disease was often the product of ignorance, and that Europeans had a right, even an obligation, to "tutor" their colonial subjects until they had assimilated the benefits of science, reason, and (Western) civilization. In the modern construction, the core of the problem in the poor world is presented as a refusal to accept the verities of international law, democratic norms like free elections, and civil liberties, rather than, as the colonialists would have had it, of Western civilization and science.

The rhetorical similarities are striking. Contemporary conservatives see this clearly. As the writer Max Boot put it in his fine study of America's "small wars," "In the early twentieth century, Americans talked of spreading Anglo-Saxon civilization and taking up the 'white man's burden'; today they talk of spreading democracy and defending human rights." And at least some contemporary humanitarians have not shied away from making the connection between their efforts and Western values almost as explicitly as their nineteenth-century forebears would have done. For example, Bernard Kouchner, the French doctor and politician who was one of the founders of Médecins Sans Frontières (MSF) and remains a leading, if controversial, figure in contemporary humanitarianism, has spoken repeatedly of the "Western ideology of human rights."

Historically, he may well have been right to do so. But the assumption on the part of Kouchner and the many contemporary humanitarians who have adopted his vision of their enterprise that they have a "right" to intervene is too close to the old colonial norms to be viewed entirely independently from them or adduced as simply an artifact of the history of ideas. Again, this establishes nothing one way or the other about the rights and wrongs of such interventions. Perhaps humanitarian military intervention, undertaken by the

United Nations if possible, but by individual great powers if necessary, is, as Kouchner has insisted throughout his career, the only moral answer in certain crises. But Kouchner and other humanitarian activists who share his view behave as if the imperial assumptions that underlie such a conclusion are self-evidently of lesser concern than the need to act to deal with a particular emergency— emergency being one of the key ideas in this interventionist humanitarianism. In effect, they present aid as an enterprise beyond criticism, one on which the moral ambiguities of previous versions of European humanitarianism should have no bearing and serve as no cautionary admonition on the certainties of present-day practice.

Obviously, humanitarian idealism has taken many forms. The contemporary secular humanitarianism that we are all familiar with is based on private voluntary organizations—the so-called non-governmental organizations, or NGOs—and upon the United Nations system, above all agencies such as the Office of the United Nations High Commissioner for Refugees (UNHCR) and the World Food Programme (WFP). Before the UN's advent, the cornerstones of European humanitarianism were the missionaries and colonial medical officers on the one hand and the Red Cross movement on the other. Like humanitarianism today, humanitarianism in the era of imperialism was very much the product of its times. To say this is not to denigrate the almost mystical idealism or the dedication of nineteenth-century Christian and colonial humanitarians, let alone those of Henri Dunant, the Swiss businessman who, between 1859 and 1864, all but single-handedly brought the Red Cross into existence, and in doing so radically altered the laws that governed the conduct of war. But it is to insist that every concept of humanitarianism, like every concept of what it means to be fully human, has a history and, more important, a historical context that we ignore at our peril.

If colonial humanitarianism could trace its origins in Christian charity, the Red Cross idea, too, was rooted in earlier efforts to codify the laws of war, limit what soldiers could do on the battlefield, and define the protections that were to be afforded to noncombatants. Already, during the American Civil War, President Lincoln had commissioned Francis Lieber, a professor of law at Columbia University, to write a manual that would govern the conduct of the Union's forces. For their time these *Instructions for the Government of Armies of the United States in the Field* were a radical improvement on previous norms, for they established categories of so-called protected persons, that is, people whom soldiers could not target. But Dunant's brainchild, the Geneva Convention of 1864, which was signed by twelve European nations, was more radical still from a humanitarian point of view. (As has been the case with most international treaties since the founding of the Republic, the United States declined to sign it.) It not only began to delineate what was lawful and unlawful in war in terms that would bind states, but it created the International Committee of the Red Cross, a neutral band of volunteer medical staff who were granted the right to care for the wounded on the battlefield. Not by accident, the flag of this Swiss organization was a red cross on a white background, the Swiss flag reversed.

It would be hard to overstate the accomplishment—or, as Dunant or his successor Gustave Moynier, who was the real animating spirit of the Red Cross movement, would doubtless have put it, advance for humanity—that the acceptance of the Geneva Convention by most European powers and the founding of the ICRC represented. The Geneva Convention was born out of the compassion and sorrow one individual, Dunant, felt when he witnessed the Battle of Solférino in 1859. It was the astonishing and unexpected influence of Dunant's book, *A Memoir of Solférino*, that provided the springboard for all that followed, and the conference at Geneva succeeded in translating the reaction to the book into a body of law. Unlike the Lieber code, it was a multilateral convention. And it also established the legitimacy of a neutral third party on the battlefield—the aid givers.

At the same time, the Geneva Convention was far less radical than it might have appeared to be at first glance. As John F. Hutchinson, the historian of the Red Cross, has shown, the great European powers were already moving toward the conclusion that the sheer brutality of nineteenth-century war—the casualties that breech-loading rifles with their immensely increased volume of fire and the new and more lethal artillery pieces imposed—meant that the status quo with regard to the wounded could not be allowed to continue. The fact that the general public was now able to learn about the horrors of the battlefield through press reports relayed by telegraph was adduced as reason enough to take action. Hutchinson quotes a lecturer to Britain's Royal United Service Institution in 1866 as putting the matter as follows: "In former days, the general results of war were made public, the knowledge of personal circumstances was exceptional, and limited to a narrow sphere; now the personal are almost as widely known as the general results." The lecturer also alluded to "all the machinery for the rapid diffusion of intelligence and personal observation, which exists in our epoch."

It is the mid-nineteenth-century version of the idea of a CNN effect, in the sense of both the democratization of information and the press's growing habit of reporting the news anecdotally. Viewed from this perspective, the promulgation of the Geneva Convention and the creation of the ICRC, far from representing developments that were not in the interests of the great powers, represented the minimum possible response to new realities. As in the past, when the interests of humanitarian action and colonialism intersected, and as in the future, when humanitarianism would serve as a cover for the agendas of powerful states in crises from Bosnia to Afghanistan, the triumph of humanity represented by the signing of the Geneva Convention was a far more complicated event morally than is commonly assumed. The enthusiastic support the fledgling organization received from states was eloquent testimony to that. The realization gave Henri Dunant pause, but Gustave Moynier welcomed it wholeheartedly. As Moynier would later put it, providing wounded soldiers with decent care is "a duty of conscience and humanity, which, by a happy coincidence, harmonizes with the acknowledged interests of the belligerents."

Over the course of the succeeding decades, as the laws of war—or, as they came to be known, international humanitarian law—evolved and expanded, the ICRC became the legally recognized guardian of these regulations. And yet, the paradox of the success of the Red Cross movement, the advance of international law, and, after World War II, the worldwide diffusion of the concept of human rights and new authority for it, is that all of these developments coincide not with a new era in which Kant's perpetual peace was ushered in, but rather with the hideous course of the twentieth century itself. No century has had better norms and worse realities. In the period from the signing of the first Geneva Convention and the subsequent conferences of 1899 and 1907 in The Hague, to the outbreak of World War I, the rights of individuals in wartime were expanded, "aggressive force" was outlawed, and protections for civilians were expanded. Then came the mass slaughter in the trenches of World War I and the Armenian genocide to make a mockery of all that.

In the aftermath of that war, in a Europe shocked by the toll exacted by gas attacks, another Hague conference in 1925 outlawed the use of poison gas and other forms of chemical and biological warfare. Three years later, in 1928, the Kellogg-Briand Pact outlawed war itself. Those the gods wish to destroy they first allow to set international legal norms. Nine years later, the Japanese army was murdering Chinese civilians by the hundreds of thousands in the defenseless city of Nanking. Four years after that, the Germans put in motion the Final Solution. Four years after that, twenty million Russians were dead and Europe was in ruins.

It is sometimes argued by human rights activists and by the many contemporary humanitarian relief workers who have come to view their enterprise as inseparable from that of the human rights international that it was precisely as a consequence of these disasters, especially the Holocaust, that international humanitarian law and the global human rights revolution that followed on its heels finally came into their own. There is no question that the absolutist conception of national sovereignty that had governed international relations since the Treaty of Westphalia (1648), in which every state, while limited in what it could do internationally, was declared free to do as it pleased to its own citizens, was utterly discredited by the experience of Nazism. Michael Ignatieff is quite right when he says that "the human rights instruments created after 1945 were not a triumphant expression of European imperial self-confidence but a war-weary generation's reflection on European nihilism and its consequences . . . part of a wider reordering of the normative order of postwar international relations, designed to create firewalls against barbarism."

But the reality is that while post–World War II documents like the Universal Declaration of Human Rights, the Genocide Convention, and the four Geneva Conventions of 1949 transformed both international law and the normative bases of international relations, the murderous twentieth century remained just as murderous. In other words, every state paid lip service to the new norms, but when those who had the power to kill thought it was time to start killing, these laws and conventions saved not a single life. As the British jurist Sir Henry Maine had pointed out in the middle of the nineteenth century, it was war and not peace that was the norm in human history. And what the second half of the twentieth century demonstrated was that while international law might have grown more humane and well-intended, it had not grown any more effective. The Cambodian killing fields and the genocidal wars of "ethnic cleansing" in the aftermath of the Cold War proved that. From Burundi to Sierra Leone to Afghanistan, the world remained the slaughterhouse that it had been since Neolithic times.

The sole exception was Western Europe after World War II, in which, at least once the bloody wars of decolonization had ended, Kant's perpetual peace really did seem likely to reign supreme and unchallenged. "He does not know war," went an old saying in the British army, "who has not fought the Germans." That bitter assertion, so self-evident in its time, makes no sense today. It is all but inconceivable that Germany, its militarism cauterized by the experience of Nazism, will ever go to war again except as part of a European Union or United Nations mission. And even the British, who retain at least some of their ancient bellicosity, increasingly justify the need to maintain credible armed forces with the argument that those forces will be called upon to participate in imperative humanitarian military interventions. When the war in Afghanistan began in October 2001, Admiral Sir Michael Boyce, head of the British Defence Staff, appeared in front of a photomontage meant to extol the virtues of Britain's military. The image was ostentatiously multicultural, with a Gurkha soldier in the foreground and another soldier, white, holding a little black girl by the hand. It was a pose that was familiar. But it was not a military pose; rather, it was the kind of image humanitarian agencies put in their appeals—the caring white adult looking after the bereft, needy black child. And as if to confirm this conflation of humanitarian and martial visual referents, the photomontage bore the legend "A Force for Good."

In reality, the British army remains an extremely efficient dispenser of organized violence. But one would never have known this from the images in which it chose to swathe itself at the beginning of the Afghan campaign. They were testimony to the triumph, in Europe anyway, of the norms Ignatieff has explicated so eloquently. To him, and those who think like him, there is no necessary reason why these new European realities cannot be institutionalized across the world just as the new norms have garnered global acquiescence. But in fact there are plenty of reasons. If indeed Western Europe has become a kind of Switzerland writ large, a place where war never interrupted business and it was safe to dream utopian dreams undisturbed by the sound of cannon fire or fighter-bombers shrieking across the sky, that is at least partly because Western Europe has already *had* its wars of religion, its genocides, its "ethnic cleansing"—year after year, century after century. The process of state formation has been accomplished; indeed, each individual national project among the EU countries is in the process of being superseded by the European Union, the most massive ceding of power by nation-states to a supranational institution in history.

Contrast such realities with those of Africa. The nations of sub-Saharan Africa are weakened by colonial boundaries that make little historical or ethnic sense. There are elites that are at best unresponsive to their populations' needs, and often actively harmful; rising vectors of poverty, disease, and illiteracy; and virtual exclusion from the new global economy. At best, the process of state formation is only now beginning in earnest. And yet so Eurocentric is the humanitarian and human rights perspective that it is somehow imagined that these agonizing processes can take place without violence, thanks to the worldwide diffusion of human rights norms.

One has only to put the matter in the context of American or European history to see how empty such hopes really are. Imagine—to expand on a fable William Shawcross developed in his book on UN peacekeeping, *Deliver Us from Evil*—that during the American Civil War a group of Martian human rights lawyers had arrived to insist that there was a better way to settle the differences over the Union and over slavery than war, or that a group of humanitarians had demanded that the fighting stop because too many young men were being slaughtered and too many civilians were being displaced and forced to live in dire conditions. Partisans of the Union and of the Confederacy would surely have argued that they had tried other methods and failed. I will not try to play ventriloquist for the Southern cause. But I will insist that a partisan of the Union would have had every moral right in the world to assert that what was taking place was not a humanitarian crisis, but a just war—one in which the humanitarian imperative had to be subordinated to the destruction of the Southern slave-holding state. After the war was over, there would be time for mercy.

In his Second Inaugural, Abraham Lincoln stated this with more intellectual rigor and more humanity than are to be found in any of the pious speeches of UN officials or contemporary humanitarians. As the classical humanitarians had done, Lincoln understood that war was sometimes inevitable, and always terrible. As a result, he did not delude himself with the idea that the highest morality would always be humanitarian. Nor did he think justice was humanitarianism and humanitarianism justice, which has been the cardinal error of post–Cold War humanitarianism. This is how Lincoln put it: "With malice toward none, with charity for all, with firmness in the right as God gives us to see the right, let us strive on to finish the work we are in, to bind up the nation's wounds, to care for him who shall have borne the battle and for his widow and for his orphan, to do all which may achieve and cherish a just and lasting peace among ourselves and with all nations." He did not say caring *is* the battle, nor that the work of winning the war was the same as the work of binding up the nation's wounds. He did not say it because it was not true in 1865, just as it is not true in 2002, whatever relief agencies may like to claim.

Obviously, not all wars are just wars. But all wars have causes. They are not humanitarian emergencies, and to describe them in this way is to distort both their reality and their significance. Rony Brauman of MSF once remarked bitterly that if Auschwitz were taking place today, he feared that both humanitarians and the mass media would choose to describe it as a humanitarian crisis. The rhetoric of the humanitarian movement—at least as it is transmitted through fund-raising appeals and the mass media, in which political and humanitarian emergencies are so easily confused—is as troubling as the rhetoric of the human rights international, in which crime and war are so easily conflated. For the humanitarian movement, the morality play is one of predators and victims to whom the humanitarians need the same unfettered access that the ICRC, from its inception, demanded to have to the wounded on the battlefield. For the human rights international, the canonical account is one of criminals and criminal justice, as if the political context in which a Slobodan Milosevic could arouse the Serbs was less important than the fact that he was guilty, as an individual, of certain war crimes.

In both cases, there is the pretense that somehow it is possible to stay outside politics. What is usually meant by outside, of course, really is above, as if a real revolution of moral concern could not be political. The rationale is easy to discern. As long as the debate is restricted to one about what the laws are, and what they should be, the moral high ground is easy to hold. The law is the law, after all. But once political arguments have to be advanced and defended, things become less cut-and-dried. It is such a saving idea, the law. The problem is that taking refuge in saving ideas rarely ends up saving anyone. To negotiate the terrain between norms and facts, there is only politics. Yes, it is a poor light, as Locke said of reason, but it is the only light we have.

But given humanitarianism's roots in the ideas of charity and philanthropy, and its history of functioning as an adjunct to imperial domination, more traditional humanitarians have had a difficult time coming to terms with the idea of a politicized version of their enterprise. In contrast, modern humanitarianism has been marked from its inception by an infatuation with and reliance upon the law, regardless of whether the statute in question was that of the colonial authority or that of an international convention. In the case of the International Committee of the Red Cross, this has led to an obsession with mandates and a fear, even on the part of relief officials whose courage and originality in the field are extraordinary, of exceeding them. The particular mandate of the organization becomes fetishized, even at the expense of both political reality and commonsense morality.

Famously, the worst example of this kind of blindness was the ICRC's conduct in Nazi-occupied Europe. Although the organization learned of the use of gas chambers in Auschwitz in 1942, it kept silent. There were a number of reasons for its decision, including some that were quite parochial. Since the ICRC was an organization dominated by the Swiss elite and viewed internationally as a Swiss institution (as, to a large extent, it remains to this day), its leaders were reluctant to take a step that would bring the anger of the Germans down on their country. Anti-Semitism undoubtedly also played a role. But the most important reason was institutional: the ICRC's main work in occupied Europe was assisting prisoners of war. The organization feared that, were it to reveal what it knew about the extermination of the Jews, the German authorities would no longer allow it to continue its work. The ICRC reasoned that nothing it said would prevent the gas chambers from continuing in operation, while, if it spoke out, the undoubted good it was doing would be curtailed. As a result, to its eternal shame, it kept silent.

The ICRC's conduct was particularly shocking because the organization had condemned the use of poison gas during World War I. As Rony Brauman put it, how could the ICRC have "condemned the use of poison gas used in combat against soldiers during the First World War and refused to do the same, during the Second, with regard to the use of gas for the extermination of civilians"?

It would be many decades before the ICRC began seriously to consider whether its acknowledged failure during World War II made it imperative to modify some of its operational norms. Indeed, it was the organization's apparent repetition during the Biafran war of 1967 of that same refusal to denounce the horrors about which it had information that gave birth to the contemporary incarnation of humanitarianism. Twenty years after Biafra, the humanitarian environment had been so radically transformed that the ICRC, which by then had also been obliged to start competing for funds with the new constellation of private relief organizations, was finally willing to think more seriously about the pitfalls as well as the advantages of neutrality and confidentiality. But to a large extent, this has remained a market-driven decision. In an environment where most humanitarian NGOs have embraced human rights as one of their operating principles, the ICRC was all but obliged to change.

To be sure, even in the immediate aftermath of World War II the ICRC was no longer the only humanitarian agency operating in the field. A few secular humanitarian agencies had already begun operating after World War I. The most notable among these was the Save the Children Fund (SCF), which was founded in Britain in 1919 with the goal of helping feed the many children then thought to be at the brink of starvation throughout the former Austro-Hungarian empire. SCF, which now has branches in a number of other countries, remains one of the most coherent and effective aid agencies in the world, in large measure because, unlike the ICRC, it has been able to combine moral outspokenness with the restricted mandate of dealing almost exclusively with issues regarding children.

And yet even in this exemplary case of one of the most effective relief NGOs in the world, the seeds of a humanitarian mythology whose destructive potential would be exposed in the crises of the 1990s were being sown. The premise of Save the Children that its function was morally unambiguous and authoritative (in the sense of taking precedence over other, nonhumanitarian priorities) made sense only if the agency was committed to helping the innocent alone. Here is SCF's official account of its founding: "At the end of the First World War a brave group of volunteers in Britain spoke out against injustice to children in Germany and Austria. They believed that these children were being punished for their leaders' part in the First World War."

Doubtless this is correct. But imagine that Save the Children had instead been called "Save the People." It would have been impossible to claim that none of the adults in need in Central Europe bore any responsibility for the war. To the contrary, most males would have fought in it, and many, as the mass following for Nazism in these countries would subsequently reveal, would have continued it had they not been defeated on the battlefield. The agency's mandate of "helping children in emergencies" may be morally uncomplicated. But relief is not. It was morally ambiguous in the heyday of nineteenth-century European colonialism, it was morally ambiguous in 1919, it was morally ambiguous in Biafra in 1967, and it has been just as morally ambiguous in the aftermath of the Cold War.

There are, in fact, striking similarities between the relief efforts undertaken in the immediate aftermath of World War I with the sanction of the great powers and those underwritten by the American government and the European Union and sometimes backed up by NATO troops that would become more and more the norm in the 1990s. The most important and effective of these was undertaken by the U.S. government and run by a future president, Herbert Hoover, to feed the starving in Russia. Once it had run its course, this initiative left no immediate institutional successor, but it did set the stage for what would become the pattern in American humanitarianism—the close link between the American NGOs and Washington. Indeed, the difficulty of knowing where Hoover's American Relief Committee (ARC) ended and the U.S. government began would find its echo during the Cold War, when groups such as the International Rescue Committee (IRC), CARE, and others were seen as being in effect the humanitarian arm of America's anti-Soviet struggle. The IRC, in particular, functioned almost as an official body in this period, when it was notable for its work with Hungarian refugees in the aftermath of the failed 1956 rebellion and with Cuban refugees in the aftermath of Fidel Castro's victory in 1959.

"IRCIA" was the way some European aid workers referred to the group. However, the IRC had begun as the effort of a few utterly committed American anti-Nazis to rescue Jews from the south of France during the period before the Germans took over the so-called free zone in 1942. Many of the most celebrated Jewish refugees got to America thanks to the heroic work of the IRC's first leader, Varian Fry. But this extraordinary campaign of rescuing intellectual, artistic, and scientific luminaries and their families was quite different from the kind of massive refugee and relief efforts the IRC would engage in after 1945.

Whatever the transformations to come in the goals, norms, and

moral ambitions of humanitarian action, World War II and its immediate aftermath was in fact the cradle of many of the leading
mainstream humanitarian groups, both secular and faith-based.
Most were started to provide relief in Europe. In the United States,
they included Catholic Relief Services (CRS), the evangelical World
Vision, the IRC, and CARE (whose name originally stood for Cooperative for American Remittances in Europe). In wartime Britain,
Oxfam, another group that now plays a central role in contemporary
humanitarian action, was founded in 1942. The acronym stands for
Oxford Committee for Famine Relief, and the organization's history
of confrontation with its own government provides a revealing coun-
terpoint, emblematic of the British humanitarian tradition generally,
to the American tradition of collaboration with government.

Oxfam was founded by Quakers and made up largely of students
and dons, including the classicist Gilbert Murray. They banded together because they were horrified by the humanitarian consequences of an action the Churchill government had taken as part of
its total war against the Germans. In the winter of 1941–1942, the
Royal Navy had mounted a blockade of Greece. It is estimated that
between November and February, 100,000 to 250,000 people in the
city of Athens died of hunger as a result of this blockade—far more
than were killed in the firebombing of Dresden. At the height of
the catastrophe, it is thought, 2,000 children died every day. What
the exact figures are will never be known. Oxfam mounted a furious campaign to persuade the British government to allow it to
send food supplies through the picket line of Royal Navy ships to
Greece, where it would be distributed through the Red Cross. It was,
understandably enough, an extremely unpopular stance, and at first
Churchill insisted that the war had to be won even if it meant the
death of innocent Greek civilians. Astonishingly, given that this was
the same period when Churchill had authorized experiments with

anthrax bombs for possible use on the Germans, Oxfam succeeded, the government relented, and eventually the food shipments were allowed through.

In the 1950s, while American aid agencies were becoming increasingly governmental, British groups like Oxfam and Save the Children were shifting their focus from humanitarian relief to Third World development. Given their ideological stance, this was hardly surprising. The connections between Oxfam and the antinuclear and anti-American Committee for Nuclear Disarmament (CND) in the 1950s and early 1960s were pervasive. And Oxfam increasingly saw its role as supporting liberation movements across the postcolonial world. Indeed, the organization's motto soon became (and remains): "Oxfam: Working for a Fairer World." Whether this ideology can continue to sustain itself is another matter. Tony Vaux, the coordinator of Oxfam's global emergency programs during the 1980s, both confirmed the original inspiration of many drawn to Oxfam's worldview and offered a caution when he wrote, "The socialist ideology of the 1960s and 1970s no longer offers significant numbers of people a philosophical basis for their relationship with the world's poor and suffering peoples."

As the American humanitarian NGOs became more deeply involved in the Cold War as adjuncts to their government, British NGOs, and later the Scandinavian governments and the quasi-official aid and development organizations they underwrote, increasingly acted from a desire to support various liberation struggles and insurgent governments as much as to undertake specific aid projects. An unintended consequence of this was that the field of humanitarian action in the narrow sense again became largely the property of the ICRC. By the time Biafra seceded from Nigeria in 1967, the ICRC was able to deploy far greater resources than Oxfam or the various faith-based relief groups that were also involved. Even so, the

ICRC was obliged to recruit outside doctors to join its effort. Many of them were young Frenchmen, some barely out of medical school, some still medical students. They included Bernard Kouchner himself, Patrick Aeberhard, and Max Recamier. But the French Doctors, as they came to be called, were hardly alone. Many of the most influential North American and British and Irish aid workers of the past thirty years, including Aengus Finucane, the founder of the Irish group Concern, and the late Frederick Cuny, perhaps the most admired American aid worker of his generation, also got their start during the Biafran war.

The ICRC expected its volunteers to adhere to the same code of conduct that bound its own delegates. When he arrived in Geneva before going on to Africa, Kouchner, like the other French volunteers, was expected, as part of the terms of his employment, to sign a statement in which he swore to "hold [himself] to the highest standard of discretion and notably to refrain, without prior authorization from the ICRC, from all communications about and all commentaries on [his] mission, even after its termination, as well as on any conclusions or information, whether direct or indirect, that might have come to [his] attention during it."

The basis for demanding this degree of self-censorship was the ICRC's conviction that its credibility as an institution depended not just on a strict neutrality but on even stricter discretion. It was, twenty-three years after the liberation of Auschwitz, exactly the approach the organization had relied upon in its work in Nazi-occupied Europe. For Kouchner, who was haunted by the memory of the Shoah, the shock at discovering in Biafra what he believed was another genocide, this time at the hands of the Nigerian government against the Ibo people who had joined the secession, was overwhelming. History, it seemed, was repeating itself, with the ICRC playing the same shameful role it had played in 1942. For Kouchner and his fellow doctors, this belief was confirmed by the dire reports they were getting from Oxfam officials on the ground in Biafra and from other aid workers, such as Aengus Finucane of Concern. Eventually, Kouchner broke publicly with the ICRC. As he recalled afterward, "By keeping silent, we doctors were accomplices in the systematic massacre of a population."

After Kouchner returned to France, he and his colleagues soon began thinking about a new humanitarian organization, one that would combine medical competence with the willingness to testify to what its volunteers saw if there was a moral imperative to do so. At first Kouchner flirted with the idea of an international medical corps that could be used in emergencies by governments or by the United Nations. But in 1971, Médecins Sans Frontières (MSF) was founded—Protestant schismatics to the ICRC's One Church, Holy and Universal—as an independent relief organization. MSF would go on to become the most important humanitarian NGO in the world. Its medical protocols have become the model for other relief organizations, and it is both envied and resented by other groups. It is, in an important sense, the conscience of the humanitarian world. For all its self-confidence (some, even within MSF, would say arrogance), it is constantly reexamining its criteria in terms of both its moral and its operational presuppositions, refusing to conform and play the obedient member of "the humanitarian community," and attempting to chart new directions for humanitarian action.

The irony is that while the existence of MSF has undoubtedly made the world a better place, in retrospect the proximate reasons for its foundation, and for Kouchner's break with the ICRC, are nowhere near as morally unimpeachable as they seemed at the time. For it is not clear that there was a genocide in Biafra. To be sure, that there was one was an article of faith with Oxfam at the time. That group's ad campaign in Britain included such incendiary claims as that "the price for a united Nigeria is likely to be millions of lives." Such exaggerations did Oxfam no harm, for one of the more startling facts about humanitarian NGOs is that, unlike, say, companies advertising their products, or, indeed, politicians, they can make any claim they wish, and retract or not retract the false ones as they see fit. In retrospect, Tony Vaux at least admits, rather half-heartedly, "the truth beyond the Biafra famine proved murky. The secessionists had used a public relations company to exaggerate the suffering."

And yet clearly it wasn't only the Biafrans who profited from such distortions. As Vaux puts it, unapologetically, "In the 1960s, the spread of TV brought the emotional impact of humanitarian disaster directly into people's homes. Oxfam rose to national prominence during the Biafra war, which was the first humanitarian disaster to be seen by millions of people and also the first to be the subject of systematic distortion."

It is almost as if Vaux can't decide whether he is pleased or sorry about the fact that Oxfam's rise to prominence was the result of this distortion. After all, if there was no famine in Biafra then the emotional impact to which Vaux alludes was a species of fraud. Although he insists that Oxfam drew appropriate conclusions from this "bitter lesson," the logic of Vaux's argument suggests that it is more important that people care about humanitarian disasters than that they be given the correct information about a particular disaster.

Unlike Vaux, Aengus Finucane seems unambivalent about the role he played, though he, too, admits, thirty years after the fact, that "the Biafrans fought a good propaganda war." But his reminiscence, like Vaux's, drives home the point of the strange symbiotic relationship between humanitarian aid workers and the Western media. "In Biafra," Finucane writes, "the many NGOs involved learned the usefulness of the media, a lesson that has stood them in good stead in winning support for their work ever since. The response to Biafra demonstrated that people do care; obtaining support is a question of getting the message to them."

In the humanitarian world, Bernard Kouchner, for all his ac-knowledged virtues and charisma, has long had a well-deserved rep-utation for being publicity-crazy. But it is hard to imagine even Kouchner putting the matter in anything like such instrumental terms. It is comments like Finucane's that have led so many critics of the aid agencies, notably Alex de Waal and the American writer Michael Marren, to insist that in order to understand the humani-tarian NGOs it is first necessary to acknowledge the depth of their commitment to defending their own institutional interests, as well as the degree to which that commitment influences the way they conceive of providing help to people in need. This question of the de-gree to which, in crisis after crisis, humanitarian groups have proved unable to distinguish, even in private, between these interests and the interests of those they are pledged to serve is one of the great is-sues in contemporary humanitarianism. So, more broadly, is the question of whether the irony that the founding moral gesture of MSF—the break with the ICRC over whether or not to speak out over Biafra—was based on a misunderstanding is just a historical curiosity, or whether it is an emblem of moral overreach, or even hubris, to which humanitarian agencies have succumbed again and again.

For Biafra was hardly the last time the NGOs got a crisis wrong. The mistakes of analysis, of political understanding, and of moral discernment made by groups such as Oxfam and MSF, not to men-tion by UN agencies such as the UNHCR or the World Food Pro-gramme, have tended to recapitulate one another, time after time after time. This led Fiona Terry, who was one of the founders of

MSF's Australian section and has written some of the most penetrating analyses of the paradoxes of relief work from the inside, to ask whether humanitarianism was not "doomed to repeat" its errors.

To insist on this point is not to condemn the NGOs. When all is said and done, humanitarianism is an impossible enterprise. Here is a saving idea that, in the end, cannot save but can only alleviate. Every humanitarian knows this. For there are, as Sadako Ogata, the former head of UNHCR, put it, "no humanitarian solutions to humanitarian problems." More than that, the pressures on humanitarian workers, whether they belong to private relief groups or UN agencies, have become all but intolerable. The prestige of the humanitarian movement and the humanitarian ideal has meant that almost everything became susceptible to being described as a humanitarian emergency, a humanitarian dilemma, or, with increasing frequency, as an occasion for humanitarian intervention. If this is not quite the same as saying "Take up the White Man's Burden," it is equally categorical and unself-conscious. This time, the battle cry seems to be, "Take up the humanitarian's burden," with that fictitious entity "the international community" taking the place of the nineteenth-century colonial power.

This explains Rony Brauman's bitter remark that if Auschwitz occurred today it would be described as a humanitarian crisis. The problem is that while humanitarians may understand perfectly well that it was not, they must deal with the crises they now face, most of which are no more humanitarian at their root than the Nazi death camps were, with only the tools of humanitarianism at their disposal. And those tools are not only almost always radically insufficient to the tasks at hand, but are often the wrong tools. Worse still, the task at hand, however urgent, may not be the most important task. Or it may be an impossible one, as relief workers themselves have increasingly emphasized publicly. But the problem begins with the words themselves. By calling some terrible historical event a humanitarian crisis, it is almost inevitable that all the fundamental questions of politics, of culture, history, and morality without which the crisis can never be properly understood will be avoided. And the danger is that all that will remain is the familiar morality play of victims in need and aid workers who stand ready to help if their passage can be secured and their safety maintained.

It would be one thing if humanitarians could bear to tell, or if the general public in Western Europe and North America could bear to hear, the truth—that the actual practice of humanitarianism is not at the center of any new international order but at its margin, and that by elevating humanitarianism in the way that it has been elevated, we delude ourselves into thinking the answer to the world's horror lies within our grasp, when the fact is that it does not. That reality is clear to anyone who watches the evening news. There is no letup in the horror, no shining new order in which refugees are treated properly and victims of war get shelter, medical care, and food. But perhaps that is too much bad news to assimilate fully. Better to say we have good intentions, we care, we want to help, and to persuade ourselves that our good wishes are sooner or later going to be transformed into good outcomes. Thus do the ambitions of relief workers (many of whom know better), the realities of what emotions seem to have to be produced in the general public in the West in order for humanitarian groups to raise funds, and the hubristic sentimentality of the West in the aftermath of the Cold War come together.

As one UN official in eastern Congo put it to me in 1998, "Humanitarian assistance has become the paradigm for North-South relations in the post–Cold War period." He said it firmly, resignation etched into his expression. But there was no doubt in his voice. He may well have been right. Perhaps this *is* the best we can do. Later, he would confide to me, "Humanitarian agencies know perfectly well that the international community doesn't really care." He was right, at least in the practical sense that Western governments were not then willing, and gave no sign that they would ever be, to do what would have been necessary to achieve lasting change in the lives of people in the poor world. Throughout the 1990s, as crisis after crisis and episode after episode of mass murder wracked the Balkans, sub-Saharan Africa, and parts of Asia, the triumphalist rhetoric about a new humanitarian order became more and more the norm in Western official circles, the United Nations, the World Bank, and the relief organizations. And yet the money that governments were willing to budget for aid to the poor world declined steadily even as the rhetorical obeisances to new paradigms and new commitments grew more florid and exuberant.

Still, it is hardly surprising, given the claims that have been advanced for it, that humanitarianism has ended up serving as a kind of moral Rorschach blot for the Western media and, through them, the public at large. We discern in it what we have come looking for, and its plasticity as a concept consoles us. There is the humanitarian as noble caregiver, as dupe of power, as designated conscience, as revolutionary, as colonialist, as businessman, and perhaps even as mirror. There is humanitarianism as caring, as in Rwanda; humanitarianism as emancipation, as in Afghanistan after the fall of the Taliban; humanitarianism as liberation, as in the case of humanitarian support for the rebels of southern Sudan; and humanitarianism as counterinsurgency, as it was in Vietnam and may yet be again in Afghanistan. All are possible; all have been true at times over the course of the past four decades. What is clear, perhaps as never before, or at least not since the foundation of MSF in the aftermath of the Biafra war, is not only that the future of humanitarianism is up for grabs, but that this confusion of roles has become unsustainable. Serious humanitarians will have to choose. And whatever choice they make, the removal of that sense of limitless redemptive possibility that humanitarianism at its high-water mark seemed to incarnate will diminish not just relief workers themselves, but all of us.

Perhaps this is the fate that must await all master ideas. Perhaps it *should* be the fate of such ideas, whether they be Communism, or globalization, or civil society, or human rights, or humanitarianism. Nevertheless, if we are indeed witnessing the drowning of this good idea in its own contradictions, humanitarianism's passing will be a great loss. That is why so many decent people hesitate to criticize the humanitarian enterprise, just as they hesitate to criticize the United Nations. "It's the only UN we have," they say. "Let's instead work to make it better." Or, to put the same pious rationalization in the humanitarian context: "The humanitarians and the human rights workers are trying to do good. To criticize them is to give aid and comfort to the cynics and the heartless of this world, and aren't there enough of them already?"

As Sergio Vieira de Mello, former UN undersecretary-general for humanitarian affairs, once remarked, what is needed is *constructive* criticism. All the rest, he implied, is nihilism. Throughout his career de Mello has had the reputation of being more open to criticism and more willing to take seriously alternative visions of humanitarianism than most of his UN colleagues. But in the end, the best answer to such invitations to stop thinking critically, even about activities that accomplish as much good as humanitarianism, is Jean Baudrillard's great remark that "the only [real] nihilism is the pious analysis of events." Certainly, humanitarianism has had more than enough of that already.

CHAPTER 3

A Saving Idea

As with so many of the saving ideas that came before it, humanitarianism's ascent now seems both improbable and inevitable. How, in less than thirty years, could an ethos that, for all its grandeur and moral ambition, was initially realistic enough to understand that it could aspire to do little more than alleviate suffering have become the principal vehicle for the moral hopes of so many in the West? Humanitarianism is not a utopian doctrine, at least in the manner of, say, Communism, with its faith in history, class struggle, revolution, and violence. Nor is it reminiscent of the more recent "irrational exuberance" in which the dawn of a single global capitalist market was expected not simply to make some people prosperous but also to make great masses of them free, thus bringing about the end of history and the birth of a universal global culture. The fall of the Berlin Wall exposed the bankruptcy of the former, but the events of September 11, 2001, showed that the latter was even more chimerical. In contrast, humanitarianism is a hope for a disenchanted time. If it claims to redeem, it does so largely in the limited sense that in a world so disfigured by cruelty and want it intervenes to save a small proportion of those at risk of dying, and to give temporary shelter to a few of the many who so desperately need it.

To be sure, what the last thirty years should have taught us is that while individual utopias may lose their adherents, and be exposed as snares and delusions by events, or fade into insignificance, the longing for salvation is all but hardwired into Western culture. Whether this is regrettable or not is immaterial. We should have known even at the height of the greatest stock market bubble of all times, during the 1990s, that consumerism, buttressed by a bogus faith in "the end of history," and an equally far-fetched belief that the rising tide of globalization would eventually make the whole world prosperous, would not be enough to keep either the mind or the heart alive. For secular Western people, at least, utopia seems almost a metaphysical necessity. Without it, there is only the passage of time, the onrush of mortality. Marx wrote somewhere that people pose only problems they can resolve. He was wrong. The point of all utopian thinking is to claim one can resolve problems that one has no rational reason whatsoever for believing one has the key to.

Of course, this does not explain why the humanitarian ethos became the reigning utopia for well-intentioned people in the West during the last two decades of the twentieth century. Why did it come to dominate the imagination of so many people for whom the crises humanitarians went off to address were at best images refracted through the media or publicized by relief groups in advertisements and mass mailings? Yes, the tone of the reporting and, indeed, the publicity campaigns were almost invariably apocalyptic, and the apocalyptic sells. The fact is that although sometimes these dire predictions were correct, as they were in Somalia in 1991, too often they were not.

One has only to think of Biafra, or of the supposed famine that Oxfam wrongly insisted was taking place in Cambodia in the after-

math of the fall of the Khmer Rouge regime in 1979. What capti-
vated the popular imagination in the West was not the authoritative
quality of humanitarian information but the authoritative quality of
the humanitarians' moral ambitions. In this sense, the truth of what
relief workers said was never the key question in the rise of humanitarianism. One can rail at the humanitarian agencies, and insist
that they are far too ready, whether out of concern or institutional
self-interest or both, to believe that the worst is about to happen and
to publicize their belief. The record of every major relief group is replete with examples of this "charity-business" at its alarmist worst.
This does not, however, get us much nearer to understanding why
humanitarianism has become so central to the Western imagination.

Utopias are moral fables. Some, like Communism, have been
drenched in the fantasy of revolutionary violence as the midwife of
the radiant future. Others have promised paradise on the cheap.
Think of *The New York Times*'s Thomas Friedman, whose immensely
influential but intellectually vacant and provincial notions about
globalization were all the rage at the end of the 1990s. Friedman
seems to think that globalization—by which he means American-
ization—is both inevitable and the only road to prosperity, and will
therefore take place whether anyone wants it to or not. And yet the
strength of both the Communists and the globalizers, at least at their
respective high-water marks, was that they claimed both to be able to
explain everything about the world and to have the key for bringing
what was wrong in it to an end. In contrast, the humanitarian project, however smug it can sometimes be, not only is fundamentally
modest in what it believes it can accomplish, but, more important,
defines itself largely in negative terms. As Rony Brauman has put it,
humanitarianism asks the question, What is a human being? and
answers, "One who is not made to suffer."

That such a cautious hope could capture the imagination of the most ethically alert Europeans and Americans is unprecedented. Viewed from one angle, it is the perfect illustration of the moral downsizing of the Thatcherite 1990s. And yet perhaps, in the aftermath of the realization by the best people in the West that Communism had been just as evil as anti-Communists had claimed, the humanitarian version of utopia was all a chastened public was willing to be drawn into. And drawn they were. A poll taken in Catalonia at the height of the humanitarian intervention in Bosnia in the mid-1990s showed relief work to be the activity most admired by people between eighteen and twenty-five years old. This was a clear index of a view commonly held in Western Europe. To be sure, humanitarianism never achieved the kind of mass following in the United States that it did in Spain, France, Germany, and the Nordic countries. But even in America, the prestige of relief work increased rapidly, particularly in the aftermath of the Cold War.

Whether they were traumatized by the failure of Communism, as was the case with many on the European left, or, in a time of political disenchantment, simply in need of a place to put their utopian longings, many Westerners found in humanitarianism something deeply in tune with their reduced moral expectations. In the past the experience of an aroused conscience had often also been a revolutionary experience in the sense that it challenged the status quo. Utopianism was a political construct. But humanitarianism was antipolitical. It challenged no established order. Rather, it called upon that order to do more, and care more. This is not to underestimate what such doing and caring would involve. Were the rich countries really to commit to the kinds of mini–Marshall Plan and nonmilitary humanitarian intervention that are so desperately needed throughout the poor world, the change would be enormous. But the basic lineaments of the system would remain the same. And of course even to attempt such a change requires the spinning of moral fables and the mobilization of utopian feeling on a mass scale.

So what is the moral fable of humanitarianism? Perhaps the best statement of it comes from Michael Ignatieff. He, too, revels in his antipolitics; his is the voice of the caring branch of the status quo. In humanitarianism, he sees the Enlightenment's dream refurbished. And what accounts for this retrofit? Human rights activists, relief workers, and development specialists, along with the constituencies they have mobilized through the media. Organizations like UNHCR, the ICRC, the NGOs, in collaboration with the media, he writes, "seized upon new facts about the modern world that have changed the very scope of modern conscience." The media, he claims, "has broken down the compartments that used to restrict our moral concerns to our immediate family, neighborhood, province, or nation." At the same time, "the revolution in jet travel and the logistics of rapid deployment made us conscious, as we have never been before, that we *can* do something—and quickly—about the disasters we see on television." Finally, "we are aware, as never before, of the sheer size of the stockpile of unused resources in the West . . . that could be put to use in diminishing the horror of the world."

Ignatieff is not wrong, at least to the degree that this "we" includes a tiny minority of Western people, who are not just exposed to these new possibilities of viewing the charnel house of the poor world, but find themselves energized rather than demoralized by the sight. But the adulation that has been directed toward humanitarian action includes many more in the West than this small, saving remnant. More important, though, is the question that Ignatieff does not ask. He identifies humanitarianism as an emblem of the modern conscience energized and transformed for the better. He rightly insists that the modern conscience is now subject to new openings and new pressures. But he does not confront the possibility that humanitarianism—indeed, his entire revolution of moral concern—is also this modern conscience given an alibi—a way of feeling better about those parts of the world without some seemingly redemptive effort, to which no decent person, once informed, could possibly be reconciled. Far from being a story of unparalleled engagement, might not the real significance of the revolution of moral concern be that the modern conscience is thereby allowed to delegate its guilt and its anxiety to the designated consciences of the world of relief, development, and human rights?

To imagine that this is a powerful event, on the order of the rise of Communism, is to take one's wishes for reality. The people who devote their lives to caring about the suffering of others are few, the institutions that do so still fewer. To his credit, UN Secretary-General Kofi Annan is almost alone among world leaders in being constantly concerned about places such as southern Sudan, Aceh, and Honduras. But while he has moral authority, he has little real power. In contrast, political leaders who do have real power—the president of the United States, say, or of France—rarely focus on such issues unless they are pressured into doing so.

While an increasingly large number of people are glad that those designated consciences, from the UN secretary-general to the individual relief worker in the field, are out there, the caring that such knowledge—or media coverage of some scene of horror—engenders is both intermittent and largely sentimental. People want something done, and they don't want to believe that these terrible things will be allowed to go on. But they haven't the faintest idea of what to do in each individual crisis. Intervene? Yes, of course. But on whose side, to what end, for how long, and at what cost? On its own, the idea of humanitarianism answers none of these questions.

This is why, as utopias go, humanitarianism—even the kind of armed humanitarianism that leads to one of Ignatieff's and Secretary-General Annan's proposed recourses, humanitarian military intervention—is a weak prescription for the world's salvation. Humanitarian military intervention is something that can take place only very occasionally. It may be unfair that we intervene in Kosovo but not in Angola, or that we send a force to East Timor but not to Sri Lanka, but the reality is that any decision to be consistent would commit the world to war without end—war waged in the name not of politics but of humanitarian need. Instead of the old 1960s-era leftist cry of "One, two, three, many Vietnams"—or, to use an earlier example, the Trotskyist dream of permanent revolution—it would be permanent peacekeeping and "One, two, three, many Kosovos." It is because they believe this to be out of the question practically that UN officials working for Secretary-General Annan have been so sanguine about raising the issue of humanitarian intervention, and so determined to make it a new norm in international relations. Privately, they tell you there is no risk because the UN will never get an army of its own and the great powers will rarely commit their own troops except when they have a political as well as a moral interest in doing so.

There are some, notably Bernard Kouchner, who ardently proclaim the need for humanitarian intervention in as many places as possible. Kouchner's celebrated break with Médecins Sans Frontières (MSF), and his departure to found another relief group, Médecins du Monde (MDM), occurred after he lost a power struggle fought over the issue of his insistence that humanitarianism should conceive of itself as being in the service of states and at the heart of state policy. "It is not so much that humanitarians must learn to be political as that states must learn to be humanitarian," was the way he once described his approach. For Kouchner, humanitarianism, along with human rights, was indeed an emblem of a revolution of moral concern.

Those at MSF who opposed Kouchner, above all Claude Malhuret and Rony Brauman, insisted that humanitarian organizations need to guard their independence fiercely. For them, inevitably, the logic of state humanitarianism is, *in extremis* at least, a logic not just of intervention but of assimilation into the established order. Kouchner's vision was one of Western states alive to their moral obligations and willing to do battle, literally and figuratively, to relieve suffering, protect refugees, and advance the cause of human rights and justice. The right of intervention on humanitarian grounds, he once said, "is our next adventure against the oppressors." But for the partisans of humanitarian independence at MSF, Kouchner was either indulging in a species of wishful thinking that would endanger the humanitarian enterprise or, worse, attempting to make humanitarianism the servant of state power.

Kouchner lost the battle within MSF, but he seems largely to have carried the day in the wider debate over the future of humanitarianism. Reading the declarations of senior UN officials, Western politicians, and NGO representatives, it is easy to get the impression that this view has triumphed. In reality, the situation is more complicated. The great and the good of this world, from the UN to the main liberal foundations in Europe and the United States, to the European Union, may routinely pay lip service to this new humanitarian perspective. But their statements carry little weight. Everyone knows the score. British Prime Minister Tony Blair might make a series of grandiose moral claims for NATO's action in Kosovo, but once the Serbs had withdrawn, Blair did not immediately call for a new intervention in Sudan or Sri Lanka. His government's much trumpeted "moral" foreign policy had its limits. And, if anything, the Blair government was far more engaged with these ideas than most other Western governments during the same period.

In practice, post-Kosovo deployments were undertaken sparingly. The British did commit a small force to Sierra Leone the following year, but they restricted its mission sharply. The force would not be sent out into the bush systematically to defeat the rebels of the Revolutionary United Front. As for the other major interventions, they were more cautious still. After hideous slaughter by Indonesian forces and paramilitaries, the Australians did occupy East Timor. But they occupied it only *after* the permission of the Indonesian government had been secured, and even then only because they had an important national interest in doing so. In the Balkans, the Germans agreed to assume command of a small verification force in Macedonia—but only after NATO and European Union negotiators had brokered a peace agreement between the government in Skopje and the ethnic Albanian rebels.

This was not war, even as it had been waged in Kosovo. Anyone doubting this would be set right by the response of the United States and its allies to the attack on the World Trade Center. What has taken place in Afghanistan, limited as it has been by the standards of World War II or even Vietnam (really, it has been more of a punitive expedition than a war, despite the assertions of the Bush administration), is what happens when states wage war in the service of goals that they view as imperative. This fighting in Afghanistan revealed that there had been less than met the eye to the much trumpeted age of humanitarian intervention. It became clear there that military force would never be used unreservedly for purely altruistic purposes.

But that hardly exhausts the symbolic significance of the notion (as it is understood by Kouchner and the Italo-French legal scholar

Mario Bettati) that there is a "right to intervention" in humanitarian emergencies. To the contrary, at the most fundamental human and societal level, the notion accomplishes the difficult task of making us feel better about ourselves even when we have no moral right to do so. If we say our idea is to establish a new norm in international relations where we commit ourselves to doing something—the something in question revealingly kept as vague as possible—then the fact that we have not accomplished very much over the course of the past half century in stopping wars or mitigating humanitarian emergencies seems far less heartbreaking or shameful. The iconoclastic German Marxist Herbert Marcuse once quipped, "If the facts don't match the theory, so much the worse for the facts." The same cynical observation might be made about the enthusiasm for normsetting among Western liberals who often act as if, when the norms don't have anything to do with the reality, then, indeed, so much the worse for the reality.

The reality? The reality is that the new belief in the transformative power of the ideas of humanitarianism and human rights arose at the same time that the enormous hopes vested in the development of the poor world from the time of the foundation of the United Nations forward were quietly being abandoned. This was understandable. Unquestionably, the development enterprise has yielded meager results. Boosters at institutions such as the United Nations Development Programme may claim that, for all the problems, things are getting better, and even put their faith in the idea that "new technologies will lead to healthier lives, greater social freedoms, increased knowledge and more productive livelihoods." But the truth is that while there has been development, and some parts of the world, notably in East Asia, have grown prosperous thanks to new capitalist development, development *aid* has largely been a failure. Not only is there a lot of evidence all over the world of increased poverty, environmental despoliation, and inequality, but it now seems clear that, even when they do their jobs properly, development organizations do not have that much effect on poor countries one way or the other. Oxfam may be working for a fairer world, but it would be rather hard to make the case that this goal is any nearer today than it was thirty years ago.

In an extraordinary book called *The Egalitarian Moment,* Anthony Low delineates the failure of land reform across the poor world, in countries whose political systems ranged from traditionalist to capitalist to Communist, during the second half of the twentieth century. All efforts at reform, he writes, proved to be "little more than blinkings at an egalitarian mirage." The same could be said of the development aid that so often accompanied and at times was meant to abet these efforts at reform. For all the money spent, little was accomplished. It is not so much that the individual projects undertaken by development aid agencies were ill conceived, although many, if not most, were. Rather, at least in the neediest areas, above all sub-Saharan Africa, outside development aid did not undertake much of lasting value but did create an extraordinary culture of dependency on the part of the general population and corruption on the part of the elites.

The failure of the so-called development decades in the poor world, and the discrediting of the "Third Worldist" ideology that went with it, is anything but irrelevant to the rise of humanitarianism. Humanitarian action begins to capture the imagination of idealistic people in the West precisely at the moment when Third Worldism and developmentalism begin to lose their authority and prestige. This is not to assert that humanitarians thought of their actions in these Machiavellian terms, or were indeed cognizant of serving any other purpose than trying to fulfill the goal of caring for those in need to which they had pledged themselves. Nor is it to insist that to those who pioneered it, humanitarianism seemed like anything other than a new and less easily corruptible form not just of striving for a better world but of living decently in an indecent world. But when a doctrine as idealistic as humanitarianism gains the degree of acceptance that it has, in a world that has little tolerance for any idealism that may threaten the status quo in a serious way, the question that has to be asked is, What other purposes does humanitarianism serve?

The first and most obvious point to make is that the 1980s, now fondly remembered by many humanitarians as the golden age of their vocation—the time before all the contradictions of the humanitarian enterprise seemed to overwhelm them—was also the era of Margaret Thatcher and Ronald Reagan. It was an age of reaction against big government, one in which the political establishment came to believe that most state functions could be privatized. Indeed, it was an age in which the ability of government to accomplish anything was challenged by the most important political leaders. And it was the age in which Western governments began first to question, and then to repudiate, many of their commitments to bilateral aid for development in their former colonies.

In development, Thatcherism uncovered almost a dream target. Bureaucratic ineptitude, poor planning, paternalism, financial mismanagement, a lack of any system of accountability, and a smug, self-regarding, and self-perpetuating culture had by then become the hallmarks of the development enterprise in the poor world. The writer Graham Hancock, who was anything but a Thatcherite, could refer in his book *The Lords of Poverty* to "a group of rich and powerful bureaucracies that have hijacked our kindness." He might have added that, having hijacked it, the overseers of official development aid had then made a shambles of what they had tried to monopolize.

At least with regard to development, the Thatcherite case was easy to make. (The privatization of such institutions as the railroads or, as we learned after September 11, 2001, of security at airports, was a different matter entirely.) Today, even most development experts will concede the point. It appeared that only in those parts of the world where private investment rather than government-to-government aid was the order of the day were there signs of any real development. There were, to be sure, realities that this dismissal of development aid swept under the rug. Much of it, after all, had been conditioned by both the United States and its allies and the Soviet Union on calculations of Cold War advantage. To cite two examples, USAID poured development aid into Mobutu's Zaire, as the Soviets did into Mohammad Siad Barre's Somalia, not because they believed the money would be used properly but because they wanted to reward client governments. Aid was a foreign policy tool—as certainly it had been in the era of the Marshall Plan in Europe—as much as it was an expression of generosity and solidarity. And since it is not only clear now, but was probably clear at the time, that the greatest challenge to development is not the lack of capital or of skills but government failure or misconduct, the development enterprise as constituted in the 1950s was probably doomed from the start, given its commitments to propping up the Mobutus and the Siad Barres of the world.

By the early 1980s, development aid came under attack both from conservatives and from liberals. The former saw it as statism run amok, while the latter simply could no longer defend a system that was not accomplishing much. As a result, there was little opposition outside the development aid bureaucracies themselves when official foreign aid budgets began to be cut. Instead, aid began to be channeled through nongovernmental organizations. The 1980s saw the start of the privatization of development aid specifically, and aid more generally. It is hardly surprising that in an era in which the dominant ethos was the repudiation of government, private agencies were thought to be more efficient, more accountable, and more appropriate conduits for the West's largesse.

With the exception of a few U.S. agencies, humanitarian relief groups did not see themselves as avatars of privatization. The political culture of European aid groups militated against such a perspective. The left-leaning idealism of an Oxfam, whose slogan, "Working for a Fairer World," summed up the activism of those committed to development aid at its best, was never going to be entirely reconcilable with such a conception. Nor was the reformulation of emergency relief work pioneered by Médecins Sans Frontières and its imitators. The difference was that Oxfam and other British agencies that shared its outlook until well into the mid-1980s, when Oxfam's failure during the Ethiopian famine forced it to reevaluate its position, had long ago come to the view that development was far more important than relief. The cliché that it was better to teach a man to fish than to give him a fish was, of course, grotesquely inappropriate to famine conditions. But Oxfam persevered in this view just the same. As Tony Vaux would recall, "The idea was revolution through development. This extraordinarily optimistic ideology . . . became so strong that aid agencies did not turn away from their developmentalist beliefs, even when poor people were suffering from the effects of famine." And Vaux is candid about the radical underpinnings of this view. "In its extreme form," he wrote, "the theory was that small development projects were going to thaw the inhuman hostility of the Cold War."

British humanitarianism, with its developmentalist bias, remained one expression of a broader tradition of left-leaning social reformism at least into the 1980s. In contrast, the founding generation of MSF, and the succeeding one, shared a common past in the hard left and in the student uprisings of 1968. For many of them, it had been the experience of the failure of May 1968 that had marked them most profoundly. As a result, they were far less interested in fighting Cold War battles, even from the "Third Way" perspective of the non-Communist British left. While, for example, Bernard Kouchner had been a militant Communist and Rony Brauman a Maoist, their move to humanitarianism was a move away from politics in the left-versus-right sense. As Brauman put it, "Humanitarian principles forbid one to [subordinate the way one thinks] of suffering to the context of history and of the political."

MSF did not make the same mistake in Ethiopia that Oxfam made. But then, its leaders had never seen their work as a vehicle for political change, or been disposed to sympathize with regimes that called themselves socialist. If anything, the reverse was true. For senior MSF officials, unlike many British aid workers for whom socialism remained an ideal, Marxism really was "the god that failed." The result was that in this, as in so many of its other approaches, despite having been founded as an alternative to the ICRC, MSF remained closer to the ethos that had informed the ICRC than to that of an Oxfam or a Save the Children. What Jean-Christophe Rufin, another major figure in MSF in its early days, said of Bernard Kouchner could be said of MSF's brand of humanitarianism generally, at least until the end of the 1980s. It managed to mobilize the until-then unutilized "energies of the demobilized militancy of the post–May 1968 period."

Brauman did not hesitate to acknowledge his debt to the left. "My first experience of collective action was political militancy," he wrote. But although this experience has certainly marked his actions, the hard certainties of the left of that era could not be further removed from the uncertainty and the recognition of contingency that distinguish Brauman's vision of humanitarianism. During his presidency of MSF, that conception of humanitarianism became the collective approach of the organization.

Stylistically, the generation of humanitarians who came out of the European left retained the same sense of urgency and moral self-righteousness (or self-confidence; it depended on one's point of view) that they had had as members of various political factions. Indeed, MSF's sense of its own importance was evidenced by the use of the term *en mission*, or going on a mission, which self-consciously echoed the language of Jesuit missions in the past. And at least some of them did undoubtedly see in humanitarianism another road to utopia, now that the road on the left had been closed. But theirs was a doctrine of contingency, not certainty; of limits, not boundless ambition—the triumph of the practical over the theoretical.

And what can be said of MSF specifically can also be applied more broadly to the Western public that became so infatuated with humanitarian aid. It was not just that development had been exposed as a dead end. The development enterprise, at least outside of Holland and Scandinavia (where it had become, by the late 1960s, almost the only way in which these countries could find a role on the international stage), had never commanded the kind of mass following that humanitarianism would come to enjoy by the end of the 1980s. The truth was starker. Except within the British humanitarian tradition—which, oddly enough, at least in the case of Oxfam, had begun as a practical response to famine, not a vehicle for political aspirations, before becoming suffused with romantic and credulous Third Worldism—it was Communism and Third Worldism that had been revealed (or, more accurately, revealed once more) to be gods that failed—malign wastes of hope.

MSF comes to prominence at almost the exact moment when

Aleksandr Solzhenitsyn's *The Gulag Archipelago* transforms the political debate in France. Many of the organization's most original and important leaders, notably Claude Malhuret, François Jean, and Rony Brauman, while continuing to work at MSF, also go on in the 1980s to found Liberty Without Borders, a sister organization with the goal of opposing totalitarian movements throughout the world. The connection between humanitarian work and an antitotalitarian perspective was probably almost unavoidable, given both the personal histories of the people involved and the long history of intellectual "fellow-traveling" with Communism among French intellectuals. In practical terms, not only are many of the leaders of MSF scarred ideologically by the revelations about the horrors of Communism, but they are directly shaped by public debates with the then still powerful French Communist Party.

Rony Brauman once partly accounted for MSF's extraordinarily efficient use of funds by pointing out that its enemies in the Communist Party would have seized upon any instance of financial malfeasance to discredit the fledgling humanitarian group. As it grew, MSF was in effect fighting two battles—the first for humanitarianism, the second against the conformist left. It has wanted to aid the victims, but has also been intent on publicizing, or, in its terms, testifying to, the plight of the Vietnamese boat people, the people of Cambodia under the Khmer Rouge, and of Ethiopia under the tyranny of the Marxist junta of Mengistu Haile Mariam.

This was the same period during which the German writer Hans Magnus Enzensberger, in a series of brilliant polemical essays, would attack head-on the kind of Third Worldism that continued to apologize for the Pol Pots and the Mengistus of the world. "We imposed upon the others [in the poor world]," he wrote, "what our own industrialized existence denied us, desires, promised lands, utopias . . . It is time to take leave of such dreams. It was always an illusion that liberation could be delegated to faraway others; today this self-deception has become a threadbare evasion."

And yet no matter how deep the disappointment, how pervasive the disenchantment, and how long overdue the reckoning with the horrors of Communism, the idea that the millenarian impulse could simply be phased out of people's hearts was never realistic. But to each time its utopianism, and whether willingly or unwillingly, the humanitarian utopia was one that did not seriously challenge the reigning preconceptions of the Reagan-Thatcher era. Indeed, in some ways humanitarian groups were exemplars of 1980s-style privatization. They were nongovernmental; they depended for their funding on what they could raise from governments, private donors, and individuals; they had no special legal status in the sense that, say, the ICRC did by virtue of its having been recognized by international treaty as the custodian of the Geneva Conventions; and their success or failure in what was, after all, a world of competing humanitarian organizations would depend largely on the degree of public recognition they managed to secure—in other words, on the way they marketed themselves, both to the public and to donors. Relief organizations were not businesses in the sense that IBM, Siemens, and Alcatel are businesses, but they struggled for market share and attention much as conventional businesses did.

The obsession of humanitarian relief groups with the media is the expression of this dependency on attention and this anxiety about their future viability. However uncomfortable aid groups are in stating this fact openly, they all know that the continuation of their programs is never guaranteed, any more than the sale of a product in the market is guaranteed. Again, structurally there was, from the beginning, something very much of their post-Communist time about the post-Biafra cohort of humanitarian NGOs, indeed something Thatcherite, even if obviously nothing could be further ideologically from MSF's radical solicitude for others than the Iron Lady's dictum "There is no such thing as society."

Predictably, this has meant that each aid agency has needed to have a telegenic star. Bernard Kouchner had, by far, the most aptitude and the most interest in playing the journalists' game, and in providing television viewers with the simple fables the medium seemed to require; he was famous for his ability to garner publicity in any and all circumstances. Kouchner always insisted that, for better or worse, such activities were integral to making the humanitarian case. In private, aid workers would report, he readily conceded that he was putting on a show. But it was, he insisted, a necessary show, for without it the public's interest would fade, and pressure on governments to intervene in humanitarian emergencies would ease. As one French aid worker who was drawn into one of Kouchner's spectacular visits to Somalia in 1991 put it, "It was almost as if he was telling us, 'I'm bringing in the media required so that you can do the work that's needed here.'"

It is easy to lampoon Kouchner. But it is by no means clear that he was wrong. Anyone who has spent any time with aid workers knows that they routinely complain in private about the superficiality and stupidity of the press and the distraction the media present at a time when they are engaged in questions of life and death. And yet, these same workers know that they are stymied. The funds come from governments, the UN (though much of that money is, in effect, only channeled through the world body by the same major donors), and the Western public. If the media are not engaged, the public won't be, either; it is as simple as that. As a result, if aid workers don't want their organizations to become completely dependent on a few major donors, as some U.S. NGOs already are, they must make their case through the media. Though some disguise this need better than others, and few are as outspoken about its necessity as Kouchner, aid workers are *in the business* of selling their organizations and the needs for aid they perceive to journalists. It is a vicious circle, one in which the viability of any given humanitarian action all too often has become conflated with the credibility of whatever story about that action the aid workers were trying to put across in the media.

Development had never exercised the same fascination over journalists. Emergencies, like wars, play well on television, whereas agricultural development programs, or micro-lending schemes, do not. This has led some development workers and UN officials to complain that the new generation of humanitarians, unlike their discreet, media-shy predecessors in the ICRC, calibrate their actions according to the kind of coverage they think they will receive. MSF, in particular, is viewed as being especially "camera hungry." But even in a media-saturated age, there are far deeper reasons why post-Biafra humanitarianism could succeed in filling the void left by the decline of development aid and liberation politics. It was not simply that the French "school" of humanitarianism was less development-minded than the British or the Scandinavian. MSF's moral ambitions were also grander and more overarching. As Brauman, whose own claims for what humanitarianism can and cannot do have always been admirably modest and antihyperbolic, once wrote, the utopian conception of humanitarian action promises "a world in which [these humanitarian] gestures of solicitude would become somehow the model of moral law in a world that might then be able to escape from its own contingency and passions."

But he added that even in his more restricted conception, humanitarian action did allow for the singling out of injustice, and what Brauman called "the designation of the unacceptable." It is here that both the moral originality of humanitarianism and the beginnings of an explanation for the breadth of its appeal begin to come into view. What Brauman is expressing is both morality at the highest and most serious level and a form of antipolitical thought. In the aftermath of Communism, and the profound shock that its fall produced in a culture where the left had enjoyed a virtual monopoly on the allegiance of intellectuals and activists for at least a century, what other direction was there to go for an ethically serious European?

One result of all this was that MSF and the groups that followed in its wake were somewhat estranged intellectually from the United Nations system. After all, from its inception, the UN had made the development of the poor world as great a priority as its original and, once the Cold War had begun in earnest, its unattainable brief of world peace and security. By the 1980s, its work as the facilitator of decolonization over, and its political role largely stymied by U.S.–Soviet rivalry, the UN was well on its way to becoming a giant alleviation machine. Few people cared much for the debates in the General Assembly; fewer still thought a system in which peace and security remained for all practical purposes in the hands of the permanent members of the Security Council—the United States, Britain, France, Russia, and China—was either fair or workable. In contrast, no matter how flawed and inconsistent it might be, the work of UNHCR, the WFP, the World Health Organization (WHO), and the United Nations Children's Organization (UNICEF) remained extraordinarily relevant. The success or failure of these organizations' programs meant literally, and still mean, the difference between life and death for tens of millions of people.

The problem is that developmentalism and Third Worldism as ideologies persisted at the UN for far longer than they should have. It was only under Kofi Annan, who became secretary-general in 1996, that the UN began to acknowledge in any systematic way what had been clear since the early 1980s at the latest: that even viewed through the most optimistic lens, development had at best had only mixed success, and, as originally imagined anyway, it had largely been a failure. Until UN officials faced that harsh reality, they were bound to be far more sympathetic to development agencies than to emergency relief agencies. Small wonder then that, although MSF had repudiated the ICRC's insistence on discretion and even what, in the field, often amounts to collusion with criminal and oppressive groups, and despite its commitment to the duty of witness and its ambition to mobilize public outrage back home, MSF remains closer in its operational conceptions to those of the ICRC than to those of UN agencies.

The differences between the continental and the British approach to relief, above all the enduring commitment to development on the part of groups like Oxfam, and the relationships of the two schools of humanitarianism to the UN humanitarian system, were important—sometimes even crucial, as in the case of the conduct of relief agencies in Cambodia in 1979 and in Ethiopia in 1984–1986. But these differences pale when contrasted with the gap that has existed since the reformation of humanitarianism in the aftermath of Biafra between European and UN agencies on the one hand and American relief groups on the other. The sorts of debates that wracked Oxfam, and MSF, and UNHCR, exposed differences, and, in private relief groups, sometimes caused splits, were almost unheard of within American humanitarian organizations during the same period. Part of this has to do with organizational structure. Many French NGOs are associations, and they attempt, with varying degrees of success, to maintain a certain level of democratic dialogue among the members. And British groups like Oxfam pride themselves on being organizations that officials will serve in for life. In contrast, American

NGOs tend to be hierarchical, and they are run more like conventional businesses than their European counterparts. In retrospect, though, it is still remarkable just how little debate of any kind there actually was in American NGOs until the 1990s, when a series of well-publicized debacles—in Somalia, then Bosnia, then Rwanda—forced a degree of self-examination that had theretofore been outside the American humanitarian experience.

Most of the mainline U.S. humanitarian agencies took cooperation with the government for granted. The deepest level of explanation for this is to be found in the abiding Wilsonianism of the American policy establishment, of which the American humanitarian leadership has always been a member in good standing. The United States is an empire. But it is a peculiar sort of empire. And Woodrow Wilson's adage, "This is an age which demands a new order of things in which the only question will be: Is it right? Is it just? Is it in the interest of mankind?" remains deeply inscribed in the minds of American officials. Obviously, Wilson's questions have never been the only ones Washington asked, and often they have not been asked at all. Nonetheless, the Wilsonian vision of a world made safe for democracy continues to resonate. And in contrast to the Western European policy establishments, the corridors of power in official Washington have always had room for this view (with the possible exception of the period when Henry Kissinger held sway). As a result, American relief officials, whether inside or outside of government, could always persuade themselves that sooner or later their views would become government policy.

In practice, this has meant that people found moving from jobs in the United States Agency for International Development (USAID) and other government agencies to jobs in the private voluntary relief groups quite effortless psychologically. And even when these officials realized they would be fighting difficult institutional battles, they almost invariably insisted that their inclusion meant they could influence policy decisions in a way that oppositional British and European NGOs could never hope to do. Perhaps this was because they shared with most government officials the belief that American power, when not misused, really did have the potential of making the world safe for democracy. From the beginning of the Cold War to the fall of the Berlin Wall, this meant that the rhetoric of most U.S. private relief agencies, again with the notable exception of the American Friends Service Committee (AFSC), was virtually indistinguishable from the Cold War rhetoric of the U.S. government. In the aftermath of the Cold War, this approach changed somewhat. But it continued to reflect the U.S. government position, which now asserted a foreign policy based on globalization, free markets, democratic openings, and human rights.

The International Rescue Committee's founder, Leo Cherne, might insist that his organization made "no distinction between terror on the left or right," but in practice the IRC, like other mainline U.S. relief organizations, collaborated so intimately with the organs of the American government that knowing where the NGO ended and the government agency began was always difficult to determine, and still remains so.

Doubtless there were considerable advantages to this on an operational level. One of the many paradoxes of the humanitarian project as a whole is that, however much individual agencies may pride themselves on their special role, or inspiration, or history, the good ones are nearly interchangeable in terms of their field practice. Certainly neither most of their beneficiaries in the poor world nor most of their supporters at home can really distinguish between an MSF, an Oxfam, or an IRC. That said, there have been tremendous moral costs to the closeness between U.S. relief agencies and the American government. Throughout the Cold War, USAID was often a front for the CIA, and, even when it was not, the U.S. government broadly expected the NGOs it funded to follow its policy directions. With the exception of a few relief groups, especially the American Friends Service Committee, American NGOs active in Southeast Asia were largely uncritical publicly of the U.S. involvement in Vietnam until very late in the war. This was not surprising. Their chief funder, USAID, played a central role in what was dubbed the struggle for hearts and minds in Southeast Asia. As a result, those Americans who opposed the war did not tend to join humanitarian groups, but, at least by the late 1970s, tended rather to gravitate toward the nascent human rights movement.

At the same time, this close relationship between relief groups and government also can be seen as one of the reasons humanitarianism was so readily accepted as the utopian special project of a nonutopian consensus about how the world should be ordered. It was as if relief groups in America were saying, "We want to change everything, but don't worry, in doing so we're not going to threaten any vested interest." To say, as a past president of the IRC, Robert De Vecchi, did, that for sixty years the institution had "served the cause of refugees, human freedom, and dignity," is to say everything and nothing, for it leaves many essential questions unasked and unanswered.

In fairness, this kind of avoidance is equally evident, in somewhat different ideological garb, in European and British agencies. As in America, the self-righteousness, even self-congratulation, that many humanitarian organizations exhibited until the great reckoning of the mid-1990s was pervasive. As Alex de Waal, who served as a consultant for Oxfam for a number of years before launching his important and in some ways devastating critique of humanitarianism, pointed out, "International responsibility for the alleviation of suffering is one of the most noble of all human goals. Nobility of aim does not confer immunity from sociological analysis or ethical critique, however . . . It is as though the sociological study of the church were undertaken by committed Christians only: criticism would be solely within the context of advancing the faith itself."

Actually, de Waal understated the problem. Until well into the 1990s, relief organizations acted as if their good intentions made any criticism of their performance in the field illegitimate. It was almost like dealing with a sect in which the interests of the group are seen as being *by definition* in the interest of truth and virtue, and, of course, one in which no one will admit to having heard of the law of unintended consequences. Motivation is everything. As a result, before the chastening experiences of the Balkans and the Great Lakes region of Africa, humanitarians usually responded to their critics by saying that they did what good they could and when they failed it was the fault of outsiders. No blame could possibly attach to them institutionally, although, sensibly enough, they readily conceded that there were good and bad aid workers, just as there were good and bad everything else.

If anything, the situation at the United Nations was far worse for far longer. Compared to UN officials, aid workers even before the great reckoning of the mid-1990s came across as a sect of medieval flagellants. For at the UN, the official culture's practice always was to take credit for every success (think of the UN's trumpeting of its accomplishments in bringing peace to El Salvador or Mozambique), while blaming the member states for every failure (think of Bosnia or Rwanda). The extent to which aid workers took a similar view may be explained by the fact that the UN in many ways has always served as a model for the private relief world. For all their differences, the often symbiotic relationship between the UN and the mainline humanitarian NGOs has led to the creation of a common culture over the course of the past five decades. At senior levels, officials move easily between private NGOs and the UN humanitarian and development agencies. And "in the field," as humanitarians say—that is, pretty much anywhere in the poor world—it is commonplace to meet UN officials who were once country directors for private voluntary agencies.

Interestingly, the reverse is less often the case. The UN is a governmental bureaucracy. It is hierarchical, and it is both self-absorbed and self-referential. The flavor of this self-absorption and resistance to criticism is illustrated by the UN official who rejected criticisms of the organization's performance in Bosnia by insisting confidently that "success should be measured in light of the goals the organization sets itself." It is less that the UN is intolerant of public or, for that matter, of private dissent so much as that it is impervious to it. Thus the world organization is marked by a particularly stable combination of an ethos of service and an ethos of conformity.

There are also dirty secrets that no one acknowledges publicly because it is not comfortable, let alone politically correct, to do so. The most egregious of these is the number of UN officials from poor countries who are timid in their posts, both in regard to writing critical reports and in allowing, at least when they control the purse strings, NGOs to take risks in the field, because they do not want to risk stirring up trouble and losing their sinecures. But perhaps their self-censorship has other motives. Many of the most perceptive and critical UN officials reject the suggestion that a UN official risks his or her career by writing an alarmist or pessimistic report. They insist that, while conformism helps, as it does in most organizations, it is much more likely that one's critical report will not be read than that one will be fired for having written it. For them, the real scandal at the UN is that it is virtually unheard of to fire anyone except for the grossest malfeasance.

That assessment is widely challenged by Western relief workers and diplomats in the field. "These guys have only one idea," a disgruntled American aid worker once said to me in Kosovo, after an endless and inconclusive meeting with a Bangladeshi UN official (the upshot was that there should be another meeting), "it's I don't want to have to go back to Dhaka, or wherever. And that's much more unlikely if your reports to UN headquarters say everything's fine than if they are critical. It may not be fine; in fact, it may all be going to hell in a handbasket. But if you value your career chances, you'd better have an awfully good reason to ring the alarm, and above all be damn sure the bad news isn't going to piss off one of UNHCR's major donors, and in turn make your bosses furious with you."

There are more down-to-earth reasons as well. In many cases, a relief organization's funding comes either from the UN or from national governments working through the UN. Thus UN agencies are dependent on their donors, and this arrangement is even formalized in the Office of the United Nations Commission for Refugees, whose executive committee is composed of many of the major donor governments. NGOs in turn are dependent on their national governments, either directly or through the various UN institutions. For all intents and purposes, agencies like UNHCR, the United Nations Development Programme, and the World Food Programme are often in charge of humanitarian operations in crisis zones. It is they who tell the relief agencies where to operate, and, with varying degrees of success, they also try to set the political as well as the operational agenda of the NGOs. In this sense, no matter how independent humanitarian organizations try to be, both institutional and funding realities often make them effectively subcontractors of donor governments and of the United Nations system.

There are exceptions. The International Committee of the Red Cross, as always, works on its own, as it must if it is to carry out its mandate under international law. And groups that are well respected within the UN system, notably Oxfam, are at times able to help shape the operational and sometimes even the political agendas of UN agencies, above all UNHCR, almost as much as they are guided by them. MSF has not made an effort similar to the one undertaken by Oxfam. Instead it has largely preferred to remain aloof. As a result, within both the UN and the world of other nongovernmental organizations, MSF is viewed as the perpetual naysayer, off on its own, unwilling to coordinate, unwilling to play by the rules that bind everyone else.

There is some justice to this claim, and not simply because the group issued from the ICRC. The more important point is that MSF's self-concept remains far closer to that of the Geneva Committee than to those of its NGO peers. Indeed, MSF almost seems to pride itself on its unwillingness to join any humanitarian consensus. In any case, to insist upon this point is not necessarily to condemn the system outright. Nor is it to repudiate the nobility of humanitarianism—a grandeur that is actually more damaged by its apologists than by its critics. If the humanitarian utopia is the product of forces outside its own realm, and if its rise coincides with the end of the redemptive fantasy of Communism, this does not make what aid does or what humanitarianism promises less relevant or less admirable.

If aid workers are seen as different by a public that, by the 1990s, had learned to view politicians with contempt, to think of journalists as beneath contempt, and to assume, in the age of the stock-market public and the drumbeat of propaganda for a world in which the triumph of globalization was assured and the business cycle in all likelihood abolished, could find few other countervailing models of behavior, they are viewed this way with good reason. Instead of getting on with their careers, aid workers chose to go off to places where they would not simply live in difficult circumstances but live to help others. They were paid almost nothing, so the best that could be said in hard-edged business terms about their choices was that they had lost a march on their classmates, and, when they finally returned home, they would have a lot of time to make up. It is not even as if, for most of those who volunteer for it, humanitarianism is a career in the proper sense of the term. The mainline relief agencies depend largely on young people who work on short contracts. Of course, some aid workers made their lives in MSF or the IRC, but most would go home and have to pull together their lives and choose another career. Save the Children (UK) and Oxfam make a greater effort to recruit staff who will make their careers within the organization, but increasingly, they, too, use workers on short-term contracts. In a sense, the challenge for MSF volunteers was the least severe, because the French system of medicine has traditionally permitted young physicians to take long leaves of absence.

In the final analysis, however, the details of how any individual humanitarian system works are only of secondary importance. The essential point is that, for better or worse, by the late 1980s humanitarianism had become the last coherent saving ideal. Its triumph, however, would prove in the 1990s to be its tragedy, for this success turned out, both morally and operationally, to be a poisoned chalice.

Dreams and Realities

CHAPTER 4

Bosnia

T HE BOSNIAN WAR WOULD EVENTUALLY become so essential to
our collective understanding of the post–Cold War world that it
is now hard to remember the euphoria that reigned in Western Europe and North America in the immediate aftermath of the fall of the
Berlin Wall. In 1989 and 1990, another war in Europe seemed an
impossibility. There was a building consensus that, after so many
wars and calamities, Europeans at last might be freed not just from
war (there had been no war on the continent since 1945), but even
from the threat of war. And it no longer seemed utopian to extrapo-
late from a Europe at peace and undivided to a peaceful order for the
world as a whole. This was the era of UN Secretary-General Boutros
Boutros-Ghali's "An Agenda for Peace," and George Bush senior's
New World Order. Liberal internationalism, with its commitments
to human rights, humanitarianism, democratic—or, as the billion-
aire investor and philanthropist George Soros preferred to call them,
"open"—societies, and the rule of law, seemed to have swept all before it. Communism was dead. We were all liberal capitalists now,
and the new political opening that the end of the Cold War had provided, combined with the prosperity that the technological revolu-

tion promised, was finally going to make the world safe for democracy, as Woodrow Wilson had said in 1918.

Beware of nature, "cynical in her sunrises," Nietzsche once wrote. He might as well have been warning about history, above all about what would prove to be the historical false dawn of 1989. The triumphalist talk, with its conceit that history had somehow come to an end, did not last long; history, the old-fashioned, pitiless, sanguinary kind, was soon back with a vengeance. In fact, the euphoria over the collapse of the Soviet Union had barely worn off when the genocidal wars of "ethnic cleansing" that would sweep through the Balkans between 1991 and 1999 began in Croatia.

The old saying "Save me from what I wish for most" could not have been more appropriate than it was to the breakup of Yugoslavia. The Western powers had wanted an end to the Cold War division of Europe. Well, now they had to deal with all the historical messes that had been festering, in some cases since the end of World War I, but had been frozen or suppressed during the half-century struggle between the United States and the Soviet Union. And the United Nations had wanted a wider role, believing, as senior officials of the world body had been insisting practically since its inception, that the potential of the UN would finally be unlocked were the superpower rivalry ever to end. Then, they said, the UN would show the world what a force for good, and above all for peace, it was, and had had the potential to be all along.

"In the course of the past few years," Boutros-Ghali wrote in 1992, "the immense ideological barrier that for decades gave rise to distrust and hostility—and the terrible tools of destruction that were their inseparable companions—has collapsed." And he insisted confidently that while "the adversarial decades of the cold war made the original promise of the Organization impossible to fulfill . . . a conviction has grown, among nations large and small, that an opportunity has been regained to achieve the great objectives of the [UN] Charter—a United Nations capable of maintaining international peace and security, of securing justice and human rights and of promoting, in the words of the Charter, 'social progress and better standards of life in larger freedom.'" The opportunity, he added, was one that must not be squandered.

Enter Bosnia, laughing. The reality was that almost no one had really expected the Soviet empire to collapse, and no government, let alone the UN Secretariat, was either prepared or really in a position to deal competently with the political aftershocks that accompanied its passing. It was not that no one foresaw the threat posed by the possible breakup of Yugoslavia. A CIA report predicted just such an eventuality in 1989. But the mechanisms that would have been set in motion during the Cold War to prevent the catastrophe from taking place—above all, pressure from both Washington and Moscow on a state that was in fact beholden to both—no longer existed in 1991 when war erupted in Slovenia and Croatia. The administration of George Bush senior offered the Western Europeans its assistance in resolving the conflict, although with what degree of sincerity is open to dispute. But the Europeans, believing themselves to be stronger and, above all, more unified than they were, told the Americans they would handle the crisis themselves. "Now is the hour of Europe," was the way Jacques Poos, the foreign minister of Luxembourg, put it as he delivered the European Union's response to Washington.

By the time the major powers realized that the Yugoslav catastrophe was something to which they would have to give priority, it was too late for conventional diplomacy. The options facing the West were simple. The first involved doing nothing and allowing Yugoslavia's leader, Slobodan Milosevic, to carve a "greater Serbia" out of the corpse of the former Yugoslavia. The second required that outsiders use force to end the fighting. But even had a NATO army intervened, or, at least, threatened convincingly to do so, the question was, what would it have intervened for? Would it have been to secure terms favorable to Milosevic, to the Croatian nationalist regime of Franjo Tudjman, or to the legitimate Bosnian government of Alija Izetbegovic, or for some democratic order that would have to be maintained from the outside? The Americans seemed not to know what they wanted, while the great European states were divided. French President François Mitterrand's government was overwhelmingly pro-Serb. The Germans were preoccupied with helping the fledgling Croatian state secure its independence. As for the British, to the extent they had a view, it was that now that the damage had been done the best thing was to arrange a partition on ethnic lines.

These political divisions among the great powers were accompanied by military anxieties. The Yugoslavs could fight, or so it was presumed, and not only by those who wanted to forestall any military move. An intervention would be costly and difficult. It was this conviction, bred of military caution and the unwillingness of any major Western government to push hard for intervention, that made the third option—containing the crisis—so appealing. In practice, this meant trying to bottle up as completely as possible all this suffering and death, and, in their wake, to contain the mass movements of refugees as completely as possible within the borders of Croatia and, once the fighting broke out there in the spring of 1992, within those of Bosnia-Herzegovina.

Only in that strange, euphoric moment that was the immediate post–Cold War period, or among people who believed the self-flattering lies that Western politicians, UN officials, and their intellectual brethren were telling about how at last we were going to live in a different and better world, could it have come as a surprise that the great powers opted for containment. European leaders did not want a war and they did not want any more refugees. Given those priorities, the choice for them must have been obvious. And yet, most educated, liberal Westerners were surprised. We thought that the world—or did we only mean Europe?—was better than it was. We thought *we* were better. Bosnia would disabuse us of both conceits, affecting us as only something that takes place in a familiar locale or context can do. Think of the destruction of the World Trade Center, almost a decade later, and how it would finally make terrorism real to Americans.

For journalists and relief workers, in particular, the reality of having to cover, or attempt to alleviate, an emergency on what for most was their native soil (for the majority of the Americans, only imaginatively so, but the effect was much the same) was deeply absorbing and deeply unsettling. Above all, it was *different*. No longer would we go "out there" to places where the customs, the look of the people, and, above all else, the poverty kept one at a distance, no matter how hard one tried to connect. Intellectually, it was easy to insist that this starving African child, this Afghan woman, or this wounded Kurd fighter was simply a fellow human being, and as such no different from us. But for most of us, on an emotional level at least, it was not true. Our sisters did not, and never would, wear burkas; our mothers would never be refused medical care because the hospital in some Taliban-controlled town was for men only; our children did not go barefoot, except at the beach or in the back garden. But more to the point, we did not come from places where people made war on one another. That period of history—it was in fact all of European history until 1945 when you thought about, but we didn't think about it—had ended.

What lies we tell ourselves. And in Bosnia, those lies came true. The driver on a UNHCR convoy wanted to talk about the experi-

mental theater company he had seen in Paris before the war. The ruined village in the Bosanska Krajina had had central heating and was
within an hour's drive of the magnetic resonance imaging machine
in the regional hospital. The young girl with her arm blown off by a
sniper's round as she played in the courtyard of her Sarajevo high-
rise had dreamed of being a contestant in the Euro Song competition. And the journalist cadging cigarettes in an underground café
had strong opinions about the relative merits of the front-page lay-
out of the *International Herald Tribune* and that of Madrid's *El Pais*.
In other words, Bosnia and its people were not significantly different
from us culturally. That was the essential point. Throughout my
time in Bosnia during the war, I heard this sense of affinity for the
Bosnians being expressed as often by black American reporters and
aid workers as by blond Swedish colleagues. For that matter, I heard
it repeated over and over by the Bosnians themselves, many of
whom felt entitled to the European "immunity" from war and want.

This deep sense of connectedness helps explain how Bosnia exerted the kind of fascination on, and engendered the kind of commitment from, aid workers and journalists that no crisis in the poor
world had ever commanded. In particular, the fate of besieged Sarajevo became more than a crisis, it became a cause. This was not only
understandable, it was justifiable, and not only because it is only human to care more about neighbors than strangers. Both morality
and self-interest justified insisting that, almost half a century after
the defeat of Nazism, the ethnic fascism Slobodan Milosevic incarnated must not be allowed its second life, and that Europe, having
emerged from the Cold War, must not be permitted to regress into
the kind of savagery that had marked it for most of its history. After
1945, Europe had to an admirable degree found a way out of its own
barbarism, above all through a commitment to education and to an
understanding between European peoples that was far more serious

than the pieties and self-congratulation surrounding it sometimes suggested. Europe had the right to prevent a slide back into barbarism, and the entire world had an interest in that effort.

This is not to minimize the grave moral problems revealed by the way humanitarians and journalists reacted to the new Balkan wars. I have come late to seeing them, and now feel that I failed to face up to them in *Slaughterhouse,* the book I wrote about the Bosnian war. One should not talk about neighborliness without conceding that this neighborliness is also a form of hegemony. The international media are dominated by Western reporters, photographers, editors, and producers, and thus a Bosnia is going to occupy the world stage, not simply that of Europe and North America. In a just world, there would be reporters and editors who cared about Angola as much as I cared about Bosnia, and those reporters would have access to the front pages and the leads on the evening news.

But to say that the world is as unjust in its response to humanitarian crises as it is in everything else is neither an excuse nor a sufficient reply to the outrage many in the poor world felt and continue to feel over the attention—journalistic, diplomatic, and humanitarian—that the wars of Yugoslav succession received. To staff their humanitarian operations in the Balkans, UN agencies and NGOs drew personnel away from programs in Africa. For journalists, Bosnia became *the* international story. Only the Rwandan genocide, in which eight hundred thousand people were killed in six weeks, managed to divert the press corps's attention from the fate of Sarajevo.

The moral challenge to the ethos of humanitarian aid was even starker. Relief workers are pledged to work on the basis of need, not of politics, and certainly not of cultural affinity. And yet the reality is that the Bosnian crisis engaged the humanitarian international, as the Kosovo crisis would engage it seven years later, to a degree that was clearly out of proportion to the purely humanitarian needs involved. Whether in terms of the monies that donor governments were willing to commit to humanitarian programs in the Balkans, or the number of NGOs that were being funded by UN agencies, the European Union, and the U.S. government—there were 250 by the time the Dayton Agreement that ended the war was signed in 1995—Bosnia was and remains a special case in the annals of humanitarian action.

The deeper question is whether Bosnia was a major humanitarian crisis at all. Was the way the crisis unfolded more the product of events on the ground, the course of the war itself, or the decisions the major donors made early in the conflict about how to manage it? In most refugee crises, even in the post–Cold War world of conflicts where refugee flows are not a by-product of fighting but the strategic goal of the war itself, what happens is that people who have been "ethnically cleansed"—to use the term we all learned in Bosnia—at least those who can make it, flee across an international border. That was just what the major Western powers were determined to prevent. There were geopolitical reasons for their concern, the fear that a flood of refugees in all directions would help ignite further conflicts in neighboring Albania and in the Former Yugoslav Republic of Macedonia, which had thus far been spared the conflict. But another, equally important reality was that Western European governments did not want to take the Bosnians in if they could possibly avoid it. For both reasons, policymakers swiftly concluded that a method needed to be devised to get them to stay where they were. That method was humanitarian action.

If the commitment to Bosnia on the part of humanitarians (and journalists) was as much an expression of self-love as it was of a more altruistic brand of solidarity, European and American politicians would prove to be far less sentimental. For them, the tragedy of Bosnia was at best a regrettable sideshow. In 1992, the American political establishment was obsessed with the economy, while European politicians and civil servants were mostly concerned with issues revolving around the European Union, above all that of a common currency. It was not that politicians such as the British prime minister, John Major, or the French president, François Mitterrand, completely agreed with Prince Bismarck, who had said that wars in the Balkans were not worth the life of "a single healthy Pomeranian grenadier." On the contrary, the French and British governments were more than willing to sacrifice troops—the French lost more than a hundred soldiers in Bosnia between 1992 and 1995—but in order to contain the crisis, not to resolve it.

Deploying and being willing to sacrifice soldiers was never intended to be the principal form of the West's response. Humanitarianism was. The idea was simple, coarse, and brutal, and it would prove astonishingly effective. Instead of political action backed by the credible threat of military force, the Western powers would substitute a massive humanitarian effort to alleviate the worst consequences of a conflict they wanted to contain. "Containment through charity" was the way one UN official put it. Boutros-Ghali would get his chance to show how relevant the United Nations could be, though hardly in the way he had proposed in "An Agenda for Peace." If the response was to be humanitarian, the moral warrant of the UN would be essential.

The world body's deeply ingrained institutional culture made it the perfect "implementing partner"—to use the phrase that UN agencies like UNHCR often use for the relief NGOs they fund—for the great powers as they looked for an excuse not to intervene militarily. Secretary-General Annan later issued a report on the Srebrenica massacre, in which eight thousand men and boys (all the males in the enclave except for prepubescent boys and a few old men who had not succeeded in escaping) were murdered in cold blood by

Serb forces after they overran the Bosnian government–controlled enclave in eastern Bosnia in July 1995. The report spoke of "the pervasive ambivalence within the United Nations regarding the use of force in the pursuit of peace" and of "an institutional ideology of impartiality even when confronted with attempted genocide."

The question was how to put this humanitarian alibi for nonintervention into operation. A UN flag of convenience already existed in the form of the ill-named United Nations Protection Force (UNPROFOR), a peacekeeping deployment whose troops were barely authorized to defend themselves, let alone the Croatians or the Serbs in the areas of Croatia in which they were deployed. But peacekeepers cannot simply be turned into humanitarian aid workers, and there was no UN agency charged with looking after the welfare of people who might, if given the chance, become refugees. UNHCR had been an operational relief agency before, but never in an ongoing conflict and never on the scale on which it would operate in the Balkans. It had been active in northern Iraq after the Gulf War, where it actually took over from Operation Provide Comfort, the U.S. military's relief effort for Kurds. But before the Bosnian war, UNHCR's principal concern since its inception in 1951 had been refugees. Its mandate included standing up for their rights—what it called "protection"—resettlement, and running refugee camps both in countries into which refugees initially fled and in third countries. It had no particular competence in running aid convoys, let alone the relief airlift that would eventually play a central part in its Bosnian programs. And looking after people in war zones had traditionally been the responsibility of the ICRC.

And yet in Bosnia, the ICRC was absent. Although to many outsiders it looked as if by emphasizing the preeminent role of UNHCR the great powers were intent on marginalizing the ICRC, in fact, as one relief worker put it, "the ICRC marginalized the ICRC." At the outbreak of the war, the Geneva Committee had only one delegate in place in Bosnia. Realizing its mistake, the ICRC sent a team of experienced officials into Sarajevo in May 1992. But the convoy was shelled, and one delegate, Frederic Maurice, was killed. The ICRC withdrew and did not really recommit to serious effort until the end of 1993. In the interim, the UNHCR began to fill the humanitarian role normally occupied by the ICRC, which was generally viewed by both UN officials and NGO workers as extremely jealous of its prerogative.

However ad hoc and almost accidental the decisions that led to UNHCR's new centrality, the agency underwent an unprecedented and astonishing transformation and, in a matter of months, became what Gil Loescher, the historian of UNHCR, has called "the world's largest relief agency." As one UNHCR official later recalled, "The preeminent role the UN and the UNHCR came to play in Bosnia was less the result of a grand plan than of the contradictory policies of different Europeans, the prevalent desire of the Europeans not to get involved, and a series of other fuck-ups. Then there was the ICRC's mistakes and ill-fortune."

A split soon developed within UNHCR between those who welcomed this new mandate and those who feared that the agency's traditional role would be swamped by its new duties and, above all, its new political centrality. According to Loescher, who cites senior UNHCR officials to back up his claim, the new high commissioner, Sadako Ogata, "perceived UNHCR engagement [in the former Yugoslavia] as an opportunity to make the agency relevant to the international community's most powerful actors." This was particularly necessary because UNHCR was in dire straits financially and on bad terms with many European governments due to its insistence on pressing them on the legal rights of asylum seekers. As Loescher puts it, here was a chance to "revitalize the organization and enable it to enhance its influence and prestige with governments—particularly UN Security Council member states—[and] also restore the confidence of European governments."

The new structures were quickly put into place. The UN would finally play a major role in peace and security in the post–Cold War world. The UNHCR would be "rehabilitated." And the great powers would have their humanitarian fig leaf for nonintervention. It was an arrangement that suited all the major players in the tragedy—except, of course, the Bosnians.

It was also a defining moment for the private relief agencies. For in an important sense, it was in the interaction in Bosnia between donor governments, the UN relief and refugee agencies, and the NGOs that a new humanitarianism was born. It was better funded (and as a result more dependent on donors), more efficient, more political, and more admired by the public at large, who saw in relief workers almost the only people in the Bosnian catastrophe with whom they could wholeheartedly sympathize. From a public relations standpoint (I speak as one of the many writers covering the war who developed a deep admiration for UNHCR during this period), Mme. Ogata's decision had been a triumph. UNHCR was soon lionized, unlike other UN agencies, and certainly unlike its Department of Peacekeeping Operations (UNDPKO, or DPKO), whose efforts in the Balkans were reviled in the press, and which seemed to epitomize what Annan's own report on Srebrenica would later concede was the institution's "inability to recognize the scope of evil confronting us."

Ogata herself came to be viewed as the one entirely admirable senior figure in a landscape otherwise dotted with failed or superannuated politicians serving as international negotiators, such as Britain's Lord Owen or the former U.S. secretary of state Cyrus Vance, and with UN officials and assorted Western leaders who seemed incapable of formulating a common policy. Indeed, her star rose so high that she was soon being whispered about as a possible successor to Boutros-Ghali as UN secretary-general, an outcome that some of her advisors played up privately and that she herself was said to wish for.

In narrow humanitarian terms, the praise UNHCR received was fully warranted. Bosnia was a place where any drunken lout with a Kalashnikov could stop an aid convoy indefinitely. A second UNPROFOR mission for Bosnia had been authorized by the Security Council in 1992. The peacekeepers' mandate was to assist, as the UN resolution put it, in "creating conditions for the effective delivery of humanitarian aid." But the UN Secretariat and the Department of Peacekeeping Operations applied this only in the most minimalist way. Above all, the peacekeepers were forbidden from using force to push the aid through. Thirty thousand UN troops were deployed by the time the mission ended, and yet they were not authorized to use their weapons in defense of anyone except themselves or any principle except that of the need to continue the mission. It was, as Jose María Mendiluce, the UNHCR's first special envoy to the Balkans, would put it, "a case study in the politics of impotence."

UNHCR officials, though unstintingly supported in their efforts by Ogata, were obviously unable to do for themselves what the UN soldiers could not do for them. And yet what was accomplished was extraordinary. While little or no aid reached the eastern Bosnian enclaves of Srebrenica, Gorazde, and Zepa, and much that did reach people in need in the northern area known as the Bosanska Krajina was stolen by the Serbs, an astonishing amount did reach those who needed it. Less than four months after the Bosnian war began, UNHCR had begun an airlift ferrying relief supplies to Sarajevo, which was by then almost completely encircled by the Serbs. That airlift would run for almost three years. By 1993, UNHCR estimated that it was getting aid to more than 2.7 million people in Bosnia (out of a total prewar population of 4.5 million), as well as 1.4 million people in other parts of the former Yugoslavia. They were spending upwards of a million dollars a day to do so.

This last figure should illustrate that the situation was more complicated than the aid tonnages delivered and the gallantry of those who did the delivering—and UNHCR officials, particularly in the early part of the war, were nothing if not gallant—might otherwise suggest. Not only were the sums involved such that only the major Western powers could provide them, but the Sarajevo airlift could be maintained only so long as NATO provided the planes and the personnel. As Eric Dachy of MSF-Belgium pointed out caustically, "The UN troops were instructed to use force to protect the aid supplies—but they were prevented from using force to protect people." Writing more generally of this form of militarized humanitarianism, Dachy concluded that "the scandal is not that the humanitarian movement is unable to prevent atrocities committed against communities. The scandal is in seeing some of the world's most powerful governments and armies playing the role of aid workers, implying their acceptance of a whole string of massacres, which they are unable to consider from a different perspective."

UNHCR officials, both in Bosnia and at the headquarters in Geneva, often grew restive in the agency's role of providing a principal rationale for nonintervention. The best of them were outraged and sickened by it. And at least once, in the summer of 1993, the agency tried to suspend its operations. But it was quickly overruled. "The international community" knew what it wanted. David Owen, the European Union's negotiator, recalled in his memoir, *Balkan Odyssey*, that "it was we as peace negotiators who had persuaded UNHCR to stay." But there was broad consensus on the subject.

Secretary-General Boutros-Ghali, under pressure from Western donor governments, quickly ordered UNHCR back into action.

For the Bosnians, UNHCR's success in carrying out the role the great powers had assigned it represented both a triumph and a tragedy. Fundamentally, the better the job UNHCR and the NGOs that worked with it did in Bosnia—and, given the appalling, impossible circumstances, the job they did was magnificent—the more cover they provided for the great powers to avoid doing anything to stop the slaughter. Had the operation been perceived as a failure, a Mitterrand or a John Major could not have hidden behind the excuse that a military intervention would harm the humanitarian effort. But since the Sarajevo airlift *was* successful, and relief convoys were able to reach large areas of Bosnia, the humanitarian alibi could be employed again and again and again by officials in London, Paris, and Washington.

As Nicholas Morris, who was the agency's special envoy in the Balkans from late 1993 through 1994, would put it later, "In Bosnia the UNHCR operation was, in a sense, a substitute for political action. Ensuring its success, and its perception as a success, was important to key governments." Perhaps this is why most UN officials hewed to the line that, from a humanitarian point of view at least, much was achieved throughout the Bosnian war. They knew what was expected of them. They also knew, just as the press did, that it was in periods when the humanitarian effort was at its least effective that the groundswell of support for military intervention would build in the West, just as it was when the humanitarian operation seemed to be going smoothly that Bosnia would begin to recede from public consciousness.

The important thing for the major Western powers and the UN was to keep control of the humanitarian operation and let in as few outsiders as possible—above all as few critical outsiders apart from the press, about whom there was not much the UN could do. To further this end, governments effectively gave UNHCR a free hand to run the entire relief effort in Bosnia. In UN parlance, it would be the "lead agency," determining not only where other UN agencies worked but where the humanitarian NGOs worked as well. Neither Jose María Mendiluce, nor Morris himself, nor his successors were hesitant about exercising this authority. As Morris put it, "In Bosnia UNHCR . . . effectively controlled access to, and participation in, the humanitarian operation." As a result, he added, with what appeared to be unintentional irony, "coordination was relatively simple."

Mark Cutts, who worked as a senior UNHCR official in Bosnia during the war, was more blunt. "The way in which UNHCR carried out its role as the lead humanitarian agency put it in the strange position of being both a 'facilitator' and a 'regulator' of the activities of other humanitarian organizations," he wrote. "As regulator, UNHCR took on the role of a quasi-government. Those operating under the UNHCR umbrella [in practical terms, Cutts meant all humanitarian organizations except the ICRC] often had to negotiate with UNHCR for access rather than with the warring parties."

Cutts said this in a study of the agency's operations during the war in Bosnia he did for UNHCR in 1999. To the extent he is critical, he follows the familiar "buck-passing" line of most UN officials and argues that "ultimately it was not humanitarian organizations like UNHCR who called the shots." This is true as far as it goes. But Cutts does not ask himself the more serious question of why an agency that, in terms of bringing relief aid, had been largely nonoperational could consider itself qualified to act as what he himself calls a quasi-government, except in the obvious bureaucratic sense that it had the permission of the UN and the major Western governments to do so. It is true, as Cutts asserts, that the major donors were more interested in the continuation of the humanitarian mission on almost any terms. The rationale was that the humanitarian mission was buying time for the political negotiations to achieve some result. In fact, as Mendiluce pointed out over and over again, this represented the triumph of the "big lie" put out by the major Western powers—a falsehood, however, in which UNHCR collaborated.

The quasi-government was more often than not ineffective in negotiating humanitarian access with the Serbs, as the catastrophe in Srebrenica would eventually demonstrate even to the UN's Department of Peacekeeping Operations. But it was extremely effective in keeping Bosnians penned in. Cutts, an official of a refugee agency whose original mandate and self-proclaimed reason for being was to protect the rights of refugees and asylum seekers, writes disdainfully of "Bosnian civilians, particularly draft age males, who applied for work with humanitarian agencies for the sole purpose of obtaining [UNHCR] ID cards which would enable them to get through checkpoints and flee the country." Such complacency gives new meaning to a phrase of the great American aid worker Fred Cuny, murdered in Chechnya, who restored the gas lines of Sarajevo in 1993 and would have restored the water in the capital as well had the Bosnian government not betrayed him. "If the UN had been around in 1939," he liked to say, "we'd all be speaking German."

The agency's conduct with the humanitarian NGOs was less morally problematic, but equally imperious. Cutts writes that UNHCR would only issue its ID cards, the so-called Blue Cards, to those organizations that "reported [to the agency] on their activities and attended inter-agency coordination meetings." For all intents and purposes, this meant that for much of the war UNHCR was in a position to determine which humanitarian organizations were allowed to operate and which were not. When Jose María Mendiluce decided that the French NGO Équilibre's effectiveness was becoming questionable, he revoked the aid workers' ID cards. More important, the sheer size of the operation meant that UNHCR was in a position not just to control the NGOs but to contribute to their success. In effect, many of these agencies, particularly the ones with less access to independent sources of funding, were dependent on UNHCR's doling out assignments and subcontracts. And success bred success. The more work an NGO had, the more likely it was that it would receive further funding, both from UNHCR and from the major donors. Small wonder that what began to take shape in the Balkans in the early 1990s was a humanitarianism that was more conformist than it had ever been before, more intent, agency by agency, on its own institutional self-preservation, and, by the end of the Bosnian emergency, more persuaded that it had to become political in order to do its job.

As for the other UN agencies, they might be resentful, but it was more a matter of institutional jealousy and competitiveness than of a principled critique of UNHCR's approach. As one World Food Programme official put it years later when asked what his agency would have done differently in Bosnia, "We would have gotten there before UNHCR." UN agencies like UNHCR and WFP had long vied with one another for the right to implement certain programs that could arguably fall under either's mandate. But this time Ogata had gotten there first. UNHCR would not only organize refugee camps, it would run the food side of the relief operation as well. By the end of the Bosnian war, UNHCR would in effect have secured a kind of humanitarian monopoly in Bosnia.

At the time, this appeared to have been what Ogata wanted. Her agency was, indeed, now as "relevant" as she had hoped it would be. And yet eventually UNHCR would be weakened, not strengthened, by Bosnia. It was suffering—to use the U.S. military's expression—from a bad case of "mission creep." Above all, its mission to protect the rights of refugees and asylum seekers—a mission that lay at the heart of the agency's raison d'etre, UNHCR officials kept reiterating, both in public and in private—was at least partly sacrificed as its frantic effort to transform itself into a relief agency gathered momentum. This was not only a question of resources, although by the end of the Bosnian war, according to Gil Loescher, something like a quarter of its staff and a third of its resources were being devoted to Balkan programs very different from the protection and resettlement issues the agency had focused on before the 1990s. The problem ran deeper than that.

By giving much-needed aid to Bosnia, UNHCR was also in effect contributing to successfully carrying out one of the major donor countries' chief priorities—to prevent more Bosnians from trying to leave. Rather than supporting its traditional role of guardian of refugee rights, UNHCR's activities were designed to prevent people from becoming refugees in the first place. The Kurdistan operation of 1991, in which UNHCR had undertaken a full-scale relief effort in a conflict zone, already provided a model for this sort of activity. As in Bosnia, UNHCR tried to prevent people from leaving or reduce the number that left. In both cases, instead of standing on international law, and above all the 1951 UN Convention on Refugees that had accompanied its founding, and insisting that asylum seekers could not be turned away, UNHCR did the work of the Western countries that wanted no more asylum seekers. This is in no sense to ignore the enormous amount of good the agency did in Bosnia during the war. Tens of thousands, if not hundreds of thousands, of Bosnians are alive today because of the relief effort. And the UNHCR's willingness to denounce not just individual Serb atrocities but Milosevic's ethnic fascism was an honorable exception to the callous refusal of most UN officials to acknowledge the difference between the Bosnian victims and the Serb victimizers.

Nonetheless, UNHCR made itself relevant to the major Western donors by serving as a buffer between the Bosnians under siege in their own country and Western countries eager to limit the flow of refugees. (Hundreds of thousands still managed to make their way to the West.) In Sarajevo, UNPROFOR and UNHCR made it virtually impossible for ordinary Bosnians to get out of the city on their relief flights. They did this, they said, because otherwise the Serbs would have shut the airlift down. Perhaps. In a moment of outrage in 1993, George Soros called Sarajevo a "giant concentration camp." That was an exaggeration. But it was a giant UN internment camp. And how an agency could be both warden and advocate posed a moral challenge that UNHCR, for all the good it did in Bosnia, was never able to resolve. Many observers of the agency have gone further, concluding that it never regained the commitment to refugee protection that had been its fundamental mission before its engagement in the Balkans.

It was a cruel dilemma, but less cruel than those that confronted UNHCR in the field. Time and again, the agency was compelled to evacuate Bosnians from areas the Serbs had conquered. UNHCR officials believed they had either to collaborate with Serb "ethnic cleansing" or stand by while people were murdered. Angrily, guiltily, they nonetheless believed they had to save as many lives as they could. What this left in the minds and hearts of officials who had to make this impossible moral choice, however, was the conviction that this was a choice they should never have to make again. Not only was humanitarian action no substitute for political commitment, it could actually be forced to serve as an unwilling accomplice to "ethnic cleansing" and fascism. Ogata might, on balance, have been pleased by her agency's newfound relevance. But in the field—and this is to their great credit—UNHCR staff were as often overwhelmed by shame and in despair as they were sustained by justified pride in what they were able to accomplish.

There were so many hidden agendas in the humanitarian operation in Bosnia—agendas that many of us who covered the war and
the relief effort did not begin to understand at the time. We were so
disgusted by our encounter, both in Bosnia and at UN headquarters
in New York, with what the former American diplomat Michael Barnett has called the "UN syndrome"—a "refusal to see themselves as
being in charge or having any real autonomy" and a "veritable petri
dish for moral amnesia and the distortion of ethical principles"—
that we sometimes lost sight of the deeper culpability of the great
powers whose agendas UN bureaucrats carried out.

Our anger was stoked by the gap between the claims the UN
made for itself—above all, as Barnett has pointed out, that it is "the
bureaucratic arm of the world's transcendental values"—and the reality in the field, in which moral imperatives seemed to carry little
weight. It was perhaps too easy to judge governments less harshly
because most governments and their supporters (with the intermittent exception of the United States) do not claim to be charged, as
William Shawcross said of Kofi Annan, with "the moral leadership
of the world." Equally, it made us almost absurdly grateful for the
moral backbone UNHCR exhibited in Bosnia. But what we did not
understand was the tremendous manipulation of relief that was taking place—a manipulation in which UNHCR was not simply a victim, as people like me imagined at the time, but, at least at Ogata's
headquarters in Geneva, a willing participant.

Under international law, the Bosnians who had not fled across an
international border were not refugees at all. Technically, they were
either internally displaced people (IDPs, as they are called by relief
workers and UN bureaucrats) or simply people who were in difficulty where they were. Why, for example, should a refugee agency
like UNHCR have looked after the citizens of the Bosnian capital?
They were not refugees; and while some would have fled had they

been able to do so, most had no wish to become refugees. What they wanted was for someone, preferably the same Western governments that were funding the aid effort, to put a stop to the shelling and sniping that would, by the end of the war, kill ten thousand people in the city, including three thousand children. Stop the war, they said, and there will be no humanitarian emergency. Let the war continue, and you will just be creating well-fed corpses. But as the Bosnians eventually realized, UNHCR was there precisely so that Western governments did not have to do any such thing.

UNHCR officials were themselves the first to admit that not only were they improvising, they were stretching both their own mandate and their own field guidelines beyond the breaking point. As Jose María Mendiluce told me in 1992, "The first thing I did when I arrived here was throw away the Blue Book"—UNHCR's operational manual. To their everlasting credit, UNHCR officials from Mendiluce on down refused to play the standard UN game of complaining off the record about being misused while boasting on the record about how many lives they were saving. Mendiluce in particular repeatedly denounced to anyone who would listen the ways in which humanitarianism, and UNHCR in particular, were being misused. "You don't reply to fascism with relief supplies," he would say, "and you don't counter ethnic cleansing with reception centers for the displaced."

Mendiluce was one of the first relief workers to opt out of the new state humanitarianism that took shape during the Bosnian emergency. The Western intervention that Bernard Kouchner would clamor for, and help unleash in Kosovo eight years later, was what Mendiluce wanted all along in Bosnia. During the time he ran UNHCR, he made no secret of the fact. That put him at odds with many of his colleagues on the ground, and with his superiors in Geneva. Exhausted, frustrated, and ill, Mendiluce resigned from

UNHCR and went into European politics, eventually gaining a seat in the European Parliament. For him, the humanitarianism to which he had devoted so much of his life was being distorted beyond all recognition. His attitude was paradoxical. Mendiluce was both justifiably proud of what he had accomplished in Bosnia and disgusted at the role he had been forced to play.

He knew that not only had Western governments taken shelter behind his efforts, but that the Milosevic regime and its surrogates among the Bosnian Serbs had realized that as long as the international response was fundamentally humanitarian, and UN peacekeepers in Bosnia would act only to assist in the relief effort, not to impose peace, let alone protect Bosnian civilians, they were free to do as they pleased. In this sense, Mendiluce insisted, the logic of humanitarianism in Bosnia, despite all the undoubted good that it accomplished, was also the logic of the Srebrenica massacre in 1995, when eight thousand Bosnian men and boys were murdered by the Serbs as the UN peacekeepers and their superiors in New York claimed there was nothing they could do to protect them. You tried to feed; you tried to shelter, clothe, and provide medical assistance. But when the Serbs started killing, you got out of the way. "Only a fool would not have expected it," Mendiluce said of Srebrenica, adding that the UN force commander "[shared] the responsibility for the genocide."

The fall of the enclave, Mendiluce wrote bitterly in its immediate aftermath, "should have taken with it the empty hopes of all the innocents still deluding themselves that they could continue the game of mediation and neutrality amid the planned slaughter of the Bosnian people."

Mendiluce had always believed there was something better. For him, his success as a relief official in Bosnia had also been a measure of his own society's cowardice. This did not mean that he dreamed of a humanitarianism that would return to an ICRC-style neutrality, or would stand aside from politics and, MSF-style, largely restrict its activism to "testimony" about what it witnessed. To the contrary, the lesson he drew from Bosnia was similar to the one Bernard Kouchner had drawn—that states had an obligation to intervene militarily when humanitarian principles were being trampled, human rights abused, and victims in desperate need. His disillusionment with the limits UNHCR was forced to work under, people close to him said, was the chief motivation for him to go into politics. For Mendiluce, the problem in Bosnia was not that humanitarianism had no business cooperating with states, but rather that states needed to act more morally. When the limits of humanitarianism were reached, it was time for the soldiers to act.

"Only if we stop being neutral between murderers and victims," he said, "if we start regarding Bosnia as our ally, if we decide to back its fight for life against the fascist horror of ethnic cleansing, shall we be able to contribute to the survival of the remnants of that country and of our own dignity."

Mendiluce's despair at the misuse of humanitarianism that he had witnessed in Bosnia was shared by many of the best, most committed relief officials from the mainline NGOs. For many of them, the age of apolitical, neutral humanitarianism that remained autonomous had passed. The so-called international community had seen to that in the Balkans. And if these were indeed the new rules of the humanitarian game, then relief workers were going to have to learn how to use them for their own purposes and in accordance with their own principles. Otherwise, the mistakes of Bosnia and humanitarianism's susceptibility to being used as a fig leaf were sure to be repeated. As John Fawcett, who had run the International Rescue Committee's programs in Sarajevo during the siege, put it,

"Since we have decided we are going to send in aid for political pur-poses, then it is incumbent upon us to look at what's happening to that aid and how it's having an impact on that society."

Fawcett was widely considered by his peers in Sarajevo, where he spent most of the war, to be one of the most creative and original thinkers in the humanitarian world. Better a savvy politicized hu-manitarianism, he thought, than a co-opted humanitarianism that was obliged to be the mute accomplice of states intent on using its prestige for their actions or their inaction. Their bitter experience in Bosnia had persuaded Fawcett and many of his colleagues that the chaos of crises like the one that had taken place in the Balkans were also opportunities for an entirely different kind of humanitarianism. It would be political. That they viewed as inevitable. But it would not be merely governmental and it certainly would not be impotent. To the contrary, the humanitarianism many of the veterans of the Bos-nian aid effort envisaged was one that might actually succeed in forc-ing governments to live up to their responsibilities and thus let the humanitarians live up to theirs. The conviction that these relief offi-cials shared was that since states were using aid to ends the human-itarians found abhorrent, relief workers themselves would have to find a way to turn the tables.

As Claude Moncorge, the president of Médecins du Monde-France, would put it later, "A positive synergy can exist between civil society, the NGOs, the humanitarian actors and the political author-ities." If it did not yet exist in Bosnia—if, in fact, the synergy there had been negative rather than positive—this only increased the need for the NGOs to try to create an alternative model of cooperation with states. Moncorge phrased the question well. "Is it possible," he asked, "to establish a link between a humanitarian diagnosis, dis-connected from all political interest, and a political diagnosis, dis-connected from *realpolitik?*" His answer, like that of a John Fawcett, a Fred Cuny, or a Bernard Kouchner, was clearly yes. But it was not obvious why it should have been.

Everyone agreed that the old modalities had failed. If UNHCR had, in the minds even of many of its best people, been forced to act in ways that were not only at variance with its fundamental mandate but were morally questionable, the other traditional responses had failed as well. In particular, the conduct of the ICRC in the early days of the Bosnian war reminded many unpleasantly of its behavior during the Nazi period. The ICRC had known about the Serb concentration camps in northern Bosnia, but had said nothing. Ed Vulliamy, the British reporter who finally uncovered the horrific truth of these camps in the summer of 1992, later reported that, rather than go public, ICRC officials had a "shockingly defensive state of mind." He went on: "There was blanket refusal to apportion responsibility or blame for these camps." And Jose María Mendiluce had much the same impression. When he raised the issue of the camps, he recalled, the ICRC "were very clearly telling me: 'Don't mess around with this. It's our area of responsibility.'"

Cornelio Sommaruga, the head of the ICRC, might say that every moment the organization spent today on "our humanitarian responsibilities to assist victims of war and political violence" reminded him of "our institution's moral failure with regard to the Holocaust, since it did not succeed in moving beyond the limited legal framework established by states." But many in the organization continued to insist that, in the words of an ICRC spokesman, Kim Gordon-Bates, there were fears "the work we were doing, probably quite well, with respect to the POWs would have been jeopardized by being too outspoken about the Nazis, with dire consequences for those we were helping, without helping those we were not helping."

But although the ICRC might have claimed to have turned over a new moral leaf, in Bosnia the arguments it used for not going public with what it knew about the Serb concentration camps were remarkably similar to those it had used until well into the 1990s to justify its conduct during the Holocaust. "In Banja Luka," an ICRC official told Ed Vulliamy, "we had to decide: do we want to continue to work with the inmates of the camps, or do we take a stand which will cost us our presence in Banja Luka?" The fact that prisoners continued to be tortured and killed while ICRC officials flattered themselves about their heroic efforts to secure visiting rights seems to have troubled these officials not a whit. To be sure, Sommaruga would make a rather nondescript speech a few months later denouncing "ethnic cleansing." (The ICRC hailed the speech as pathbreaking, which it was, but only in internal institutional terms.) But on the ground, his delegates acted as they had always acted, with ironclad discretion.

Trapped between a state-imposed misuse of humanitarianism and the ICRC's unacceptably rigid notions of neutrality, the most creative, diligent, and morally responsible relief workers began to dream of a humanitarianism that would become a force for change, a species of democratic activism. These aid workers thought they saw the way out of the humanitarian dilemma in the language of rights, above all the language of the UN's Universal Declaration of Human Rights, which they interpreted as guaranteeing them access to the victims of war, and guaranteeing the victims access to relief. To the Western powers' politics of substituting relief for rescue, the humanitarian international proposed a politics of human dignity that would force states to live up to their obligations under human rights law and the laws of war. Given what had taken place in Bosnia, such a response was understandable. It was more than understandable; it was, to use a most unfashionable word, noble. But it was not coherent, and, as events would prove, it was probably not wise.

This was a humanitarianism that thought it could change the

world, or at least, by insisting on the rights of the victims, turn the world toward thinking about crises in the same way that it did—not simply in terms of altruism, or philanthropy, but in terms of a human solidarity grounded in binding legal norms. But there was no reason to believe, just because certain international legal documents and conventions existed (no matter how binding on states they were in theory), that the world had changed. No reason except that mixture of hope and despair that had always animated the best humanitarian relief workers. In fact, international law was no better respected at the end of the Bosnian war than it was at the beginning. And no amount of ad hoc war crimes tribunals, or integration of human rights concerns into the daily practice of relief workers, could change that fact. Indeed, as Françoise Bouchet-Saulnier, MSF's resident expert on international humanitarian law, would point out, compliance with the law plummeted in the 1990s, even while Western governments and the NGOs themselves paid lip service to its authority as never before at the UN.

Some thoughtful UN humanitarian officials agreed. For example, Sergio Vieira de Mello, who spent most of his career as a UNHCR official before going on to run the UN's Office for the Coordination of Humanitarian Affairs and then becoming the UN's proconsul in East Timor, put it starkly. "Recent history may suggest that evil is prevailing," he said in a speech. "The body of international law is under severe challenge, particularly in the humanitarian sphere. It is, in fact, being systematically flouted and disregarded . . . deliberately violated. Does this mean a breakdown of these norms? I don't think so. What it means is a breakdown of respect for those norms."

Despite the gap he correctly identified between norms and realities, de Mello remained enough the career UN official to insist that this "behavioral breakdown," as he called it, could be addressed successfully. Unlike Bouchet-Saulnier, who, despite her lifelong commitment to human rights, was brave enough to recognize the gap between admirable norms and vile facts, de Mello was too much the conformist international civil servant, pledged to optimism no matter what the intellectual cost, to entertain profoundly the possibility that things were getting worse, not better.

For humanitarians in the field, however, the distortions produced by the Bosnian experience, above all the increasing dominance of the notion that since aid inevitably had political consequences, relief workers always needed consciously to adopt a political approach, even if this meant violating the principle of neutrality and taking sides, were very much the product of the Bosnian—i.e., the European—experience of relief work. Of course, what they meant by this was far more than the obvious and unarguable point that all actions in the public sphere are in some sense political. Relief workers were talking about policy. As John Fawcett had rightly said, in the Balkans aid was systematically used for political ends.

Moreover, in Bosnia most, though by no means all aid workers believed that in the Milosevic regime and its Bosnian Serb creations the world was facing a new fascist threat. Bosnia had something of the same moral significance that the Spanish Civil War had had sixty years earlier. It was this conviction, along with the belief that humanitarian emergencies paradoxically offered opportunities to change societies for the better—an idea Fred Cuny spent his entire professional life trying to demonstrate—that had inspired George Soros to make a fifty-million-dollar grant to the humanitarian effort in Bosnia and hire Cuny to administer his programs. Soros always adamantly insisted that he was not a humanitarian, and had no interest in relief for relief's sake. But if humanitarian aid was the best mechanism to support an "open society" in Bosnia against the Serb fascists who wanted to destroy it, he would drape his democratic activism in the flag of convenience of humanitarianism.

Soros and Cuny were not alone in believing that humanitarian action could be honorably "borrowed" for such purposes. The rightness and urgency of the Bosnian cause alone seemed to justify such a conviction. But leaving aside the issue of the rightness of the Bosnian cause—and despite the disappointments of postwar Bosnia, I still believe that people like Soros, and Cuny, were right that the Bosnian government had justice as well as victimhood on its side—what many of us failed to see was how singular and nontransferable the Bosnian model was. The reality is that most conflicts in which humanitarian relief workers are needed do not have a clear-cut right side and wrong side. Indeed, the UN peacekeepers' routine insistence that all sides were villains in the Balkans, while false in the instance, was right about any number of other conflicts in the world, from Tajikistan to Burundi.

In particular, things looked that way in Africa, where often there was no "right" side. Moreover, by the standards of an Angola or a Liberia, the humanitarian needs that had existed in Bosnia, grave as they were, seemed comparatively minor. To say this is not to try to establish some idiotic and morally repellant hierarchy of want. Rather, it is to underscore that it was in sub-Saharan Africa that the most terrible and intractable humanitarian crises were taking place. Was the impartiality that had been so inappropriate in Bosnia really so wrong in the African context? Most relief workers who had served in Africa but had not served in the Balkans did not think so. Nor did the ICRC's approach seem nearly so open to reproach as it had in southeastern Europe in the early 1990s. Even events in Rwanda, which came closest to the "Bosnian" norm, would demonstrate how different the humanitarian imperative looked in the Great Lakes region of Africa from the way it did in the Balkans.

There is a sense in which the lessons drawn by relief workers from the Bosnian experience were the right lessons for Balkan wars but the wrong lessons for humanitarianism. As Françoise Bouchet-Saulnier put it, "The particular became general. Humanitarianism legitimized the containment of refugees who themselves became human shields either around or at the heart of conflicts."

What the Bosnian catastrophe seemed to have demonstrated was that the possibility of a kind of humanitarian action that could remain apart from politics and reasons of state was a pipe dream. Even Médecins Sans Frontières, which unlike almost every other mainline NGO continued to remain steadfastly loyal to this conception of humanitarianism, was haunted by its own complicity in the illusion of safety that the presence of UN peacekeepers *and* relief workers had created in the minds of the people of Srebrenica. "The continued presence of MSF in the midst of [the population of] the enclave contributed to maintaining the illusion of international protection in the zone." To a considerable extent, MSF's own subsequent engagement in making sure the full truth about Srebrenica was revealed, especially the French government's complicity in the disaster, and above all its secret dealings with Bosnian Serb forces, was an act of contrition for its inadvertent collusion in the lie that was the humanitarian effort in the Bosnian war.

And even MSF did not come out against humanitarian intervention that protected civilians against aggressors. "Our demand," it said in its statement calling for a French government commission of inquiry into Srebrenica, "is not an anti-militarist crusade. On the contrary, we hope the commission draws the [right] lessons so as to avoid in the future deploying soldiers who would be tied hand and foot as they confront criminal policies against a [civilian] population."

Other agencies went further. Bosnia had been a failure, but henceforth humanitarianism would be one element of the response to such outrages by an "international community" sobered by its failures and alive to its responsibilities. That community did not yet exist, but it was in the process of being born. "If humanitarianism knows that it is political," Bernard Kouchner wrote in 1995, just as the Bosnian war was drawing to a close, "and if it can succeed in constructing a new humanism," humanitarian action would be an integral part of that better world.

Was it realistic hope? Even in the Bosnian context, it presupposed political clarity, the commitment of donors, the engagement of the Western public, and the possibility of rescue. In those practically utopian conditions, the kind of politicized intervention a Fred Cuny or a Bernard Kouchner favored was at least possible, although eight years later Kosovo would demonstrate just how problematic the construct was. But *none* of these conditions prevailed in Africa. The public tended to be indifferent; the donors tended to be unwilling to spend the sums needed on alleviation, let alone intervention; and the aid workers and UN officials usually were correct in believing that between guerrillas and governments there was little if anything to choose.

In such a context, the sacrifice of humanitarian neutrality, even if it came wrapped in an appeal to international humanitarian law and a commitment to upholding human rights, was likely to be dangerous if not actually fatal to the humanitarian enterprise. For if Africa could not hope from the world what Bosnia or Kosovo could expect—attention, money, even the willingness to establish international protectorates—had the humanitarianism that had turned its back on neutrality taken a necessary step forward or, instead, seized upon what the French so aptly call a "false good idea"? A humanitarianism that would right wrongs rather than alleviate them. It sounded marvelous. But it sounded marvelous because it was only a dream.

CHAPTER 5

Rwanda

T HE RWANDAN GENOCIDE WAS the worst thing to happen in the 1990s, and one of the vilest things to happen in the entire vile twentieth century. This catastrophe of unimaginable proportions was made ineradicably shameful and sorrowful by the fact that at least some of the up to eight hundred thousand people who died in fewer than nine weeks in the late spring and early summer of 1994 could have been saved had either the major Western powers or important African countries with the capability of doing so, such as Nigeria and South Africa, cared enough to send troops. Does this seem like special pleading? Can anyone say with certainty that the Tutsi and moderate Hutu victims of the Forces Armées Rwandaises and the Interahamwe militias would definitely have been rescued had UN peacekeepers been allowed to do their jobs by their nominal bosses at UN headquarters in New York (for instance, the then head of the peacekeeping department, Kofi Annan) or their real bosses, the powerful member states to whom Annan and his colleagues reported? That would be claiming too much. But at the very least, some of those who died might have been saved. Just knowing this is horror enough, shame enough, tragedy enough.

The season of cowardice that accompanied this season of blood had started before the killing began. There had been a UN peacekeeping force in Rwanda since 1993. It was known as UNAMIR (United Nations Assistance Mission for Rwanda), and it was commanded by a Canadian general named Romeo Dallaire. He and his peacekeepers had been sent to Rwanda to help oversee a peace accord between the government and the Tutsi-led rebels of the Rwandan Patriotic Front (RPF) that had been brokered by the UN in the Tanzanian town of Arusha in late 1993. But their mandate did not include preventing further slaughter, which, in any case, the UN was persuaded would not take place (as were development agencies like Oxfam). After all, the regime of Major General Juvénal Habyarimana had signed a peace accord, hadn't it? And if it had signed, in the presence of UN officials and representatives of the international *community*, then surely that meant it was committed to peace.

In other words, as had so often been the case at the UN, it was a triumph of form over substance, legalism over reality, hope over experience. And UN officials charged with overseeing events in Rwanda seemed as complacent about their ability to see no evil as their opposite numbers in the Balkans were. "One has to be a little Pollyannaish to be in this business," Hedi Annabi, the UN desk officer for Rwanda at the time, would later tell me. Why he and his colleagues assumed that warring sides that had been trying to murder each other for several generations, who had grown up in a political culture that knew little except massacre and the zero sum game, were at last committed to peace, Annabi never made clear. But whatever the reasons, the UN was determined to operate its UNAMIR peacekeeping force under the assumption that it could rely upon the good-faith cooperation of both the Rwandan government and the RPF. It was a decision that the Rwandan people would pay for, even if Kofi Annan was still defending it at the time of his first visit to

Rwanda after the genocide. Asked by a reporter in Kenya shortly before his arrival if he would have handled things differently in the pregenocide period, Annan replied that he would not.

Of course, after Bosnia this was becoming standard operating procedure at the UN's Department of Peacekeeping Operations. As a Belgian colonel attached to the force would recall, "I had not come to Rwanda as a para-commando to fight but as a Blue Helmet, a symbolic presence to help the Rwandans . . . My perception of classic UN operations was that the UN does not fight . . . I believed in the assurance [as the genocide was beginning] . . . of the command of the Rwandan army that they would help us to assure security and order . . . I was blinded by this logic, paralyzed by it."

As was the case in Bosnia during the same period, there was the conviction that the UN did not fight, whatever the moral dimension and whatever humiliation it had to undergo in order not to do so. UN peacekeepers, whether in Sarajevo or Kigali, found themselves in thrall to the same moral syllogism, which, in fairness, was imposed on them by Annan's peacekeeping department headquarters in New York, that the UN, as Yasushi Akashi, the secretary-general's special representative for the former Yugoslavia, put it, was an organization committed to "the logic of peace, not the logic of war." To UN peacekeeping officials, fulfilling what the Belgian officer rightly characterized as this "symbolic function" was to do their duty.

However, the UN's commander on the ground in Rwanda was neither naïve, nor careerist, nor cynical, nor morally obtuse and politically misguided after the fashion of so many of the commanders selected by the UN Secretariat and the powerful member states to lead the UNPROFOR detachments in the Balkans. General Dallaire had begun receiving reports that the Rwandan government was planning a preemptive campaign of mass murder against the Tutsis in late 1993, and that it was gathering the weapons it needed in caches in the Kigali area. He was not only horrified by the information he was receiving, he was determined to do something to prevent the slaughter. He cabled the UN's Department of Peacekeeping Operations asking for permission to raid these caches.

Dallaire was a man almost uniquely driven by conscience. He could never accept, and perhaps had not understood, that in the aftermath of the UN's disastrous experience in Somalia, the organization was unwilling to take any risks in Rwanda. His colleague from the Canadian military, General Maurice Barril, who was the DPKO military advisor during the Rwanda crisis, tried to set him straight. Michael Barnett describes the exchange in *Eyewitness to a Genocide*, his definitive book on what he calls "the ethical history of the UN's involvement in Rwanda." Barril told Dallaire that from the UN's point of view the "planned raid had Somalia and 'mission creep' all over it." Another debacle like Somalia, UN officials believed, might destroy UN peacekeeping. As a result, they committed themselves in Rwanda to what Iqbal Riza, a senior DPKO official, would later describe as a "cautious interpretation" of the UN's peacekeeping mandate in Rwanda. "We could not risk another Somalia as it led to the collapse of the Somalian mission. We did not want this mission to collapse."

Most other peacekeeping generals would have understood the argument. The commanders of UNPROFOR in Bosnia—Canadian, French, Belgian, and British alike—either embraced or acceded to the rules of the game of UN peacekeeping. Neither the siege of Sarajevo, nor the "ethnic cleansing" of northern and eastern Bosnia, nor even the Srebrenica massacre led them to question fundamentally their commitment to "impartiality." Indeed, the memoirs of Major General Lewis Mackenzie, General Francis Briquemont, and General Sir Michael Rose all insist on the fine job they did under such difficult circumstances in the Balkans.

But Dallaire was not content to stand by and watch the heavens darken while consoling himself that his mandate precluded doing what he could to stop the catastrophe. It was a stance that availed him nothing in terms of career. As Michael Barnett puts it bitterly, "There was a nearly inverse relationship between the extent to which UN staff fulfilled their responsibilities and their subsequent professional fortunes." Kofi Annan became UN secretary-general; Iqbal Riza his *chef de cabinet*. But after Dallaire retired from the Canadian forces, the thought of the Rwandan lives he had been unable to save would lead him to the brink of suicide.

As head of UN peacekeeping at the time, Annan was responsible for the decision to authorize or forbid Dallaire to proceed. His response was not long in coming. He instructed Dallaire firmly that nothing was to be done. Preventing such an eventuality—assuming, Annan added dampeningly, the information was actually correct—was not part of UNAMIR's mandate. As Dallaire recalled it, Annan cabled him that "such a raid could only be viewed as hostile by the Rwandan government." He was to go on as he had before, overseeing the Arusha settlement.

Annan did not just stop Dallaire from acting. Whether it was in consultation with his boss, Secretary-General Boutros-Ghali, or on his own initiative (Boutros-Ghali would later insist Annan had kept him in the dark), Annan also chose not to inform the members of the Security Council about what its own mission commander was reporting from the ground in the Rwandan capital of Kigali. Pollyannaish? There are other words for such conduct. Asked on the occasion of receiving the 2001 Nobel Peace Prize whether he had considered resigning at the time, Annan replied that he would have but only had he believed it would have done any good. His share of responsibility in what the UN's own inquiry into the Rwandan genocide would describe as the "wider picture of failed response to early warning" was, it seemed, not a compelling reason to do so.

Whether it was for fear of failing, or overstepping its mandate, or undertaking an action the powerful member states might disapprove of, the UN did nothing except inform the ambassadors of the major Western powers in Kigali of Dallaire's information. The matter was never brought before the Security Council, let alone made public. Far from overstating the threat, as some UN officials claimed at the time, even Dallaire had not begun to grasp its magnitude.

On April 6, 1994, the genocide began. A Falcon 50 executive jet, the gift of French President François Mitterrand to Juvénal Habyarimana, the Hutu president of Rwanda, was shot down as it approached the Kigali airport. Habyarimana and his counterpart, Cyprien Ntaryamira, the president of Burundi, and their staffs were killed. It has never been established who shot down the plane, although blame has been affixed variously to Hutu extremists and the RPF. But within a few hours, the genocide had begun. All over Rwanda, regular Rwandan troops and the Hutu extremist Interahamwe militia (the name in Kinyarwanda meant "those who struggle together") began to hunt down every Tutsi they could find—as well as many Hutus who had opposed Habyarimana and his supporters' extremist, racist creed—and kill them. In the nine weeks during which the slaughter continued unabated, more people died in less time that in any other massacre in modern history.

Western states were determined not to get involved. In a brilliant investigation laying out the American role in this disgrace, the American writer and human rights activist Samantha Power has shown that it was not that the U.S. government did not know what was going on. It did. Rather, it did not want to do anything. Here was another demonstration of Françoise Bouchet-Saulnier's point that the lip service Western governments paid to international law had no correlation to their actual disdain for the obligations it supposedly imposed. Under the Genocide Convention, a finding that a genocide is taking place anywhere in the world imposes on signatory states the affirmative obligation to do whatever is in their power to bring it to a halt. The United States could have acted. The truth is, it did not care enough to do so.

And yet, if the authority of international law did not extend to forcing great powers like the United States to live up to their treaty obligations, it nonetheless had a certain negative authority. The United States was not so contemptuous of international law that it was willing simply to thumb its nose at the Genocide Convention. Rather, through the person of its then UN ambassador and future secretary of state Madeleine Albright, the Clinton administration made sure that the word "genocide" was never applied to what was taking place in Rwanda while the killing was actually going on. The goal of U.S. policy was *not* to have to do anything about the mass slaughter in Rwanda. The means chosen was to ensure that what was taking place was called a "humanitarian crime," not a genocide. And when that position became untenable, the U.S. State Department retreated to the stance that while "acts of genocide" might be taking place in Rwanda, "genocide" was not. Asked by a Reuters correspondent named Alan Elsner how many such acts would be needed to add up to a genocide, Christina Shelly, a department spokeswoman, answered, "That's just not a question that I'm in a position to answer."

It is unlikely, without the availability of a humanitarian alibi honed in Bosnia, that the Clinton administration would have been able to sustain its own alibis for so long. Examples of cynicism, but also of anxiety over the totemic quality of the word "genocide," abounded. As Samantha Power reported in *The Atlantic*, Susan Rice, an Albright protégée who would go on to become assistant secretary of state for African affairs, demanded of her then colleagues on the National Security Council, "If we use the word 'genocide' and are seen as doing nothing, what will be the effect on the November [congressional] election?"

The realpolitik point of view that Rice's comment exemplified emerged victorious from the policy debate within the Clinton administration. National security advisor Anthony Lake held out the hope to human rights activists that if they could mobilize enough support for a U.S. intervention, this might change. But in reality the administration had made its decision, and that was to treat Rwanda as an intractable problem—"a problem from hell," as one former aide put it to Power—and, as such, one to be avoided. Small wonder then that the U.S. government did everything it could to present what was happening in Rwanda as a humanitarian crisis, when in truth it was a planned campaign of mass murder by the Rwandan government, which, almost uniquely in sub-Saharan Africa because of the centralized nature of power there, was able to marshal the organs of state power to carry out the killing with an efficiency comparable to that of Hitler's Germany.

Obviously, this was not the humanitarians' fault. What is unfortunately all too likely, however, is that the humanitarians' powerlessness in resisting the appropriation of their own prestige by Western governments, and their ever-increasing dependence on those governments for funds and logistical support, did make them inadvertent accomplices in the cruel deception.

For if any slaughter in the 1990s justified military intervention, it was the one in Rwanda. And yet despite the best efforts of some humanitarians and a core of international human rights activists, for the Western public as a whole it soon came to be regarded as yet another horrifying case of something incomprehensible, awful, and intractable where all that could really be done was provide aid for the victims. The British journalist Lindsay Hilsum remarked that a reporter who came to a place like Kigali in the killing time and thought

that what he or she was witnessing was sheer anarchy had understood little or nothing. Nothing could have been further from the
truth. As MSF's Jean-Herve Bradol, who worked in Kigali throughout the genocide, put it, "There was no anarchy, no chaos" in the
Rwandan capital. To the contrary, though they might be using ma-
chetes, rocks, and firebombs to do their killing, those carrying out
the genocide were acting according to a well-rehearsed plan.

Once the killing had started, the UN became only a minor actor
in the disgrace. It is true that Secretary-General Boutros-Ghali went
on parroting the French government's line that, if indeed a genocide
was taking place, it was, as he put it, a "double genocide," with "the
Hutu killing the Tutsi and the Tutsi killing the Hutu." The most
powerful African states behaved unconscionably. Nigeria was nowhere to be seen in the crisis, but at least it was possible to rationalize this by saying that it was a dictatorship and thus little more could
be expected of it. But what of newly liberated South Africa, which by
then had as its president the revered Nelson Mandela? South Africa,
too, turned its back, when it had both the firepower and the airlift capability to intervene, as a number of senior officers of its defense
forces urged Mandela to allow them to do.

But at the center of things was French backing for the radical
"Hutu Power" regime that took over after President Habyarimana's
death, and America's refusal either to intervene itself, help materi-
ally those smaller African countries like Ghana that had shown
some readiness to go in themselves, or even smooth the way for a Security Council resolution authorizing such an intervention. If responsibility is to be apportioned for the Rwandan genocide's making
a mockery of that great phrase of the post-Holocaust era, "Never
again," it is the United States and France that deserve the lion's
share, not the Africans, and certainly not the careerist bureaucrats at
UN headquarters. U.S. politicians were convinced that their elec-

torates were indifferent to what was going on in Rwanda. That made taking action seem too risky, especially to the poll-driven Clinton administration.

Of course, there were reasons besides political calculation for the lack of response from the major Western powers. Events on the ground in Rwanda had helped see to that. The Interahamwe had begun their campaign by torturing, killing, and mutilating ten Belgian soldiers who had been part of the bodyguard of Agathe Uwilingiyimana, the Rwandan prime minister and a Hutu moderate. (Belgium was the ex-colonial power in Rwanda.) All that Belgium and the other Western countries seemed to want, once the full horror of the killings had sunk in, was to evacuate their troops and their resident nationals. The last thing they were thinking about was returning in force to stop the genocide. Significantly, among those evacuated were not only Western embassy personnel and the expatriate business community, but also the international staffs of the major relief and development organizations, whose headquarters in Europe and North America had determined that the situation in Rwanda had simply become too dangerous. The sole exception was the ICRC itself and some individual doctors from MSF who put themselves at the Red Cross's disposal. It was ironic. Humanitarianism seemed almost to have come full circle. Just as in Biafra in 1967, the French doctors were, in the absence of a better alternative, volunteering to work for the ICRC.

But the deeper reality that Western aid workers were Westerners first, aid workers second, could not have been plainer, above all to the Rwandans. One of the buried traumas of the humanitarian international that is a searing legacy of that killing time is that when the major agencies redeployed they found that most of their Tutsi local staff had been murdered. As the killing gathered pace, the great powers dithered. To its great credit, little Ghana offered to send more troops into Rwanda. But its forces did not have either the airlift capacity or the armored vehicles that were required for an effective deployment. And the U.S. government, which obviously had equipment to spare, refused the repeated requests of a belatedly but at last fully committed UN bureaucracy to lend the Ghanaians some of them, and stalled as the Pentagon debated what fees it would charge if it made the equipment available.

In such a context, even to focus on what effects the Rwandan experience had on humanitarianism may seem a moral solecism. Humanitarianism was anything but the most important casualty of the Rwandan genocide. Asked by a reporter whether his faith in God had been shaken by the experience of living through the genocide, a foreign priest replied: "No, my faith in God is intact. But my faith in human beings has been shattered forever."

To borrow that familiar bit of U.S. military newspeak, given the scope of the disgrace, the losses the humanitarian international incurred in Rwanda could be considered simply "collateral damage." And yet the cost to the dignity and sense of self-worth of the aid world is almost incalculable. Every one of its most cherished ideals came to dust in Rwanda. And when the crisis finally ebbed in 1996, humanitarians were left with a profound sense of impotence. There was the nagging fear, based on bitter experience, that the relief effort in eastern Congo, western Tanzania, and Rwanda itself in the aftermath of the genocide, heroic as it had been, had contributed to making things worse, not better. There was also the realization that, once again, the nobility of purpose of aid work and the bravery and dedication of so many individual aid workers had been used to cover up the fact that those outside powers that could have stopped the genocide had chosen not to do so.

If Bosnia turned humanitarianism on its ear ideologically, Rwanda broke its heart. Alex de Waal summed up the challenge the relief organizations faced: "How were organizations dedicated to the relief of suffering to deal with a government whose *raison d'etre* was the infliction of suffering?" Rwanda exposed the powerlessness of aid agencies. For many aid workers, it offered definitive proof that, at least in the most extreme situations, humanitarianism makes sense only as part of a larger international response. As a French reporter put it, "Hell cannot be administered." By the same token, relief workers felt that they could not be left out on a moral limb as well as an operational one, having to substitute for states that did not want to get involved, without having the power or the resources to do so either effectively or without causing political or social harm.

And in Rwanda, there were so many opportunities to cause harm. Even providing the outside powers and the UN with the ability to say that "something" was being done for Rwanda as the killing went on and on was disgrace enough. Despite itself, humanitarian action occluded the reality that everything that took place in Rwanda from the late spring through the summer of 1994, including the refugee exodus, was the result of the genocide. It is not just that to call what happened there a humanitarian emergency was a grotesque misrepresentation of what was taking place. It proves, if proof is needed, that Rony Brauman's bitter suggestion that Auschwitz would have been called a humanitarian crisis had it occurred in the 1990s was not hyperbole. Rather, it was that the participation of humanitarians in that crisis, for all the considerable good they did, carried the risk of giving the Western public a false impression of what was going on, and Western governments a way of saying that they were not simply standing by, since "their" relief workers were in the field saving lives.

It was a case these governments did not have to work hard to make. One of the things that the Rwandan genocide established was that this distortion had already been integrated into the imagination of the West. Revolution of concern? Humanitarianism as an all too efficient impediment to understanding would have been a more accurate diagnosis. Obviously, there were those in the West—most were human rights activists but a significant number were relief workers—who kept repeating in the media or to any politician who would listen that Rwanda was a political problem, not a humanitarian one. "In Rwanda once again," Philippe Biberson, president of MSF-France, told a news conference in early May 1994, at the height of the genocide, "humanitarianism is serving as a cover for the inaction of states . . . We have [already] known humanitarianism as alibi, but now we are entering into the humanitarianism of impassability and of the dead end." He warned that, in the absence of some political resolution, the humanitarian aid that was so needed in so many places in Rwanda risked wrongly being seen as a solution to the crisis. Instead, it was being used by both the Rwandan government side and its enemies in the Tutsi-dominated Rwandan Patriotic Front to feed the war. "One cannot halt a massacre with medicines," he said. "The genocide must stop, and those responsible for it be brought to justice!"

MSF had opposed American humanitarian military intervention in Somalia on the grounds that the mixing of humanitarian and military imperatives was bound, given Somali realities, to degenerate into real war. In the name of helping the Somali people, MSF officials feared, a so-called humanitarian military intervention would end up making war upon them, even if it did so in the name of halting a famine. In Mogadishu, the organization's worst fears had been realized. Later, MSF had refused to take a position officially about how the Bosnian slaughter should be halted. But in Rwanda, it called for military intervention from any outside power willing to undertake it. This was genocide—"absolute evil," to use Rony Brauman's accurate phrase—and thus constituted a special case for MSF.

Brauman was well aware of the trap MSF risked falling into. "Ambiguity and the confusion of roles," he would write later, "are in the very nature of humanitarianism, whose special area remains that where social and political violence [reign] . . . [This] is one of the constitutive paradoxes of humanitarianism: On the one hand, we are held to act on a certain level as if it was the suffering of populations and not political reality that should be our principal concern. On the other, we have a duty to be lucid politically. That has led us to draw a line beyond which the necessary negotiations and compromises with local authorities become unacceptable."

For Brauman, the compromises MSF had been obliged to make with the remnants of the Khmer Rouge in the refugee camps along the Thai-Cambodian border, after the fall of the Pol Pot regime in Phnom Penh in 1979, had been necessary, at least at the height of the refugee emergency. (Unlike some other agencies, MSF subsequently withdrew from these camps.) So was its determination to remain in Taliban-ruled Afghanistan despite the constraints put upon it. But Rwanda was as far on the other side of MSF's "line" as it was possible to be. In a situation where, as Brauman put it, the purpose of the conflict was the extermination of the Tutsi population, humanitarian aid had a very limited utility. Increasingly conscious that it could not play a useful enough role, MSF began campaigning in the West to see to it that what was taking place in Rwanda was recognized internationally as a genocide and calling for a military intervention to stop it.

The humanitarians could do nothing. And yet, while nothing could have been further from what they wished, the prestige of relief workers was so high in the West (above all in Western Europe, but increasingly in North America as well) that the public could be persuaded to believe, at least initially, that the fact that relief workers were on the scene might mean that all was not lost. This credulity should not have been surprising. It was a by-product of twenty-five years of humanitarian action, twenty-five years of media manipulation and media adulation. A poll done in France in 1997, *after* the Bosnian and Rwandan calamities, would find that there was more support for the idea that humanitarians were better suited to prevent conflicts than NATO, the European Union, or the French government. But all was lost. That was the reality of Rwanda in April 1994, at least so long as no great power sent soldiers.

Most relief workers in the field in Rwanda, as in so many other crises, had enough experience to realize what was taking place once the killing started to accelerate. They might be horrified, but they did not lie to themselves about what was going on, as Western governments and the UN continued to do. But having the courage, as Oxfam did, to go out on a limb and use the word "genocide" was not the same as knowing what to recommend or how to describe what was going on to their donors in the West.

Critics of aid have routinely pilloried the NGOs for seizing on crises for fund-raising purposes, and there is some truth to that, though by no means as much as these detractors tend to suggest. A far more crucial problem, exposed by Rwanda and Bosnia, was that the humanitarian mode of understanding as it was popularized in the 1980s and early 1990s was not conducive to understanding. Worse still, humanitarians found themselves trapped in the contradictions between their most cherished principles. MSF had started as an organization dedicated to testifying; its sophisticated technical expertise came later. Oxfam was for a long time principally a development agency. And the IRC was principally concerned with refugees. By the same token, the United Nations agencies like UNHCR and WFP faced the challenge of transforming themselves into relief organizations as the humanitarian disasters of the 1990s piled up one after the other and powerful states insisted the international response needed to be humanitarian first, political second (if it came at all).

By the time the Rwandan genocide started, it was already something of a vicious circle. The slaughter would begin. To the Western public, the crisis was far away and unreal, a matter, as the British government liked to say about Bosnia, of "ancient ethnic hatreds," or, about Rwanda, of African "savagery." Since the great powers did not want to intervene militarily or politically, they did everything they could to support and confirm this alienated, despairing analysis. They pointed to victims with humanitarian needs. The needs were real enough. But they served to immunize the public against any political questioning or analysis of what was going on.

At best, the false morality play that this engendered was one that presented wicked warlords and innocent victims, and conveyed the impression that the actions of those warlords were stopping well-intended humanitarians from helping. In the case of a Rwanda, the result was far worse. For the availability of the humanitarian alibi actually allowed the great powers, above all the United States, to prevaricate until it was too late for military intervention to succeed. As Brauman put it, the presence of the humanitarians, "far from representing a bulwark against evil, was in fact one of its appendages." And he added pointedly that "the social and political role of humanitarian aid was simply to stage-manage goodwill, to organize the spectacle of compassion."

In fact, it was not the presence of relief workers—how could it have been?—but only the success of the Rwandan Patriotic Front on the battlefield that prevented the Hutu extremists from slaughtering every Tutsi in the country. And the best relief workers were painfully aware of the humanitarian trap into which they had fallen. MSF was not alone in calling for an intervention. The IRC had demanded one also. Oxfam's approach was more problematic. To its credit, it had been either the first or among the first relief groups to identify what was taking place as a genocide. But its response was confused. It simultaneously demanded an end to the killing, a UN military intervention, humanitarian access (as it would do in Afghanistan in 2001), and an immediate ceasefire. And though Oxfam does not appear to have realized it at the time, these demands effectively cancelled one another out. In particular, as Alex de Waal has pointed out, had a ceasefire been put into effect at the moment Oxfam called for it, the result would have left half of Rwanda in the hands of those perpetrating the genocide and thus allowed them to finish what they had started in the zone they controlled.

In calling for a ceasefire, Oxfam only meant to make it possible for relief workers to reach people in desperate need of its assistance. But the mistake highlighted the degree to which relief groups may be knowledgeable about their own imperatives but, in focusing on what they require in order to carry them out, may be blind to other implications of what they are calling for. The tremendous moral authority of a group such as Oxfam, above all in Britain, only compounds the problem. In this case, the NGO's correct decision to demand action became more problematic when the organization began to detail just what kind of action it had in mind. Oxfam's expertise was in relief and development. What made its political views worth taking seriously? Why, for example, call for a ceasefire? In World War II, Oxfam had not called for Churchill to stop the war in the Greek theater of operations; it had demanded that he allow relief supplies to get to the Greek civilians who were suffering as a result of the British blockade of Athens.

The difference testified to the growth in the importance of humanitarianism in the minds of its practitioners over half a century. The reasons for this hubris, for that is what it was, are anything but discreditable. Understandably, relief workers are convinced of the rightness of their own actions, and they believe it imperative that the relief they provide get through. It is a matter of life and death for the people they are trying to assist. Bosnia had demonstrated, and Rwanda would establish beyond any argument, that humanitarianism not only could not address the root causes of most emergencies, but could not even operate effectively in its own sphere of alleviation without political engagement. This did not necessarily imply supporting a humanitarian military intervention. Often, it might mean lobbying and advocacy.

In countless academic studies, relief officials, human rights activists, and UN officials appear to assume that it is possible to remain faithful to the fundamental mission of humanitarianism, which is the impartial alleviation of suffering, while also taking policy positions about how best to address the underlying causes of conflicts. But is this true? Relief is a coherent idea, both morally and operationally, because it is universal and impartial. But no political stance, even one largely inspired by humanitarian concern, is likely to be so unimpeachable. And one of the defects of the humanitarian approach to politics is that it tends to spin a fable of warlords and innocent victims that has little bearing on the actual choices that are available, *even* when the will to intervene can be mustered among those states in a position to do so. The relief agencies accept the need to be political, but what does this mean in practice?

The case of Rwanda illustrates these dilemmas painfully. At first glance, arguing for an intervention to stop the genocide seemed like all that needed to be done. But of course, it wasn't. In reality, such a prescription begs more questions than it answers. Yes, the killing needed to be stopped. But was such an intervention to be in support of the Rwandan Patriotic Front that was also pledged to stop the genocide? Or was the RPF, which would itself go on to murder massive numbers of civilians, not worthy of support? If that was the case,

then the goal of any intervention would probably have to include setting up some sort of international protectorate that would respect
the wishes neither of the old Hutu Power regime nor of the RPF. But
what this meant in practice was a new humanitarian colonialism.
It might prove to be the only answer; certainly it was the answer
Western governments chose in Bosnia, Kosovo, and East Timor.
But it was not clear, when they advocated intervention in Bosnia
and Rwanda, that relief agencies fully understood the political as
opposed to the humanitarian implications of what they were calling for.

Indeed, most aid workers in the field, and, for that matter, most
relief officials at headquarters, had no special political expertise or
historical insight into the crisis zones in which they were operating.
That was hardly surprising. Why should a doctor from Narbonne,
France, who had been working in a regional hospital there before ar-
riving in the Great Lakes region of Africa, or a water and sanitation
engineer from Sausalito, California, have been expected to know
much about Rwanda? Most were young and had never been in the
region before. And they were not political experts. In fact, had they
been, it is unlikely an MSF, an Oxfam, or an IRC would have hired
them in the first place, since it was their technical skills that were
needed, not their historical acumen.

To say this is not to deny that some humanitarians are politically
astute. But given both the highly specialized nature of aid work and
the peripatetic nature of a relief worker's career, the chances are that
the worker will be transferred to another continent at just about the
time that he or she becomes conversant with the culture and politics
of a current posting. Even if the worker remains, it is not clear that
this familiarity will have brought with it any special authority with
regard to the essential policy issues that have to be addressed. It is
true that many of the major NGOs have policy units, and that some

of these, above all the ones set up at Oxfam, Save the Children (UK), and MSF-France, are particularly sophisticated. But of necessity, these units focus mainly on the interrelationship between politics and aid, not on politics in its own terms.

Relief and development workers in Rwanda had a very strong reason to be modest about their insights into the place. As Peter Uvin has pointed out in a brilliant and unaccountably ignored study, *Aiding Violence: The Development Enterprise in Rwanda,* before April 6, 1994, "almost none of the foreign experts living and working in Rwanda expected the genocide to occur . . . For most of these people, up to the end, Rwanda was a well-developing country—facing serious development problems, but dealing with them much more effectively than were other countries."

Tony Vaux, who was Oxfam's coordinator of global emergency programs, offers telling firsthand testimony of these confusions. "The Rwandan genocide," he writes, echoing Uvin's point, "was particularly shocking for longer-term aid workers because it happened in a country where development had once appeared so successful." But he adds, with a naïveté that is saddening, "The genocide seemed to deny everything that humanitarians stood for."

Can Vaux be serious? Here is an aid official who is a veteran of the Khmer Rouge genocide in Cambodia, and of the government-created famine in Ethiopia, and of ethnic cleansing in Bosnia, who is still surprised by the horror of the world. It would be one thing if he were just a *contributor* to Oxfam, but he is a senior official of the organization. And yet he appears unable to accept the fundamentally tragic context of his own vocation. How else to account for the way Vaux concludes the chapter on Rwanda in his memoir, *The Selfish Altruist,* sunnily insisting that Oxfam had "a sense of space still left, an ability to challenge and protest, to fight against the cycles of oppression and impoverishment"? He is tormented by the fact of the

Rwandan genocide. But his faith in his organization's ability to know what is the right thing to do remains unshaken. It is reminiscent of the priest's remark about the genocide not having shaken his faith in God. For a priest, such a response may be appropriate. Relief workers are not priests. But Vaux's language illustrates the degree to which humanitarianism has come to see itself as a secular religion (much as the United Nations and the human rights movement do). What is this conclusion, anyway, if not a credo, an affirmation of belief?

Vaux's approach invites skepticism about whether the political solutions relief agencies call for should be accorded any particular authority. Vaux's moral commitment radiates from every page of his book, but it is almost devoid of political intelligence. And for every Rony Brauman or Bernard Kouchner in the humanitarian world—people whose understanding of politics, for all their differences, is profound—there are, in my experience, a dozen Tony Vauxes. To question the legitimacy of NGOs' claims that they have the answers to what should be done politically, as they do to how to deliver relief effectively, is not to suggest that the humanitarians were solely or even principally to blame for the weakness and folly of the Western and UN response to the genocide. If an Oxfam tried to carve out for itself a position that was central, it could try to do so only because that position had been vacated by the great powers. The reality was that at the beginning of the crisis in Rwanda, and for the entire period between Habyarimana's death on April 6, 1994, and the deployment of a French expeditionary force on June 23, 1994, the humanitarians were on their own.

Of course, the humanitarians were no more "to blame" for what was happening in Rwanda than they were for what was happening in the Balkans during the same period. They had not actively discouraged action, as Kofi Annan had done, nor had they blocked it, as the Americans were to do. Nor had they called for military action as in Somalia but, to use Michael Marren's fine formulation, promptly repudiated that action when they discovered that soldiers were behaving like soldiers. Humanitarianism nonetheless found itself hurtling toward an operational and moral impasse. Given the uses it had already been put to in Bosnia, perhaps this was to have been expected. The great powers had learned that when they did not know how to respond, humanitarianism offered an attractive stopgap or fallback position. And these great powers were the humanitarians' major donors, the government departments or Western-funded UN agencies that the NGOs depended upon for their institutional survival (the United States, for example, has long been UNHCR's largest donor).

There had been, in any case, no chance that Washington, Paris, London, or Brussels would let the relief agencies off the hook. While they were determined not to intervene militarily to stop the genocide, from a political standpoint it was impossible for these great powers to do absolutely nothing at all. This was partly because of the images of slaughter that were appearing on television. But while the general public felt genuine shock and dismay at what was going on in Rwanda, at no time during the crisis did that translate into a groundswell of calls for action. The sight of all that killing broadcast live on the evening news does seem to have been as disturbing to the amour propre of Western policymakers as it was to the public at large. There was a feeling, inchoate to be sure, that something should be done—but something not too politically, let alone militarily, risky. Something, well, yes, *humanitarian*. For the great powers, humanitarianism did indeed seem to provide a way. Above all, it afforded them an opportunity to be seen as responding seriously. Thus the path that had been laid down in the Balkans now turned out to be at least as useful in the Great Lakes region of Africa. The Western powers were quick to seize the opportunity.

Western governments did not act in lockstep or even in concert. The French government had supported the Hutu Power government until the last possible moment. The Habyarimana regime had been a French client. In 1990, Paris had intervened militarily to prop it up against an invasion by the Rwandan Patriotic Front that might otherwise have succeeded. And the loathing the French military felt for the RPF was real: the "Khmer Noir" was what French officers called them. And yet it would be too simple to claim, as the RPF and its foreign supporters did, that when, in late June of 1994, the French launched Operation Turquoise, they did so only to rescue their erstwhile clients. That was certainly part of the story. French units deployed in the southwest of Rwanda and in some cases engaged the RPF on the battlefield. But if the deployment was far from being classical peacekeeping (though, interestingly, a number of the French commanders had served tours with UNPROFOR in Bosnia), its humanitarian dimension soon came to the fore.

Some French officers later said this was because they were genuinely shocked to discover that a genocide had indeed taken place, and that their Hutu clients were still trying to kill any Tutsis they could find. For them, the mission was transformed almost in spite of itself. Others said that the French government had acted out of mixed motives—one of which had always been humanitarian. The truth will probably never be clear. What is undeniable is that while some of the architects of the genocide escaped justice thanks to the French deployment, literally thousands of Tutsis were saved by French soldiers. It is also true that while the French were deploying troops, the other great powers were still dithering, and the Americans were still trying to block the use of the word "genocide" at the UN Security Council.

Perhaps this is why the French intervention divided the relief agencies. By and large, those humanitarians who, like Rony Brauman, were most pessimistic about what aid could do in the political sphere tended to favor Operation Turquoise. In contrast, Oxfam, which traditionally had seen itself as a vehicle for social transformation and whose brief included development as well as relief, was more appalled by France's shielding of Hutu Power's mass murderers in its zone than heartened by the Tutsi lives that French soldiers might be saving at the same time.

Relief workers did agree that the Rwandan genocide had provoked a full-fledged crisis. The crisis was in part the result of almost complete operational failure once the killing started. Indeed, by the end of April, all the mainline NGOs had withdrawn their expatriate staff. The ICRC struggled on alone, its efforts in this instance made singularly effective by the brilliance of its head of delegation, Philippe Gaillard. It was Gaillard who had coined what early in this book I described as the most eloquent formulation of the traditional view of humanitarian aid. The humanitarian enterprise, he said, was "an effort to bring a measure of humanity, always insufficient, into situations that should not exist."

During this part of the crisis, the ICRC's classical humanitarian doctrines showed their utility to its fullest. For all the moral problems that come with neutrality, when there is no hope of effective political action a politicized humanitarianism makes no sense. For this brief period, then, humanitarianism reverted to what it had been at the time of the Biafra war. In Rwanda, too, the ICRC was aided by a number of French doctors from MSF, including MSF-France's future president, Jean-Herve Bradol, and MSF-International's future president, James Orbinski. Given the difficulties, what the ICRC managed to do was extraordinary. But by the standards of post-Biafra humanitarianism—standards subscribed to as fervently by the partisans of MSF-style independent humanitarian action as of the state humanitarianism of the U.S. NGOs or of Bernard Kouchner—it was a failure, even a humiliation. For here, in all its tragedy, was the humanitarianism that could "merely" alleviate.

For many aid workers, that sense of defeat would only grow deeper as the challenges of trying to provide humanitarian aid in Rwanda in the aftermath of the genocide proved, if anything, to be more daunting than those they had confronted during the killing time itself. Part of the blame for this could properly be laid at the door of donor governments. But at the same time, relief agencies were finally forced to confront their own internal demons, and face the full extent to which, under the wrong circumstances, their efforts could do harm to the societies if not necessarily to the individuals—after all, a vaccinated child is a vaccinated child—they were struggling to assist.

Part of this was the result of the way the killing finally stopped. The Rwandan genocide did not end because of anything Western governments, the UN, or the NGOs had done. Rather, it was RPF's victory on the battlefield that brought the slaughter to a halt. Had the RPF not attacked, and had its commanders, notably Rwanda's future strongman, General Paul Kagame, not been able to seize power, it is probable that every Tutsi in Rwanda would have been murdered.

Given the vast crimes General Kagame's regime committed after taking power, which at a conservative estimate included tens of thousands of Hutus killed during the RPF's advance on Kigali in 1994, the massacre of several thousand internally displaced Hutus in a camp near the town of Kibeho in 1995, and the murder of between 30,000 and 150,000 Hutu refugees in eastern Congo in 1996 (the figure is simply impossible to determine by anyone who does not have access to secret U.S. satellite intelligence), it is important not to fall into the trap of the Great Lakes equivalent of Nazi revisionism. The RPF ended a genocide when no other power was willing to do so. This fact cannot be denied just because the Kagame regime turned out to be far worse than many of us imagined, and that some writers—including myself, to my everlasting regret—excused its conduct long after there was any justification for doing so except, precisely, gratitude for its having ended the genocide.

It was, however, the nature of the genocide itself and the fact of the RPF's victory, rather than the wickedness of the RPF regime, that would determine the nature of the second act of the Rwandan crisis. Unlike the Nazi extermination of the Jews and Gypsies, the genocide of the Tutsis had involved the majority population as enthusiastic participants—great numbers of Hutus had taken part in the slaughter. The demographics of pregenocide Rwanda tell most of the story. When the killing started, Rwanda's population was between seven and eight million. There were about a million Tutsis. Their murderers numbered some 250,000, which seems at first glance like a comparatively small fraction of the Rwandan population. But the average family size in Rwanda was between six and seven people. This means over a million and a half Rwandans belonged to the immediate family of someone who had killed. If one counts extended family just to the level of first cousin, the number is several million. There is no question of attributing collective criminal guilt to these people. But Karl Jaspers's famous argument that while the German people did not bear collective criminal guilt for the Holocaust, they did bear collective political responsibility is just as applicable to the Hutu masses of Rwanda.

The great flight out of Rwanda in the aftermath of the genocide bore witness to this. Fear of retribution was the biggest goad. As the RPF advanced and its victory became inevitable, the terror among Hutus about what the rebel front would do understandably became more and more intense. But guilt, both in the direct sense, for that sizable number of Hutus who were guilty of mass murder, and in the indirect sense, among the relatives and neighbors of the killers, loomed large as well.

The size of the refugee influx into neighboring Congo and Tanzania and the speed with which people moved across those international borders were unprecedented. Even as the genocide was going on, there had been massive movements of populations. But on July 14 and 15, 1994, after the RPF decisively defeated a Rwandan army force near Ruhengeri, more than 1,200,000 Hutus crossed into the Congo around the town of Goma in the province of North Kivu. In the period between the launching of Operation Turquoise and the withdrawal of French forces, hundreds of thousands more moved into the area around the Congolese town of Bukavu, in South Kivu. In all, more than two million Hutus were refugees in the Congo by the end of the summer. As Samantha Bolton, a press spokeswoman for MSF, would recall, "It was as though the whole country was emptying."

Many of those fleeing were in appalling health and incapable of moving farther away from the border, as UNHCR norms for refugees customarily would have required that they do. Indeed, every standard of humanitarian and refugee practice was violated in eastern Congo that year. The refugee camps were filled with armed Hutu fighters, both regulars and militia. Aid workers were in no position to disarm them; indeed, what relief they could provide depended on the acquiescence of the gunmen. At the same time, a cholera epidemic and massive dysentery had broken out, and the relief agencies scrambled to cope. (The vast majority of the residents of the camp were women and children whose health was especially precarious.) There had been no significant pre-positioning of supplies, and the UNHCR, while nominally the so-called lead agency, had not yet decided on its strategic goals in coping with the crisis.

But what was a disaster for the refugees—and, as events would demonstrate, for the security of the Great Lakes region—was an opportunity for the Western powers that had stood by while the genocide took place to leap into the humanitarian breach. Now, the crisis really could be called "humanitarian." The media abetted this confusion of genocide and humanitarian crisis. Almost effortlessly, it moved from showing images of Hutu mobs hacking Tutsis to death to showing those of babies dying of cholera in the Goma and Bukavu camps. The Western powers, above all the United States, responded by mounting a massive aid effort, the American portion of which was dubbed "Operation Support Hope." To an understandably confused public, that seemed like the appropriate response, even though in the context of the genocide it could not have been more inappropriate.

President Clinton's announcement that the United States would join the relief effort encapsulated all this perfectly. "The world's most powerful nation," he said, "must not turn its back on so many desperate people and innocent children who are now at risk." And he added that what was going on in eastern Congo was the worst humanitarian crisis in a generation. In saying this, Clinton distorted the facts, papering over the reality that if so many people were now at such risk, this was partly the result of his administration's decision both not to intervene and to block all efforts to halt the genocide that had created this crisis in the first place. It was *because* the United States had turned its back on these people that the crisis was as bad as it was. This is not to imply that there was a conspiracy on the part of the U.S. government. Did Clinton know he was lying? Somehow, I doubt it. I am persuaded that most Western leaders fell as comfortably into thinking of a human disaster in humanitarian terms as they would have resisted taking the political roots of such a calamity to heart. That, too, was the legacy of the rise of humanitarianism in the West.

For the humanitarians themselves the refugee crisis that played itself out in eastern Congo between the midsummer of 1994 and the late fall of 1996 was an institutional and moral calamity. The RPF rolled into Congo, destroying the camps, forcing most of the refugees back into Rwanda, and hunting down and killing many of those who tried to flee west, further into Congo, rather than return. All the pathologies of aid were on display during this period. There were many blunders in what relief workers themselves began to refer to as the "humanitarian circus" of Goma and Bukavu.

But the issue was less technical and operational—agencies continuing to send doctors after there was no more need for doctors, or doubling each other's efforts in shelter or sanitation programs, or sending inappropriate or useless supplies—than it was whether, on balance, the humanitarian effort was doing more harm or more good. This is not to underestimate the concrete problems. The World Health Organization estimated that 15 percent of the drugs its aid workers received were unusable and an additional 30 percent unnecessary. To want to help is, even from a technical standpoint, not the same as helping. And then there was the famous case of the American relief group, AmeriCares, that sent ten thousand cases of the drink Gatorade to the camps with the peculiar idea that this would help rehydrate people stricken with cholera. But instances of inefficiency or even malfeasance were trivial compared with the political blunders, however unintentional, that marked the aid effort in eastern Congo.

Because the dictatorship of Mobutu Sese Seko was not a legitimate state in anything but the most legalistic sense, but rather a family kleptocracy, the Congolese authorities could never have been expected to police the refugee camps, as the Tanzanians policed theirs. And Western powers like the United States that had been willing to commit enormous military resources to providing clean water for the refugees, combating the cholera, and setting up the camps were not willing to commit a single soldier to policing the camps. The result was that the elite of the old genocidal regime, which had more weapons at its disposal than any other force in that part of the Congo, was able to take charge of the camps. Rwanda had been a highly organized society, its people divided into groups and subgroups, down to what were called cells, each with its chief. The architects of the genocide quickly reestablished these structures in the refugee towns of eastern Congo, and UNHCR and the aid agencies were helpless to stop them.

Relief groups were forced to work through these structures, in effect becoming logisticians, medics, and civil engineers for those who had committed mass murder. Many aid workers realized this only later. An American engineer named Tim Schmaltz, who went to eastern Congo for the IRC at the height of the emergency, told me how he had been recruited over the phone from his home in northern California. "I didn't know anything about Rwanda," he recalled. "I had just read that people were in trouble, and I wanted to help. So I went to Goma and worked there for three solid months. But it was only later, when I finally went to Rwanda on a break, that I found out about the genocide, and realized, 'Hey, I've been busting my butt for a bunch of ax murderers!'"

Schmaltz's ignorance of the context of the calamity into which he had volunteered to throw himself was all too typical, and not just of Rwanda or of American aid agencies like the IRC where new staff are rarely briefed properly. Usually within weeks of volunteering for "an emergency," newcomers find themselves in the field, where they are obliged—or even worse, not obliged, as Schmaltz had not been—to learn as they work. In the Rwandan crisis, aid officials simply could not or would not make serious training a priority. An Oxfam official who had been involved in sending staff to Rwanda and had told me that often he was "just trying to plug holes with bodies" was describing the standard procedure of most mainline agencies. In some crises, such ignorance, while a drawback for an aid worker, would not have been so important. In Goma and Bukavu, the political effect of deploying ill-informed young people, no matter how brave, committed, and serious, in situations where their technical proficiency could be misused was to prove calamitous.

For all the good they did, the aid efforts bought the old genocidal Rwandan regime enough time to reconstitute its institutional structures and rebuild its morale. In effect, as the Kagame regime rightly insisted, the camps became the rear echelon for those who had committed mass murder to plan their return to power. The old Rwandan elite used the massed refugees both as human shields and as potential cannon fodder. Much as it might have wished to do so, UNHCR had no means to separate out those who had committed or had been complicit in genocide (though what this would have meant, given the ties of blood between them and the other refugees, is debatable), even though under international law it was the agency's obligation to do so. And before too long, the attacks on Rwanda from the safe haven of these purportedly internationally administered refugee camps began to mount. In the meantime, the aid provided the old regime with new sources of income. Many of the supplies were purloined and sold in the markets that sprang up in the camps. And much of the rest could still generate income, since aid agencies, which needed local staff to do their distributions (few aid workers, after all, spoke Kinyarwanda), tended to hire educated Rwandans, who tended to be themselves members of the old Hutu Power elite.

Some relief agencies tried to ignore what was going on. Others tried to mitigate the effects of the old regime's control over the camps by attempting to get relief to vulnerable populations in other ways. One NGO tried to use its own "scouts" to distribute aid. But the first time one of these employees refused a request from the killers who really ran the camps, he was killed. Then, within the space of a few hours, the militiamen who had murdered him killed most of his fellow workers one by one by one.

It was an impossible situation. In the first three months of the emergency, while they were still fighting the cholera epidemics in the camps and before it had become clear that the RPF would be able to consolidate control over Rwanda, the NGOs and UNHCR could ignore what was going on. But as the dying ebbed, and the emergency became, as, paradoxically, they always do, in a certain way routine, the humanitarian international came face to face with the realization not only that compassion was not enough, as *New York Times* reporter Raymond Bonner pointed out at the time, but that in the Rwandan case it was at least as destructive as it was helpful. Some aid workers accepted this, and insisted that, absent an international protection force, there was little they could do. "Of course, it's lose-lose," the assistant high commissioner of UNHCR, Soren Jessen-Petersen, told me at the time. "If we stay, we contribute to the horror, but if we leave, many, many people will die, and many, many more—children, pregnant women, old people especially—will suffer unnecessarily. I don't want to have to make such a choice, of course. But if I must, then I choose to stay. I choose to *be* a humanitarian."

Some of the agencies could not accept such complicity. The IRC and MSF, in particular, soon concluded that they simply could not continue to work under such conditions in any way that was morally defensible. It was then that Rony Brauman began to speak of relief agencies' "right of abstention" from crises in which they cannot act effectively. And eventually, IRC and MSF did withdraw. It was a complicated gesture, at once principled and hollow. For while it was important that NGOs take such a stand, the reality was that in the humanitarian circus that was eastern Congo at the time, with donors all but throwing money at NGOs, there were other relief groups already poised to take the place of those that withdrew. (Over the course of the two years of its operation, the relief effort would cost almost $1.3 billion.) The real question, and it was one that, fortunately for them, neither IRC or MSF had to face, was whether they would have withdrawn in a situation that was analogous politically, but in which they were the only aid groups on the scene. And that is only one of the deep dilemmas of even the most principled and politically and ethically alert humanitarianism that the Rwandan emergency revealed.

Another impossible situation: In Rwanda, too, aid was being misused. Many outsiders, including myself, were far less alive to this reality than to what was occurring in eastern Congo. It was easy to see the genocidal Hutu leadership in the camps for the scum they were. But we deluded ourselves about the RPF. At the time, I was personally so ashamed and angered by the role that the United States had played in the genocide that I could not, or perhaps would not, see that General Kagame and his colleagues were not some new and better group of African leaders—as their apologists in the West kept insisting—but old-fashioned African big men, as willing to kill to retain power as most African leaders in the postcolonial era had been. The fact that they were not authors of a genocide did not make them what people like me pretended to ourselves and insisted publicly that they were—leaders worthy of support. It was a failure of judgment, of moral common sense, and of political decency.

The Kibeho massacres in 1995 put paid to the illusions of most supporters of the Kagame regime. Thousands of Hutus had gathered in a camp near the town of Kibeho. Unquestionably, there were Hutu Power activists among them. But they hardly posed a threat to the Kagame regime. Still, in retrospect it is clear that the RPF was intent on demonstrating its power. When a riot started in the camp, the RPF began firing, in full view of aid workers and UN peacekeeping troops. The shooting went on all day. No one knows how many died, but the figure is certainly in the thousands. And Paul Kagame was almost proud of what he had done. "I could have killed many more had I chosen to," was the way, after cursory expressions of regret, he later put it to an American writer. It was in the wake of the massacre that MSF-France pulled out of Rwanda. Later most of the French agencies were expelled by the Kigali authorities, who viewed them as extensions of a hostile French government. For independent humanitarianism, it was "lose-lose" again. The needs in the country were profound, and yet the moral price for continuing to work there was to become an onlooker to slaughter. No, Kibeho was not genocide, but it was mass murder, and no amount of rationalization, or special pleading for the Kagame regime on the grounds that it had brought an end to the genocide, can change that fact.

But no matter how great the crimes of the new government in Kigali, its claim that the "alternate Rwanda," the Rwanda of the old regime, that was flourishing in the refugee camps in eastern Congo presented a mortal threat to the surviving Tutsis of Rwanda was absolutely true. In 1996, the attacks on Rwanda from the camps multiplied. UNHCR, which had appealed for an international force of ten thousand soldiers and been rebuffed, was unsure of what to do. And the option it chose, far from mitigating the crisis, actually provoked the decision of Kagame and his colleagues to attack the camps and force the refugees back into Rwanda.

For reasons that he has strenuously defended ever since, but has never satisfactorily explained, Sergio Vieira de Mello, then the assistant high commissioner of UNHCR and charged with dealing with the Rwandan crisis, negotiated an agreement with the Congolese government of Mobutu Sese Seko to send troops to police the camps. UNHCR would pay them. According to some UNHCR officials, the project was the brainchild of Sadako Ogata herself. Ogata had apparently concluded that using local troops to improve security in the camps was the only option left to her after a renewed effort to get international peacekeepers failed in early 1996. That may have made sense to her because, under international law, this function was normally the responsibility of the authorities in the state into which the refugees had fled.

Congo was not a normal state. Nor was the history of the Mobutu regime's involvement in Rwandan affairs one that could have provoked anything but alarm in the minds of Kagame and his colleagues. And, it appeared, Ogata and de Mello did not understand the force that history still exerted on the minds of the Rwandan Patriotic Front's leadership. For them, there was nothing decisive, or particularly provocative, about the decision.

But for the Rwandans, it seemed to represent a mortal danger. After all, the Presidential Guard that UNHCR wanted to contract to police camps run by Hutu Power *génocidaires* was the same one that had intervened along with Belgian and French forces to block the RPF's offensive in Rwanda in the earlier war in 1990. Through his efforts at that time, Mobutu had regained the standing among the major Western powers that he had lost when, at the end of the Cold War, the Americans had virtually severed their ties with him. And Mobutu had been a consistent backer of the Habyarimana regime.

The decision to subcontract the security of camps, in which the final chapter of the genocide was being plotted, to forces loyal to

Mobutu—a man whose links to Hutu Power dated back decades—seemed to the Rwandans like the final betrayal by the same "international community" that had stood by as the Tutsis were almost exterminated. For these Congolese soldiers were, in reality, the allies of the genocidal leadership in the camps, as well as their business partners. From the Rwandan perspective, de Mello might as well have asked the veterans of the genocidal Interahamwe militias in the camps to police themselves. As they saw it, a deployment by the Congolese army would make little difference to the security of any group within the camp except the aid workers themselves, while strengthening the killers immensely. The reinforcement was sure to bring about an escalation in their campaign to complete the extermination of the Rwandan Tutsis.

And so, goaded almost beyond sanity, the Rwandans attacked the camps. UNHCR had predicted the refugees would not return peacefully. It was wrong. Most, in fact, walked back home, and far fewer died than NGOs such as Oxfam had predicted. But the RPF also exacted a savage vengeance, killing, at a conservative estimate, tens of thousands of Hutus who chose to flee west into Congo rather than return to Rwanda. The Kigali authorities claimed that those who died had been part of the genocide. Doubtless many had. But again, the truth was not the vile but understandable truth of retribution, but rather the logic of mass slaughter. The RPF hunted down anyone who fled their advance. The United States, which by then had moved from preventing action to halt the genocide to supporting the RPF, covered up the slaughter. For its part, UNHCR refused to go public with the anecdotal evidence of mass killings that its field workers had collected. Such reticence is hardly surprising in the conformist world of intergovernmental bureaucracies and international organizations. The United States was the UNHCR's largest donor. The agency's one attempt, several years earlier, to criticize the conduct of the Rwandan Patriotic Front, in a report by the human rights activist Robert Garsony, had led to a stinging rebuke from the UN secretary-general and the decision by Ogata to claim the report "did not exist."

Thus the Rwandan catastrophe, which had begun in blood, and had never been a humanitarian emergency in any useful sense of the term except during the initial phase of the mass flight of Hutus from the advancing RPF and the cholera outbreak in the Congolese camps, ended in blood. The humanitarians remained as helpless to affect the outcome of the crisis at its ending as they had been at its start. The effect this had on aid workers is difficult to gauge. Endless studies were written; institutional changes were made; and relief agencies endlessly (and correctly) reproached the major donor governments for their cowardice. It seemed as if the humanitarianism that emerged was both more chastened and more ambitious than ever.

The fact that the logic of melding human rights concerns and humanitarian ones had been shown to be completely incoherent passed unnoticed. Perhaps the idea was too uncomfortable for many relief agencies to contemplate. For if the old regime in Rwanda was guilty of genocide, and its successor murderous (the full extent of the Kagame regime's nihilism and self-absorption would only be revealed in the Congo war of 1998, which, by 2001, was estimated to have led to the deaths of two and a half million people, most of them civilians), then the only coherent international response along the interventionist lines most NGOs were now coming to support was humanitarian recolonization, as would occur later in Kosovo. In the mid-1990s, most NGOs were not prepared to go that far. Or, at least they were not prepared to face what the logic of their evolving position implied.

Of course, there were those who—conscience-stricken and un-persuaded by the consoling fiction that next time, with the proper "lessons learned," improved coordination, and more timely and responsible state action, a disaster like Rwanda could be averted—chose to reconsider every dimension of the humanitarian vocation. Many of those who did not drop out simply lowered their expectations and soldiered on. But a surprising number of relief officials remained optimistic—too often unreflectively so—about aid work. For them, Rwanda seems to have been more a "learning experience," as politically correct Americans say, than a disgrace, and more a confirmation of why they were desperately needed than an intimation that what they could accomplish was limited, *even* when they were working at their best, when coordination with the UN and other NGOs could be undertaken successfully, and when there was ample funding.

In the fall of 1998—that is, long after the full extent of the failure of UNHCR in Rwanda had been made clear in study after study, and less than a year before the agency would face and fail the test of the Kosovo refugee emergency—Julia Taft, then the U.S. assistant secretary of state for population, refugees, and migration, would tell an audience in New York City that "the thirteen million refugees who are around the world . . . are probably the lucky ones because there is an incredible support system through the UNHCR and through the NGOs and through the protection of the UN." In reality, all three institutions had failed both the Rwandans and themselves during the genocide and the refugee emergency that followed. What is more, they knew perfectly well that they had failed. Taft had no answers. All she could do was repeat the post–Cold War humanitarian mantra that humanitarianism and development aid were basically already success stories, but that there needed to be more advocacy, more emphasis on human rights, more promotion of civil society.

One might have thought that Rwanda would have compelled her, and humanitarians like her, to question their cherished assumptions. But it had done nothing of the sort. If anything, the Rwandan debacle seems to have made her more determined. And chillingly, this official of the U.S. government even spoke of the need to do "whatever we can"—and who the "we" in question meant was clear enough—"to overturn the ultranationalism which seems to be a feature [of the world situation] right now."

Taft's call for what would have constituted, if not endless wars of altruism, then at least endless state interventions, was advice that none of her superiors in the Clinton administration were likely to take to heart. But to those with some historical memory, it would have been apparent that, for all the self-lacerating studies, the advocates and administrators of state humanitarianism did not blame themselves for what had happened in Rwanda any more than the UN did. They were still behaving like the proverbial doctor whose response to any imputation that he did not actually know what to do for a patient dying of cancer was that medicine was making advances all the time, and that one day there would be a cure. This does not mean the patient's death is the doctor's fault, any more than the crisis in the Goma camps was the humanitarians' fault. But the limits of medical knowledge do not excuse doctors when they make the wrong diagnosis or employ the wrong treatments, nor does it permit them to tell a patient that they have an idea of what to do when in fact they haven't a clue. That is what the Hippocratic principle of "Do no harm" requires. And yet, though Rwanda had demonstrated the tragic limits of both humanitarian practice and humanitarian understanding, many humanitarian agencies continued to tell the media, their donors, and, perhaps worst of all, themselves that they saw the way forward.

The Death of a Good Idea

CHAPTER 6

Kosovo

I̶T WAS IN Kosovo in the spring of 1999 that the battle for an independent humanitarianism was probably lost. The Bosnian experience had been scarifying enough. But if humanitarianism had served in Bosnia as a pretext for the refusal of the great powers to intervene, in Kosovo the misuse of humanitarian action was taken a step further. In Bosnia, the great powers refused to intervene because, they claimed, to do so would be to imperil the humanitarian effort. In Kosovo, humanitarian efforts were deployed for the opposite purpose, as a pretext for what was essentially a political decision by the great powers—taken in haste and as much in the interests of restoring their credibility, which had been so damaged in Bosnia, as out of any higher principle—to put an end militarily once and for all to Slobodan Milosevic's fascist rebellion in the European backlands. By the time the NATO military campaign was over, and Serb forces had withdrawn from the rebellious province, Milosevic's days were indeed numbered. But the political instrumentalization of humanitarianism was also nearly complete.

This is not to oppose what the West did in Kosovo. Almost no one now doubts that had NATO intervened as the Yugoslav Federal

Army laid waste to eastern Croatia in 1991, the Bosnian genocide with its 250,000 people dead and its millions displaced would not have occurred. Even wars that have been fought successfully in the name of far less just causes—here the British campaign to retake the Falklands comes to mind—often have had the salutary consequence of forcing tyrants from power. Had NATO not acted in Kosovo, it is entirely possible that Milosevic would have remained in control in Yugoslavia for many years and, even had he been replaced by another leader, that the apartheid state he had created in Kosovo would have continued. For that reason, many humanitarians supported the war on moral grounds. But just because individual humanitarians and, for that matter, some humanitarian NGOs were for the war, this did not make what took place a *humanitarian intervention,* although that was precisely what the major NATO powers tried to claim it to be.

"It is clear," said Clare Short, the British secretary of state for international development, "that [in Kosovo] our political and military objectives are completely intertwined." In making such a claim, and linking it to the humanitarian operations her own department was undertaking in collaboration with the British military, she probably only meant to inject into the language of humanitarian action the pseudo-Churchillian rhetoric of her boss, Prime Minister Tony Blair, who had said that, for the first time in NATO's history, its powers had gone to war "in defense of our values, rather than our interests." Blair's statement was in fact entirely defensible, whereas only in the context of a humanitarianism that was no longer pledged to maintain the divide between itself and political and military action was what Short said even partly defensible.

There was ample reason finally to put an end to Milosevic's depredations. It was in Kosovo that he had begun his bloody campaign for "greater Serbia," this Communist banker-apparatchik who had never given the slightest evidence, before the collapse of Yugoslavia, of having a Serb nationalist bone in his body. What Milosevic cared about was Milosevic. Once embarked on the murderous voyage toward "greater Serbia," he shied away from no atrocity. It was hyperbole to claim that Milosevic was the new Hitler, or to claim that he represented a threat to the peace and security of Europe as a whole. Still, the kind of ethnic fascism he represented was something that Europe, even fifty years after the end of Nazism, had every reason to fear and to believe it must suppress. And it was not as if Milosevic had agreed to mend his ways after the 1995 Dayton Agreement that brought the Bosnian war to an end.

To the contrary, it seemed to many at the time that the decision of American and European negotiators to treat Milosevic as a legitimate interlocutor without whom peace in the Balkans would be impossible not only prolonged his political career, but gave him reason to believe he was indispensable enough to his Western interlocutors to go on getting away, quite literally, with murder. But conditions in Serbia had changed after the end of the Bosnian war. Those restive paramilitaries who had grown used to easy plunder in Croatia and Bosnia were back home now, and, if left to idle, they could pose a threat to the stability of Milosevic's rule. So he again turned his attention to Kosovo, setting loose upon the province the Arkans, the Seseljs, the "Major Mausers," and the other genocidal thugs who had committed many of the worst atrocities of the Croatian and Bosnian wars, from Vukovar to Srebrenica.

This time, the West had had enough. It had long ago grown tired of the Balkans, but it was more tired still of Slobodan Milosevic. He had been let off the hook for Bosnia, because Richard Holbrooke, the architect of the Dayton Agreement, was convinced the agreement could not be secured without the Serb leader's assent. That view was shared by British and French officials, whose ample connivance with the Milosevic regime only became clear six years later as researchers and parliamentary commissions began uncovering the details of the negotiations between the Serbs and British and French officers at the time of the Srebrenica massacre. But going after the Albanian Kosovars *again* was too much for Washington, Paris, and London to tolerate. It was therefore all but inevitable that, after the failure of last-ditch negotiations over an end to the violence and the future of the province in the French town of Rambouillet in February 1999, NATO would intervene militarily.

I believed then and I believe now that the war was worth fighting, even though the struggle in Kosovo was far less clear-cut morally than Bosnia had been, because, for all the assurances of opposition politicians in Belgrade—assurances they had been offering since the mid-1990s—that Milosevic was on the brink of being forced from power, I was convinced he could be stopped only by force. But what was astonishing—perhaps even more so to a supporter of the campaign than to a doubter or an opponent—was the unwillingness of the British and the Americans to frame their decision finally to counter one of Milosevic's campaigns of "ethnic cleansing" in terms of *political* rights and wrongs. Instead, it appeared that the only sort of just war these leaders were disposed to present to their electorates was one entirely innocent of politics. They placed less emphasis on their fears of the conflict spreading to Albania and Macedonia. Still less were they prepared to say, "We are intervening because Milosevic poses a clear and present danger to peace and order in Europe, and, while we should have acted earlier, we are determined to teach any would-be Milosevics the lesson that Europe is not prepared to tolerate ethnic fascism as a basis for legitimate regimes."

Instead, the West's "new" new world order was insistently humanitarian. It involved not the politics of just war, as it had been understood in the West for a millennium, but the politics of rescue. War, in this dispensation, was simply the ultimate mode of enforcement in a brave new world of human rights—a world in which sovereignty is conditional on the rulers treating the ruled decently, and in which, if they abuse that privilege, they are properly condemned as having forfeited their right to rule and are laid open to military intervention from the outside. The NATO powers did not go quite so far as to use the Orwellian newspeak of the new muscular humanitarianism—they did not talk of "peace enforcement." But they were not all that far away, either.

As Eric Dachy, the operations director of MSF-Belgium, put it, "One could have hoped that [in Kosovo], politics would finally reclaim its rights, even in its most extreme form, war, and one could have hoped for a more intelligent delineation of the field of humanitarian intervention and the field of political, diplomatic, and military decisions . . . [Instead], we witnessed on the one hand a war that would not call itself by its right name, and on the other the creation of a militaro-humanitarian space whose strategic priorities reflected more the interests of the great powers than of the populations being helped."

Nonetheless, this was not the way things appeared in the media or were understood by the general public. To the casual observer, NATO seemed to be recapitulating the arguments of the human rights movement. The rhetoric—above all the critique of state sovereignty employed, as in Kosovo, in the service of oppression and injustice—was remarkably similar. Human Rights Watch's *World Report 2000*, written in the aftermath of the international interventions in Kosovo and East Timor, begins by asserting: "Sovereignty loomed less large in 1999 as an obstacle to stopping and redressing crimes against humanity. Governmental leaders who committed these crimes faced a greater chance of prosecution and even military intervention."

But what may, indeed, have begun in part as an effort by NATO to stop Milosevic from denying the Albanian Kosovars their rights and to force him to dismantle the apartheid structures he had established in the province during the decade since 1989, when he had stripped it of the political autonomy Tito had granted it in 1974, ended as being described by Western leaders and understood by the Western public as one more humanitarian crisis—the next stop on that nightmare ride that had begun in Biafra in 1967. The reasons for this are both complicated and controversial. It seems clear that, as soon as he got the chance, Milosevic had always intended to expel at least part of the ethnic Albanian population of Kosovo to "redress," as Serb nationalists liked to say, the ethnic balance of the province. This plan, dubbed "Operation Horseshoe," has been described in Serb documents that passed into the hands of German intelligence officials. It was also confirmed to me privately by several Greek diplomats whose good relations with the Serb authorities allowed them to come in and out of Kosovo during the war.

But there can be no doubt that NATO at least inadvertently also helped create the humanitarian emergency. By opting initially for a campaign of strategic bombing designed to force Milosevic to back down, NATO provided the Serbs with the time to counter with a vast campaign of forcible deportation, mass killing, and mass rape, which, given the way they had acted in eastern Croatia and then in Bosnia, was predictable. Having gone to war in an effort to become the master of what was taking place, rather than a passive onlooker, NATO ended up, at least temporarily, making an appalling situation even worse. By the time the Serbs were forced to withdraw from Kosovo, eight hundred thousand Kosovars had been forced to flee into neighboring Albania and Macedonia. The humanitarian needs that had been a small element of the political crisis in Kosovo before the bombing began on March 24, 1999, now came to occupy center stage. Whether it liked it or not, NATO found itself in the humanitarian business—as it had not in Bosnia, where it had delegated those obligations to the United Nations.

There were practical reasons for this. Albania was the poorest country in Europe and had itself gone through a low-intensity civil war in 1997—an event that had provoked the slightly opera buffa Operation Alba, an Italian-led, again ostensibly humanitarian intervention whose real purpose was to restore order and prevent a mass migration of refugees across the Adriatic to Italy. Albania might be willing, out of ethnic solidarity, to let in hundreds of thousands of refugees. But the consequences were sure to be catastrophic economically, and, eventually at least, socially, without massive amounts of aid—not just relief, but the kinds of improvements to infrastructure, economic credits, and the like that only governments, and certainly not NGOs, can provide. Macedonia was in a different fix. It was poor, but not destitute. Its problem was political. At least 30 percent of the population was ethnically Albanian, and was centered in the west of the country along the Albanian and Kosovo borders. An influx of hundreds of thousands of Albanian Kosovars terrified and angered not only the Macedonian Slavs who ran the country but their constituencies as well. If the Macedonians were to be prevailed upon to take the refugees in, more powerful voices than Kofi Annan and the UNHCR, let alone the private humanitarian agencies, would be needed. Again, only the great powers—the United States and the European Union—had enough influence to compel the response needed to cope with the crisis.

If the Western powers had stopped at exerting pressure on the authorities in Macedonia and underwriting the efforts of the Albanian government, and had then underwritten the aid effort, leaving the essential decision-making to the relevant UN agencies and relief groups, the Kosovo emergency would still have been a humanitarian crisis. But it would not have become the crisis *for* the humanitarian movement that it did. That development was the direct outcome of the fact that, as the tragedy unfolded, it rapidly became clear that the NATO powers wanted as much control over the humanitarian strategy as they did over their own military operations. They might pay lip service to the classical division of labor between governments and humanitarian organizations, as when Javier Solana, NATO's secretary-general, wrote to UNHCR's Sadako Ogata that "NATO fully recognizes the leading role of UNHCR, which is not only reflected throughout NATO's operational plan, but is currently being implemented as a working operational reality on the ground in Albania." But the reality was closer to an off-the-record remark a UNHCR official made to a reporter from *The Guardian*. "NATO not only builds the refugee camps and ensures their security," he said, "it sets the humanitarian agenda."

In any case, not all Western officials were as discreet as Solana. Two weeks after the bombing campaign over Kosovo began, the French minister of defense, Alain Richard, stated bluntly, "As has been the case in many [other] crises, French soldiers are both the most efficient at putting humanitarian aid in place and are the first to do so."

The question of efficiency was at least debatable. But on the question of why NATO soldiers almost immediately took charge of the humanitarian operation in Macedonia and Albania, Richard's assertion obscured far more than it clarified. Lieutenant General John Reith, the British officer who was placed in charge of a large force of NATO troops in Albania whose mission was explicitly humanitarian, has since described the objectives for that mission as laid down by NATO's American supreme commander, General Wesley Clark, in the following way: "To synergize [sic] International Organization/ NGO efforts [i.e., those of the UN agencies like UNHCR and the private NGOs] to maximize the value of in-place resources. To improve the flow of aid into Albania. To house the refugees. To maximize a positive media image of NATO to counter the negative effects of NATO's unpopular bombing campaign [in Kosovo]."

Few people within NATO militaries now deny that this last point was the most important one for NATO officers, let alone for their political masters in Washington, London, Paris, and Berlin. As would be the case in Afghanistan more than two years later, for the first month of the campaign, the bombing of Kosovo seemed to be producing the opposite result from the one the American president and the British prime minister had promised. What was already a bad situation was being made worse, at a tremendous cost in civilian lives. Public opinion in some NATO countries, notably Italy and Germany (not to mention Greece, where outright support for the Milosevic regime and for the justice of the Serb nationalist cause, as opposed simply to doubts about the war, remained overwhelming), was beginning to turn against the war. There is no question that much thought was given at NATO headquarters in Brussels as to how to turn the tide against these doubters, nor of the priority of doing so. And it is not surprising that the NATO countries so quickly turned to the humanitarian justification for what they were doing. After all, the moral ground for this had been well prepared, by governments, by Kofi Annan's UN, and by many of the relief groups themselves.

Part of the reason for this, of course, was simply the immense prestige humanitarianism had acquired over the previous two decades—something that inevitably came to have something of the moth-to-a-flame quality for poll-obsessed, chameleonlike politicians such as Clinton and Blair. But whatever the motivation, between the end of the Bosnian war and the beginning of the Kosovo campaign, an enormous amount of effort and energy had been devoted by the major NATO military powers, UN specialized agencies, and many mainline relief organizations to cementing and improving coopera- tion in planning for emergencies and in field operations between civilian aid workers and soldiers. Military universities in the United States were cranking out theses with titles such as "The U.S. Mili- tary/NGO Relationship in Humanitarian Interventions (1996)" and "U.S. Military Interaction with Humanitarian Assistance Organiza- tions during Small-scale Contingencies (1998)." Similar studies ap- peared in military journals and as dissertations in the comparable institutions in Britain and France.

If anything, there was far less enthusiasm within NATO military establishments to participate in what, in the American armed forces, had been dubbed "operations other than war" than there was among the NGOs to coordinate their relief operation with the military. Offi- cers from these countries who wrote on humanitarian operations worked in an institutional context where making a career as a hu- manitarian intervenor was a much more doubtful path to success than pursuing the trajectory of the warrior.

Nonetheless, things were slowly changing even in the usually re- sistant U.S. military, as influential officers like General Anthony Zinni, one of the architects of the Gulf War, and the then chairman of the Joint Chiefs of Staff, General John Shalikashvili, threw their weight behind these new peacekeeping and humanitarian roles. The underlying assumption, as Eric Newsom, the assistant secretary of state for political-military affairs, would put it after Kosovo, was that the U.S. armed forces' much touted "revolution in military affairs" had to include a "full spectrum of military operations." Significantly, Newsom meant far more than war-fighting. For him, the spectrum ranged from "major theater warfare" to "peace enforcement, hostile and non-hostile non-combatant evacuations, [and] humanitarian and disaster relief."

By 1998, representatives of the mainline relief NGOs were regular participants in military exercises designed to improve the performance of U.S. forces in these operations other than war. As General Shalikashvili put it, "What's the relationship between a just-arrived military force and the NGOs and PVOs [private voluntary organizations] that might have been working in a crisis-torn area all along? What we have is a partnership. If you are successful, they are successful; and, if they are successful, you are successful. We need each other."

From the U.S. military's point of view, then, there was no problem except that of coordination and improved understanding between soldiers and relief workers. In fairness, it is difficult to see how senior military officials could have believed anything else. For NGOs were more gung-ho than the soldiers were. Not only had many of the groups been pressing, usually behind the scenes, for more humanitarian military interventions, but their think tanks were also producing numerous texts on how to improve civilian-military cooperation in crisis zones. It is true that these texts raised the question of which group would have primacy. But if ever something could be called an academic exercise in the derogatory sense, this was it. The idea that agencies dependent on funds from governments that had dispatched their own militaries into a crisis zone would ever be in a position to dictate policy to those militaries was the purest wishful thinking. After Somalia, Rwanda, and Bosnia, it would have been reasonable to expect reality to have set in. For a few groups, notably MSF, it had. But then, MSF had never been more than ambivalent, except, and even then reluctantly, in the case of Rwanda, and had usually been hostile to the militarization of humanitarianism. Most other relief groups were eager to get a seat at the table.

As usual, the Americans were the most convinced of the need for civilian-military collaboration. The degree of their investment in state humanitarianism would become clear after the Kosovo campaign, when MSF's American branch decided to withdraw from the disaster response committee of InterAction, the umbrella organization that included all mainline, U.S.–registered NGOs, on the grounds that humanitarian action and military intervention had to be kept separate. The response was not long in coming. The assistant secretary of state for population, refugees, and migration, Julia Taft, who had previously headed InterAction, wrote angrily that if MSF saw no reason to be a part of this committee, she wondered why MSF should be part of InterAction at all. The message was clear: Either one played the game of state humanitarianism or one risked forfeiting one's status as a bona fide humanitarian actor.

Taft's letter is an astonishing combination of conformity and confusion. It is not that she rejects the idea of an independent humanitarianism; yet in practical terms, it is alien to her. She repeats the fiction with which so many NGOs console themselves: that humanitarian work will not be compromised by working with national militaries because InterAction believes these armed forces will "support, not substitute for, the work of humanitarian organizations and see their coordination efforts as a means to this end." She points to the "major gains in international coordination." Taft ends by proposing a vision of an international response to humanitarian emergencies that is utterly uncontaminated by any notion of reason of state other than that of states committed to doing good. It is as if, for her, the UN, the NGOs, and the NATO powers and their armed forces are all just working together to try to meet humanitarian needs.

For Taft, the anxieties of the type that drove MSF to withdraw have little substantive merit. And yet her letter was written more than a year after the end of the Kosovo war. Had she learned nothing from the experience? Certainly, she is consistent. NATO's participation apparently still appears to her as an unmixed blessing—further progress along that road to a better world that Secretary-General Annan kept outlining in his speeches. And closer relations between humanitarian NGOs and NATO can only improve the functioning of both. Underlying these assumptions, of course, is the view that there is no reason why, if people work together in good faith, the humanitarian and military systems cannot be made relatively compatible. For Taft, it is the humanitarian autonomy put forward by MSF that is the utopian fantasy.

As an official who had spent her entire career moving back and forth between the American government and U.S. NGOs, Taft might seem an extreme case. She wasn't. Indeed, by the time the Kosovo war started, her views were the norm rather than the exception in the upper echelons of most NGOs. They might differ about what kind of military intervention was necessary. And some in Western European NGOs, perhaps out of vestigial loyalty to the left-wing dogmas of their youth, were reticent about the use of U.S. forces in particular. To distinguish, as Mike Aaronson of Save the Children (UK) did, between military "logistical support to humanitarian operations, which is fine, and military co-ordination of a humanitarian operation, which is not fine" might have been comforting. But it did not come close to reflecting reality as it existed in the humanitarian world in 1999.

Blaming states for this is unfair. Over the previous decade, humanitarianism had been transformed, and had transformed itself into something that readily lent *itself* to this official interpretation of a Tony Blair, an Alain Richard, or a Julia Taft. It had all but begged for the chance to be used as a moral warrant for warfare. Or, rather, as relief workers preferred to think of it, humanitarian military intervention. The distinction was crucial, both cognitively and morally.

There were deep reasons why intervening "on behalf" of victims was almost never described as warfare. If the conscientious critiques of groups like Human Rights Watch about violations during the war over Kosovo tended to be restricted to insisting that all countries, including the humanitarian interveners, had to obey the laws of war and refrain from using prohibited weapons and tactics, the humanitarians tended to take refuge in far more sanitized descriptions, along the lines of Philip Johnston's statement that it might be necessary to "fight" (not kill, or bomb, or raze) in order to save lives in Somalia, or Bernard Kouchner's declaration that humanitarian military intervention was a great "adventure." This kind of rhetoric allows little room for the recognition that war always is a descent into barbarism.

Human Rights Watch seems untroubled by the ambiguities accompanying the fact that now "the international community" had military force as one of its resources in the battle to "stop atrocities" and protect and promote human rights. It is haunted by the difficulties of getting right the new global architecture it calls for. But the possibility that the "right of intervention" might be the modern version of Kipling's "white man's burden" does not resonate with most human rights activists, just as many nineteenth-century abolitionists were untroubled by the notion that abolitionism went hand in hand with European domination. Bring in the rule of law, they argue, and you are bound to get closer—no matter how far there remains to go—to a world in which, as the American legal scholar Anne-Marie Slaughter puts it, there may finally be "order and peace in human relations."

For their part, most relief groups, even those, like MSF, which have tended to be skeptical about the real intentions of Western powers, still in practice usually look forward to the day when these interventions will provide them with enough security, after the conflict has ended, to get back to doing their life-saving work among the victims. What haunts so many of them is the anguished sense that some means has to be developed so that they do not find themselves, as they did in Sarajevo, only able to keep people alive, with their medical and shelter needs at least partly attended to, while the Serb gunners on the hills fired on and on, or being forced, as they had in Rwanda, to watch as massacre (in 1996) followed genocide (in 1994). Understandably, many aid workers have become more interested in anything that would change these malign equations than in fighting for their autonomy.

The historic compromise with national militaries has seemed to get them part of the way past the dilemma. Improvements in technical standards, financial accountability to donors, and moral accountability to beneficiaries, as embodied in internal covenants for nongovernmental organizations like the SPHERE program, assuaged anxieties about whether NGOs were performing as they were supposed to. Finally, and this was hardly surprising given that the prestige the human rights movement now enjoyed rivaled that of humanitarianism itself, collaboration with human rights organizations seemed to provide a new moral grounding for the humanitarian enterprise—something that, after the failures in Somalia, Bosnia, and Rwanda, the times seemed to cry out for.

By 1999 the rhetoric of humanitarian military intervention had already muddied the distinction between humanitarian and human rights concerns in the minds of most people in the West anyway. Intentionally or not, many humanitarian organizations contributed to this confusion by some of their initiatives. At the time the Kosovo war started, several were deep in the process of trying to figure out how to collaborate more effectively with human rights organizations. Memoranda of understanding were being signed, for example, between the International Rescue Committee and Human Rights

Watch, and studies, many of them backed by the major American left-liberal entities like the Ford Foundation, were being undertaken to see how human rights norms could be assimilated into humanitarian practice. A 1998 internal report on the human rights effects of CARE's programs in Sudan went so far as to insist that "CARE is a human rights organization." After all, the report said, the organization's mission was "to assist the disadvantaged to attain their right to food, health, shelter, and freedom from poverty—all human rights."

But was this a realistic expectation for an NGO? As Eric Dachy noted acidly, "Because we deal with destitution and injustice as humanitarians and human rights activists does not in any way mean that we represent a factor of progress and evolution."

Even assuming the CARE goals did not, in fact, embody the most terrible hubris, it is difficult to understand why CARE didn't close its field programs and work flat-out for debt relief for countries like Sudan. This would probably have had a far greater effect on the securing of these rights than all the relief and development programs CARE could possibly have managed. But this is not what aid groups tend to mean when they talk of human rights. Usually, they mean two things: their beneficiaries' right, guaranteed under international humanitarian law that seeks to secure minimal rights for noncombatant civilians in wartime, to the services they can provide, and *the NGO's* right of access—state sovereignty or no state sovereignty—to provide those services.

It was this understanding that lay at the root of the conviction of so many humanitarians, in the aftermath of Somalia, Bosnia, and Rwanda, that the political-humanitarian divide no longer needed to be maintained. Rather, it needed to be bridged, as the student demonstrators had liked to say in the 1960s, "by any means necessary." Working without soldiers in Goma had meant acceding to the imperatives of the Hutu *génocidaires* in the refugee camps; "just" giving aid in Bosnia had meant feeding people without doing anything to put a stop to the causes of the war that had brought them to this state of miserable dependency in the first place. And, crucially, most aid workers believed that dealing with Kosovo in a similarly passive and conventional way, respecting the sovereignty of the Milosevic regime and the need of aid workers to restrict themselves to their traditional role, would have a similarly disastrous outcome both for the Kosovars themselves and for humanitarianism.

Small wonder, then, that as the crisis deepened in the latter part of 1998, a number of aid agencies facilitated the activities of a number of Western human rights rapporteurs by pretending to the Serb authorities that they were relief workers. The danger in this confusion of roles is obvious. But the problem goes deeper than that. There is no question that the reports by NGO officials of the massacres, pillaging, and rape that Serb paramilitary forces were committing in Kosovo prepared the ground for military intervention. The fact that these NGOs were also issuing reports about similar atrocities in places like Brazzaville, Congo; Liberia; and the Indonesian province of Aceh does little to alter the significance of what the NGOs did in Kosovo. For they knew perfectly well what the effects of their reports would be in a crisis on which, for once, the Western powers had focused their attention.

Many of the relief workers in Kosovo had worked in the Balkans before. Given the frustrations they had felt in Sarajevo, and then, most desperately, as the slaughter in Srebrenica took place, it would have been a human and moral impossibility for them to have kept silent. In the case of Médecins Sans Frontières, such testimony was actually part of the organization's charter. And yet was it the job of NGOs such as MSF that were not supportive of humanitarian military intervention to question whether they needed to take into consideration the effects of their actions? It was a question MSF adamantly and, in my view, arrogantly refused to entertain seriously.

Indeed, when the bombing campaign began, and it became clear that, bad as the refugee crisis was in Albania and Macedonia, the Albanian Kosovars in most desperate need were those who were still in the province, MSF called a press conference in Tirana to demand action. But when pressed on what exactly that action should be, James Orbinski, the young Canadian pediatric AIDS specialist who was then the international president of MSF, refused to be drawn out. "That is not our responsibility as humanitarians to determine," he insisted. "We're not going to say if the bombing should go on or stop, if there should be a land war or a truce. That's up to governments. We are simply calling on them to live up to their obligations."

It was this self-declared right of abstention from the political dimension of the crisis that made many aid workers in Kosovo lose both sympathy and patience with MSF. As John Fawcett, then the head of the IRC's operations in the region, put it, "You can't defeat fascism with humanitarian aid. Fascism has to be hit with military force. When it goes violent, you have to use violence."

For Fawcett, one of the bravest and most creative humanitarian aid workers I have met, humanitarianism was in crisis in Kosovo, all right. But the crisis was not one of the end of humanitarian autonomy, but rather of a humanitarianism that would either impotently play the game of warlords and tyrants like Milosevic or would stand for human rights. If it did not, he predicted, the major powers would turn to their own national militaries and to corporations to get the humanitarian job done. After all, construction companies could build refugee camps just as efficiently, if not more so, than relief groups.

At his gloomiest, Fawcett would predict that the Kosovo crisis would be the last one in which NGOs and UN specialized agencies would be at the center. In the crises of the future, he said, donor governments would hire private companies to do what an IRC or a World Food Programme was doing now. "Maybe they will be more efficient," he said, "but it will be terrible because a Bechtel or a Siemens can't deal with human rights. They can only be service providers."

Fawcett was well aware of the risks both of humanitarian military intervention, which in practice he knew to be usually weak and insufficient, and of the alliance between human rights and humanitarianism. "Advocates of humanitarian intervention," he told an interviewer, "base it upon the universality of human rights . . . The rights of the individual become a higher priority than the political ordering of geographic space, of the international system of states. From this liberal perspective, current dictatorships or oligarchies are modern manifestations of feudal landlords abusing people to the benefit of the few. Intervention with a covert or overt use of force is intended to stop the abuse of universal rights (life, body, property). The hurdle liberals often miss is that they are asking the current system to be cannibals, that is, turn on its own members and eat them."

Knowing that this meant that humanitarian military intervention would take place, to continue his analogy, only against the weak members of the tribe, such as Milosevic's Serbia or the Taliban's Afghanistan, and not against strong members such as Russia or China—Chechnya or no Chechnya, Tibet or no Tibet—Fawcett was nonetheless convinced that humanitarianism and military intervention had to go hand in hand. But in the hands of a humanitarian practitioner whose political understanding was less subtle than his and whose moral resolution was less firmly grounded, this doctrine became a pretext for scrapping the autonomy of the humanitarian

enterprise and for a kind of naïve triumphalism that discerned in the
NATO intervention in Kosovo the first inklings of an extraordinary
transformation of international order.

As usual, Bernard Kouchner took the lead in singing the praises
of this humanitarian new world order. He was named by Kofi Annan
to run the UN protectorate that was installed after the Serb withdrawal from Kosovo. Kouchner had lobbied hard for the job. "The intervention in Kosovo," he declared, "signifies that we have to forge a
new ideal for European and world youth based on a constant rejection of wars, a strong-hearted world democracy, and the means to
implement those goals without constantly relying on America to
provide the basics . . . Interventionism can be summed up quite
simply . . . Auschwitz never again, Pol Pot never again, Kosovo and
Rwanda atrocities never more. Intervention is the protection of minorities and of the essential species: man, the potential victim."

The statement is as breathtaking in its moral ambition as it is
contradictory in its expression. Kouchner did not go so far as one
similarly minded American advocate and describe humanitarian
military intervention as "the 'peace movement' of the '00s." But he
did manage simultaneously to assert that in the future the prosecution of humanitarian war will be a moral imperative, while at the
same time claim that what he is offering young people is the rejection of war. It is a vision emblematic of the moral inconsistency and
political myopia to which the advocates of humanitarian intervention have been prone. In Kouchner's rhetorical landscape, war,
which even when it is just is always horrible, becomes sanitized as
"brute force intervention." The image evoked is one of a burly man
breaking down a door in a burning building, rather than of an action that even in the best of circumstances is inseparable from the
slaughter of innocents. He makes the rejection of war the corner-
stone of his vision of the future, and then revels in the prospect of

the right of intervention being put into practice wherever there is a dictator oppressing or expelling an ethnic minority.

For Kouchner, the essential point about Kosovo is that "might is on the side of human rights." In this, he spoke for many. Kofi Annan was careful neither to endorse nor to condemn the NATO action in Kosovo in 1999 (although many of his aides whispered at the time that privately he applauded it, especially given the UN's inability to act). But in many ways, Annan had played at least as important a role as Kouchner in creating the intellectual atmosphere in which an operation like the intervention in Kosovo could go forward. His critique of sovereignty seemed to echo and complement Kouchner's idea of might in the service of human rights and of victims in dire humanitarian need. "Why was the UN established," Annan had demanded at a speech at Ditchley Park, "if not to act as a benign policeman or doctor? Our job is to intervene . . . That is what the world requires of us [and it is also] what the [UN] Charter expects of us."

Importantly, Annan was not restricting his argument in favor of humanitarian intervention to military operations undertaken beneath the UN's blue flag. Privately, he was said to favor the proposal of Sir Brian Urquhart, the former UN undersecretary-general for political affairs and, along with Canadian Prime Minister Lester Pearson and American diplomat Ralph Bunche, for all intents and purposes the inventor of UN peacekeeping, for a standing UN army. But Annan was realistic enough to know that is unlikely to be agreed to for the foreseeable future by the permanent five members of the Security Council. In his Ditchley Park speech, he therefore contended that the Security Council's "unique legitimacy . . . does not mean that [any particular] intervention itself should always be undertaken directly by the United Nations." For, he added, "in the foreseeable future [such] operations will have to be undertaken by Member States, or by regional organizations."

The problem, however, was less with the mode of the intervention—a coalition of the willing under a UN Security Council resolution, UN force, or regional force—than it was with the implications for policy for the secretary-general's image of the benign doctor or policeman. He will talk about crime, he will talk about medicine, he will talk about the protection to which civilians are entitled when their governments either abuse them or cannot protect them. But the one thing Annan will not talk about is the thing he is calling for: war. And war, precisely, does not principally require policemen or doctors, but warriors—people licensed by their states to kill legally.

This is not to disagree with Kouchner's claim (and perhaps Annan's as well) that sometimes wars are necessary to right injustice. It is to emphasize two further points. The first is that any new international order worth supporting must not traffic in lies, however well-intended, and pretend that war is police work, and police work war. The second is that those who want to go to war to stop human rights abuses should not use the moral warrant of humanitarianism to justify their actions. Just wars do not need any such pretext, nor should they have it available. The recourse to a moral imperative like humanitarianism puts war beyond debate, when war should never be beyond debate. It is in this sense, however inadvertently, a totalitarian construct. All dissent from the war is stifled, because the humanitarian imperative is held to trump all other considerations. I say this as one who supported military intervention in Bosnia, in Kosovo, and, later, in Afghanistan.

And the role of humanitarianism is key. There is nothing conspiratorial about insisting that in Kosovo it did not occupy the center by accident. By the time the crisis began to spiral out of control at the end of 1998, humanitarians had become the public image of what was now self-servingly and misleadingly called "the international community." Aid agencies themselves boasted of the fact before and

after the crisis. The annual report of the American branch of Médecins du Monde (MDM) boasted, "Doctors of the World's seven-year
commitment to those suffering human rights abuses on a massive
scale gave the organization unique expertise and credibility in addressing the needs of war-ravaged refugees in 1999."

Such a statement, typical of the public rhetoric of humanitarian
NGOs in the post–Cold War world, was incoherent in almost every
possible sense. To begin with, why had an organization of medical
doctors been expending substantial portions of its limited resources
on a human rights emergency rather than a humanitarian emergency? In the case of an extreme emergency such as a cholera
epidemic, or for that matter long-term health projects that were ap-
propriately thought of as development work, MDM could undoubtedly play a key role. But in Kosovo, the real problem was the
apartheid state the Serbs had set up. The policy of exclusion had created some medical needs among the Kosovar Albanian population.
Those needs were real. But they were paltry compared even to those
in many countries in sub-Saharan Africa that were *not* at war, let
alone the countries that were or where the health system was col-
lapsing or had collapsed. For example, while the incidence of tuberculosis in Kosovo was said to be the highest in Europe, at 77 per
100,000 people, it was a fraction of Namibia's 480 per 100,000 or
Djibouti's 597 per 100,000. Even MDM's claim that Kosovo's rate
was the highest in Europe was false. In 1998, peaceful Lithuania's
rate was 82 per 100,000.

The deepest reason for MDM's profound involvement in the
Kosovo crisis (and, in fairness, the agency was typical rather than exceptional in this regard) was not need but rather the fact that major
donors wanted it there. They were willing to fund programs in the
province. Of course, in any poor country there are always needs. The
refugee crisis in Albania and Macedonia was another matter. Al-

though it was, by sub-Saharan African standards anyway, a "privileged" crisis, the emergency was real. But MDM's deployment before the Kosovo war and in its aftermath had not, despite what was claimed in its annual report, been simply a case of "working to meet demands as conditions worsened."

The reality was that MDM's claims made far more sense in human rights terms than in humanitarian ones. The agency might have been justified in trumpeting its "expertise" and its "credibility," but these were hardly the same thing. MDM had no special expertise in human rights; it had medical expertise. And the credibility it boasted of was with the Albanian Kosovar population. Doubtless, the agency was effective in addressing its needs after the Serbs withdrew. But what about the needs of the Serbs in the province, which, in humanitarian terms, were supposed to be alleviated with the same commitment? How did MDM's "credibility" with the Kosovar Albanians affect its credibility with the Serbs? It is a safe bet to say, not very well. In short, everything MDM boasted about in its annual report was in one way or another incompatible with, irrelevant to, or undermining of the traditional understanding of the humanitarian vocation.

And this kind of confusion was what so many relief workers and UN officials viewed as a great step forward. To be sure, far graver distortions were being imposed on NGOs by their major donors than they were imposing on themselves. This was as much a matter of underlying assumptions as of specific decisions, which is why what might have appeared to be harmless and well-intended—if somewhat naïve and oversimplified—rhetorical stances were in fact far more important in practice than UN officials, Western government officials, and relief workers were willing to admit. Above all, at key points in the Kosovo crisis, these major donors took the collaboration between NGOs and NATO governments further than even most interventionist NGOs had wanted it to go, until the distinction between UN agency, NGO, and Western government became all but impossible to draw. Kosovo provided any number of illustrations of this, but the case of CARE Canada is probably the most instructive.

Several months before the bombing campaign began, CARE was approached by the Canadian International Development Agency (CIDA) and given a $3 million grant to recruit people to work for the mission of the Organization for Security and Co-operation in Europe (OSCE) to monitor peace agreements and report on human rights violations in Kosovo. But this mission turned out to include reporting on troop movements and, more generally, providing intelligence information, as well as its more mundane verification activities and responsibilities with regard to human rights. The contract was kept secret. In its press releases and on its website, CARE continued to emphasize its role of bringing relief to people in need in Kosovo, although it did state clearly that it understood that role to include working for human rights.

Shortly after the bombing began, two members of CARE's expatriate staff, Steve Pratt and Peter Wallace, and one of its local employees, Branko Jelen, were arrested by Serb forces and accused of espionage. There was an international uproar. Both Kofi Annan and Nelson Mandela appealed for the men's release. Pratt and Wallace were Australian, and their government appointed a special representative to work for their freedom. The problem, however, was that while Pratt and Wallace may not have been spies in the strict sense the Serbs alleged, they had been working for the Canadian government. And CARE officials, after initially prevaricating, were at a loss to say where the monitoring mission had ended and the humanitarian one had begun. As Malcolm Fraser, the former Australian prime minister who was then chairman of CARE Australia, put it later in an interview, "I thought CIDA was purely a humanitarian organization and then I discovered that CIDA had a non-humanitarian funding window."

Of course, CIDA was no more a purely humanitarian organization than USAID was. No government development agency ever is. But Fraser made the strongest possible justification for what he was the first to concede, over the bitter and public opposition of many on his staff, had been an error of judgment. "The program was designed to keep the peace," he said, "designed to help stop incidents in which people got murdered, or beaten up, or killed. The program itself was a good program . . . The error of judgment was attaching a different kind of good program to a humanitarian organization."

It was the best case that could have been made for what had happened from the point of view of a traditional understanding of the humanitarian enterprise. But in fact Fraser's scruples, and his outrage over having been deceived, were not widely shared in CARE Australia or CARE Canada. And this was by no means simply the result of a decision to cover up what had happened. To the contrary, what had occurred was congruent with the instrumentalization of humanitarianism that had taken place over the course of the 1990s. States saw humanitarian action as an element of their response to crises in places like the Balkans or the Great Lakes region of Africa.

Foundations, such as Ford or, for that matter, George Soros's Open Society Institute, saw in it a vehicle through which their real agenda—human rights, for officials at Ford; the building of pluralistic societies, for Soros—could be expressed. That had been Fred Cuny's entire pitch to Soros. Humanitarian action, he had told him in effect, could be a device with which you could either protect failing democratic polities, like Bosnia, or encourage fledgling ones, like Albania after the fall of Communism, or Tajikistan after the breakup of the Soviet Union. After Cuny's death in Chechnya, Soros and the president of his foundation, Aryeh Neier, had become more skeptical about the emancipatory potential of humanitarian action, even as a flag of convenience for other agendas. But most foundations had not, and neither had most NGOs.

Whatever humanitarian NGOs might say after an incident like the CARE Canada debacle, they were not simply being used. By assiduously seeking funding from these rich donor countries for programs in these places—funding upon which they had come, increasingly, to rely—they were all but begging to be exploited for these realpolitik purposes. The fact that they knew perfectly well, in the words of one American aid worker, that they were the "one percent solution," and that whatever they did would be insufficient, seemed to give them little pause.

Still less were many of them troubled by the view expressed by Fiona Terry, then head of MSF-Australia, in her response to what CARE had done in Kosovo: "This whole mission creep that humanitarian aid organizations are going into at the moment is a hugely retrograde step. I think we need to go back to basics. I think we have to look at the fundamental principles of impartiality and be very careful of independence from governments."

But it really was too late. As Alex Morrison, the president of Canada's Pearson Peacekeeping Centre, put it, "We don't use the term mission creep. We use the term mission reality. By that we mean civilians and military must work together to use resources to the maximum extent."

By the end of the Kosovo campaign, the takeover of the humanitarian ideal by state humanitarianism was all but accomplished. It had not been hostile, it had been friendly. There were limits, but most of these were more aesthetic than substantive. Other humanitarian agencies, for example, might wince when they discovered that Henry Kissinger was on the board of the IRC. But that was only because Kissinger was despised by many people.

The presence of less controversial Western politicians on the boards of aid groups was taken as a matter of course. Besides, they helped the NGOs get access to the donors. Having a David Owen, or a Michel Rocard, or a Richard Holbrooke on your board meant your views would be heard. Why would one not want to include them, just as why would one not want to be included in military training exercises, ministry planning sessions, and United Nations policy reviews? Surely it was better to have a seat at the table than continue as a powerless outsider. In any case, it was difficult for many humanitarian NGOs to remember even what the debate over an autonomous humanitarian space had been about. The different imperatives between relief groups, governments, the UN, even NATO military forces had come to seem trivial compared to the imperative of saving lives and righting wrongs.

In a report issued in the aftermath of the Kosovo war that reflected this line of thinking, two British defense analysts wrote that one of the most important things separating the NGOs and armies was "the use of different 'language' and terminology [that seemed] to obscure any understanding of common objectives between the actors." Putting the word "language" in quotation marks spoke volumes about how little importance either NGOs or governments now attached to such questions. The distinct principles that had given rise to humanitarian groups in the first place were no longer to be seen as either central or as inhibiting civil-military cooperation. Instead, what seemed to matter most was learning how various and very different institutional cultures could mesh more smoothly. A report to the U.S. military put the matter more succinctly. One section was entitled "Does Anyone Here Speak Civilian?"

As far as most NGOs were concerned—it was a comment one heard particularly from officials of British agencies such as Oxfam—the response of groups taking MSF's stance reflected little more than a humanitarianism trapped in its self-involved adolescence and refusing to grow up. As one senior UN humanitarian official put it to me, "The MSF style was all very well in the 1970s and early 1980s, but now it just looks like sheer bloody-mindedness. I think it's groups like Oxfam, agencies that managed to neither fall into the trap of total dependency on their own governments like the U.S. NGOs, nor insist on independence at any price, including the price of getting the job done, like MSF, that are the humanitarian wave of the future. They have consciences but they know how to cooperate, know that we are all of us—governments, the UN, the NGOs—all in the same boat."

But were they? Kosovo had revealed enormous fissures within the humanitarian movement itself. UNHCR had found itself marginalized. In part this was because, despite its vast experience in the Balkans, it had been caught by surprise by the amplitude of the crisis—a dereliction that reportedly led Secretary-General Annan to exclaim that the one thing he thought Sadako Ogata could be counted on to follow closely was the Balkans. But even after UNHCR began to catch up, and replaced the third-tier officials it had posted in Kosovo, Macedonia, and Albania with its best and brightest, it was unable to influence events even to the extent it had done in Bosnia.

National militaries were acting as humanitarians, and NGOs were reporting to NATO officials. It was the first time the humanitarian international had, for all intents and purposes, wholly identified itself with one side of a conflict. That identification did not mean that there were not fissures within the humanitarian movement. On the contrary, what was remarkable was the degree to which nongovernmental organizations tended to follow the same ideological path as their national governments, with U.S. and British NGOs largely for the war, the French ambivalent, and a few groups, notably the Greek sections of MSF and MDM, aggressively pro-Serb.

Odysseus Boudouris, the president of MSF-Greece, who unlike most of his colleagues in the Greek section was courageous enough to recognize that Greek humanitarians had often given in to "Greco-Serb solidarity," overstated the case when he insisted that during the Kosovo war the Western humanitarian movement went "where NATO wanted it to go, did what NATO wanted it to do, and said what NATO wanted it to say." In fact, NGOs *said* a great deal that NATO cannot have welcomed. But most of what they complained about was that NATO was not doing *more*.

In many cases, these complaints amounted to lamenting that NATO was still bombing, when what was clearly needed was a ground war. Boudouris's call for the renewal of real humanitarian impartiality may have been partly special pleading, since MSF-Greece was for a time suspended by the association's International Bureau for its abandonment of humanitarian neutrality in Kosovo. But his idea of a "subversive impartiality," one that insisted upon a genuine independence for humanitarian organizations from those in power in their own societies, was utterly alien to the conduct of the NGOs in Kosovo. As Boudouris said, quite correctly, "the instrument"—humanitarianism—"had ceased being used in service of the idea." Instead, "the idea had become the pretext for [the deployment of] the instrument."

Boudouris's motives were viewed skeptically in the other sections of MSF. Given MSF-Greece's extraordinary rationalizations for Serb abuses, this may have been correct. But there can be no question that Boudouris was right in insisting there was no real effort on the part of the NGOs to maintain an autonomous humanitarian space in Kosovo on the political and moral level. He might have added that there was no effort on the practical level, either. For when the Kosovo crisis erupted, the humanitarian circus that even the NGOs themselves would later concede had been such a disgrace in eastern Congo in 1994 was immediately reproduced.

There was the same unseemly rush to deploy; the same competition for funding in Washington, Paris, London, and Brussels; and the same advertising campaigns insisting that if only one would give generously to MSF, or Oxfam, or the IRC, or CARE, the lives of the Kosovars could be made whole again. Aid agency representatives trumpeted their worst-case scenarios, the same ones they had put forward in each crisis that preceded Kosovo. And all worked under the seeming assumption that the absence of their particular organization would condemn the Kosovars to disaster. It was a conceit that lasted through the war and beyond.

At the end of the war, UNHCR tried to persuade the various NGOs that were nearly hysterical with anxiety to get back into Kosovo to agree to go in slowly. Having been marginalized during the war, partly because NATO wanted to be in charge, but at least as much because it had largely botched its response in the initial stages of the refugee emergency and behaved as unimaginatively in Kosovo as it had acted creatively in Bosnia, UNHCR was attempting not just to bring some order to the chaotic humanitarian situation but to regain a measure of control.

MSF, finding that it had not been selected to be among the first to go in (the competition had been fierce and relations between MSF and UNHCR on the ground were tense), decided to go in anyway. Its motives were mixed. The ostensible rationale was that some of the work that needed to be done, notably mine awareness training, was not going to be done by anyone else. But while it is debatable (despite what some UN officials asserted at the time and continue to believe) that it was the lure of the media coverage that would await them in Kosovo that accounted for their impatience, there can be no doubt that the spirit of competition played a significant role in MSF's decision.

As one MSF-Belgium official put it to me later, "It was virgin territory." Still later, he would write me that the truth, whether I or anyone else wished to accept the fact or not, was simply that MSF was better in its particular domains of expertise than any other agency. He was not just boosting his own agency, he said. Had the problem in Kosovo been principally nutritional, ACF rather than MSF would have had the right to make the same claim. I have no doubt he was sincere; perhaps he was even right. But the story was more complicated.

For everything that happened during the Kosovo war and after seemed to confirm Alex de Waal's point that for all the NGOs' supposed new spirit of self-criticism, the same old result kept getting produced every time a crisis erupted for which massive funding from donors and massive opportunities for fund-raising from the public presented themselves. In the increasingly business-oriented cultures of U.S. relief groups, this was being referred to as the need for acquiring a substantial "market share" of each humanitarian crisis.

Reynold Levy, an AT&T executive who had succeeded the former foreign service officer and longtime humanitarian aid official Robert De Vecchi as head of the IRC, was generally agreed by U.S. relief workers to be particularly fixated on this notion. But the views of other mainline agency officials were not really all that different. And if the European agencies simply operated differently, and, at times at least, with less shamelessness, the goal was much the same. And, in reality, there was little in any of this to distinguish NGOs such as MSF that had remained faithful to the dream of independent humanitarian action from those such as CARE that were comfortable collaborating with states and committed to at least a partial merger with the world of human rights activism.

In the fifteenth century, the armies of Venice symbolized their conquests by the ceremony known as *piantare il leone,* or "planting the lion," the symbol of their republic. In 1999, in Kosovo, the NGOs, too, wanted to plant their flags, whatever harm such a rush might do to the humanitarian ideal.

But at most, given the degree to which humanitarian organizations had become subcontractors to governments, and had been willing to declare that they would not defend the specific gravity of their own enterprise, it was a fairly minor matter. For Bernard Kouchner, it was the Europe of "human rights and fraternity, [the Europe] we love" that had been born out of the Kosovo intervention. He would be disappointed. But at least Kouchner had always known what he wanted.

In contrast, relief workers would leave the Kosovo emergency less sure than ever about what their roles were and were not, what they could hope to do, and what they would be allowed to do. Kosovo had resolved nothing. Meanwhile, Africa still burned. So did Afghanistan.

CHAPTER 7

Afghanistan

AFTER SOMALIA, BOSNIA, RWANDA, and Kosovo, after Kouchner and Bettati's "right of intervention," and the United Nations' championing of military campaigns in the name of humanitarianism and human rights, if there was much left of the idea of an autonomous humanitarianism, it was all but put out of its misery in Afghanistan in the fall of 2001.

As in Kosovo, the challenge that confronted the humanitarian actors—the UN agencies, the NGOs, the various aid bureaucracies in Western governments—stemmed not from being marginalized but rather from being elevated to a central role in providing a moral rationale for the conflict. This had been a general tendency for some time. As Eric Dachy of MSF has put it, the new importance given to humanitarianism and human rights in the post–Cold War world testifies "first and foremost to the desire within the Western world to affirm that its relationship with the rest of the world is characterized by generosity and altruism. But it in no way reflects the effectiveness of the humanitarian approach, nor the real influence of the relief and/or human rights organizations on the societies in which they intervene."

When the war in Afghanistan began, this desire to appear altruistic was wedded to a need on the part of the United States to use the
humanitarian gesture to demonstrate that its fight was with the Taliban and Al Qaeda and not with the people of Afghanistan. Non-
governmental organizations and UN officials had warned repeatedly
that an American attack might push a people already hungry into
famine. The casualties inflicted by the U.S. bombing were expected
to be far greater than in Kosovo—this in a country already ravaged by
two decades of war. The inevitable result was that, out of this combination of calculation and compassion, American policymakers soon
began offering a humanitarian rationale for their actions, as well as
those of self-defense, military necessity, and the demands of the
"war" against terrorism.

The problem was obvious. The United States was well within its
rights under international law, thanks in no small part to a UN Security Council resolution crafted by France in late September 2001
that basically gave the United States carte blanche to wage the "war"
on terrorism. But within days of the onslaught of the bombing campaign, people all over the world began to grow indignant over the
deaths of innocent Afghans from the American bombing—Afghans
who were as much victims of bin Laden and the Taliban as were the
dead of the World Trade Center.

It was all very well to speak of this, as the Pentagon did, as being
the regrettable "collateral damage" of war, but it was also largely irrelevant, at least to the more privileged sectors of those societies,
above all in Western Europe and to a lesser extent in the United
States, above all within the universities, which had lost their tolerance for war on the deepest cultural and moral level. That was where
humanitarianism came in. The commitment of the U.S.–led coalition to live up to what it presented publicly as its humanitarian obli-

gations to the people of Afghanistan went a long way toward reassuring a public that it was feared would be, and in Western Europe soon proved to be, increasingly disturbed by images of civilians killed by errant American bombs and missiles.

Almost from the moment the bombing started, U.S. officials went to considerable lengths to point out how the military mission and the humanitarian one were parts of the same campaign. They pointed both to their new long-term commitment to helping the Afghan people and to the emergency effort to airdrop relief supplies to hungry people. Paula Dobriansky, the influential undersecretary of state for global affairs, gave a speech in Kazakhstan entitled "Humanitarian Assistance and [the] Battle Against Terrorism Go Hand in Hand." She said, "The media coverage of the military response to the terrible events of September 11 has tended to overlook another crucial aspect of the Bush administration's strategy—addressing both immediate and long-term problems plaguing the people of Afghanistan."

By "addressing . . . long-term problems," Dobriansky meant the promise of development aid and democratic openings for Afghanistan once the fighting stopped. These are the standard prescriptions of the U.S. government in the era of globalization under both Republican and Democratic administrations. By "addressing . . . immediate . . . problems," she meant humanitarian assistance. "Compassion," she declared, "is an integral component of President Bush's foreign policy, and it motivates America, even in these trying times, to continue to lead the international effort to provide humanitarian relief to those [Afghans] most vulnerable." And, as she pointed out correctly, this was not a departure from past practice. For two decades, America had "consistently been the largest donor of humanitarian assistance to the Afghan people." It would step up those efforts now. The international coalition's efforts would be multifaceted—military above all, of course, but also diplomatic, economic, and, crucially, humanitarian.

There is no reason to doubt Dobriansky's sincerity or that of the Bush administration. The connection Dobriansky made with pride might have revolted many aid workers, who even claimed, erroneously, that the same planes that had dropped bombs then went on to drop food rations—a tactic one MSF official called "after-sales service." But, like globalization, or civil society, humanitarianism has become so much a master idea in the rich world that it cannot be viewed, even in the context of war, as merely an instrument policymakers deploy when it suits their purposes but to which they have no loyalty.

The fact was that policymakers had become at least as enraptured by the idea of humanitarianism as the general public, and for entirely understandable reasons. Along with human rights and an idealized conception of civil society, humanitarianism has become the emblem of a genuinely different and preferable world order—one whose moral bona fides are beyond question. Conservative critics of this view, like the American political scientist Michael Mandelbaum, might mock this tendency as "foreign policy as social work." But in fact this vision is far more attractive to the public at large than Kissingerian realpolitik.

The cynical interpretation of all this would be to conclude that without moral warrants like human rights and humanitarianism, most contemporary policymakers who are not pure careerists could no longer rationalize all the filthy things they have to do and the compromises they need to make on a daily basis. That, more than anything else, I would argue, accounts for the iconic power of humanitarianism. As a disgruntled UN official once put it to me, "If you can't believe that what you're doing when you preach globalization is bringing democracy, human rights, rule of law, [and] humanitarian assistance, then how can you, if you're a decent person, even go to work in the morning? No, you believe that by furthering the interests of Microsoft, you're also furthering the interests of the International Rescue Committee or Human Rights Watch. And what's more, so for the most part do they!"

On a deeper level, this turn to the humanitarian justification is simply an expression of the pervasive Wilsonianism that unites American relief workers and U.S. government officials. Most aid agency officials in New York, Westport, or Baltimore believe passionately that there is no incompatibility between an activist humanitarianism and a successful U.S. foreign policy. Indeed, their view is that, properly construed, America's vast wealth and power bring with it an obligation to reform the world and move toward the goal of what Wilson called "an organized common peace." More important, many American government officials are drawn to the same moral vision of international politics. In the end, for all the talk of the new realism or the new isolationism in post–Cold War America, Wilsonianism has remained, at least sentimentally, the most comfortable stance for policymakers. It is hardly surprising that in a crisis like the war in Afghanistan, U.S. officials should so easily have gravitated toward it. As Strobe Talbott, the deputy secretary of state during the Clinton administration, wrote, "American values and interests reinforce each other." And what better expressed these values than the humanitarian project itself?

Oddly enough, the more cynical rationale for the need for humanitarian aid to be part of the war effort in Afghanistan came not from the Bush administration, but from representatives of American humanitarian groups. In a letter he sent to President Bush only eight days after the World Trade Center attack, Kenneth Bacon, a former Defense Department spokesman who had recently become the head of a Washington-based humanitarian advocacy group called

Refugees International, put the matter bluntly. In this campaign, he wrote, "The U.S. requires the support of moderate Muslims around the world and this necessitates maintaining the moral high ground. A humanitarian disaster in Afghanistan, if attributed to U.S. military operations, could leave the American people even more vulnerable to terrorism in the future."

Bacon's view, reflecting, as it did, that of most mainstream American NGOs, carried considerable weight. But it is unlikely that the United States acted solely out of such prudential considerations. To be sure, the need to inject this humanitarian dimension into the Afghan conflict—the imperative, from both the international and the domestic standpoint, of being seen as doing something besides killing people—doubtless played a role in the initial U.S. decision to undertake a campaign of humanitarian airdrops in Afghanistan, as it had done in Kurdistan in 1991, in Bosnia in 1993, and in Kosovo in 1999. Secretary of State Colin Powell all but admitted as much in a speech on October 26, 2001. "The NGOs," he said, "are such a force multiplier for us, such an important part of our combat team."

On a practical level the effort was always bound to be more symbolic than substantive. Short of a massive commitment of airplanes, not to mention relief personnel on the ground to organize distribution of the supplies, airdrops almost never work well in humanitarian emergencies. In Kurdistan, they were a disaster. In Bosnia and Kosovo, they were largely ineffective. American planners claimed they had remedied the flaws in these previous operations. Afghanistan, they promised, would be different. It wasn't. The planning was clearly so ad hoc that not only was the actual beneficial effect minimal, but it soon turned out that the rations being dropped, while carefully complying with Muslim dietary requirements, came in yellow wrappers that made them virtually indistinguishable from the yellow bomblets of the cluster bombs the U.S. Air Force was dropping at the same time.

On Capitol Hill during the same period, however, there seemed to be more concern about the U.S. getting the credit it was due from the Afghan people for the food aid it was delivering than about any other issue, including safety and efficacy. In the course of the colloquy that followed the testimony of the United States Agency for International Development (USAID) administrator, Andrew Natsios, before the Senate Foreign Relations Committee—a colloquy that was all the more ludicrous because neither Natsios nor the senators seemed conscious of the other interpretations that could be put on their words—Senators Christopher Dodd of Connecticut and Bill Nelson of Florida kept asking why the meal packets did not identify the food more clearly in the local languages as a gift of the people of the United States. Natsios's response was revealing. He agreed that this was important. Food clearly labeled as a gift of America, he said, had made a lot of people in North Korea the year before realize the United States was not their enemy, but rather that their own government was at the root of their troubles. The same thing, he suggested, might well work in Afghanistan.

Natsios is a skilled humanitarian operator. He was a far cry from the officials who had dealt with humanitarian issues during the Clinton administration, like Hugh Parmer, a former mayor of Fort Worth, Texas, whose main qualification for his post appeared to many to be that he was an "FOB" (friend of Bill Clinton). Natsios had been a vice president of the immensely powerful and controversial evangelical relief organization World Vision, a group whose undeniable competence was, in the opinion of many secular relief workers, tarnished by the way it combined proselytizing with help. He had also led the U.S. NGO umbrella organization InterAction, and was a former assistant secretary of state for population, refugees, and migration. He was himself a controversial figure, in no small measure because of his reported sympathy for the Christian guerrillas of the Sudan People's Liberation Army (SPLA). (Roger Winter, the man Natsios appointed to run the Office of Foreign Disaster Assistance within USAID, was even more committed to that cause.) His stance on the need for massive aid to North Korea was also controversial, particularly for MSF, which believed the food aid was being misused, and in certain circles within the American government, which believed reports of starvation were exaggerated.

But no one questioned Natsios's competence or his commitment. He was a professional, and he was a man with a strong political and moral vision that was rare in humanitarian circles. Where Natsios, in other ways so untypical, remained in the mainstream of the American humanitarian tradition was in his belief in a governmental vision of relief. And from the moment he took up his new post, he made it clear that his vision of USAID would be one of humanitarian aid and development firmly in the service of U.S. foreign policy goals.

In Natsios, there was joined a deep belief in the inherent rightness of humanitarian action and an apparent lack of anxiety over whether instrumentalizing that action in the service of U.S. foreign policy was morally problematic. Not for him the conception of an autonomous humanitarian space. He exemplified perfectly the mindset that the disgruntled UN official had been referring to. There was something syllogistic about this: Humanitarian aid is good; the United States is good; therefore why shouldn't the two be twinned? As Natsios had put it on May 8, 2001, "As a great power, I believe America's foreign assistance both serves to accomplish our foreign policy objectives, and expresses the deep humanitarian instincts of the American people." USAID, he went on, is "a key foreign policy instrument." It would respond to natural disasters and man-made humanitarian emergencies, as it had always done, but it would also expand its "democracy programs."

Natsios concluded: "Foreign assistance is an important tool for the President and the Secretary of State to further America's interests. In fact, it is sometimes the most appropriate tool, when diplomacy is not enough or military force imprudent. Foreign assistance implements peace agreements arranged by diplomats and often enforced by the military; [it] supports peacekeeping efforts by building economic and political opportunity; [it] helps developing and transition nations move toward democratic systems and market economies; [it] helps nations prepare for participation in the global trading system and become better markets for U.S. exports. All of these activities help build a more peaceful, stable, and prosperous world—which is very much in the interest of the United States."

Natsios's rhetoric mixes a confident view of globalization that in the 1990s came to be associated with the Davos conference of world business titans and the view from the U.S. embassy in Saigon, circa 1965, in which great claims were routinely advanced for the U.S. campaign of winning hearts and minds. In it, panegyrics to globalization reminiscent of those penned by its most energetic publicist, *New York Times* columnist Thomas Friedman, blend with fantasies of a new world order secured by humanitarian and development aid intelligently deployed. Of course Natsios could hardly have anticipated that his agency, along with private relief groups and UN agencies such as the World Food Programme and the Office of the United Nations High Commissioner for Refugees, whose programs in Afghanistan had long been disproportionately dependent on U.S. government funding, would have to operate in a full-scale war. And yet within days of the beginning of the bombing campaign, it had become clear that his conception of humanitarian action was easily adaptable to wartime conditions. A decade of humanitarian military interventions in which the distinction between aid givers and war fighters had been fundamentally elided had seen to that.

For this, one probably has to credit the synergy between the traditional, comfortably collaborative assumptions of the American humanitarian tradition in its relations with the U.S. government; the efforts of Bernard Kouchner in promoting the idea of the right of interference; and the enthusiasm of Kofi Annan, at least once he became UN secretary-general, for the military intervention on humanitarian and human rights grounds that had become a staple of serious discussions on international relations. Yes, there were instrumental grounds for emphasizing the U.S. commitment to humanitarianism. But matters ran deeper. It was as if war had become impossible for a modern Western country to wage without describing it to some extent in humanitarian terms. The Americans could have said: "We've been attacked. We have the right and the will to avenge our dead and make sure this never happens again. And we're grievously sorry about the civilian casualties, but even our technology is not foolproof, and the sad truth is that war always entails the killing of innocents, so unless you're a pacifist, your criticisms have little or no legitimacy."

But the Bush administration did not say this. Nor was its commitment to humanitarianism merely window dressing or a cynical effort to mollify public opinion in Western Europe. This should not have been surprising. To some extent at least, the rhetoric that accompanied the bombing of Afghanistan recapitulated what had been said during the Kosovo conflict in 1999. Already then, British Prime Minister Tony Blair's "Doctrine of the International Community," as he called it in a speech in Chicago on April 22 of that year, had sought to lay out the case that the great powers could not turn their backs "on the violation of human rights if we want to be secure."

As in Kosovo, the United States and its allies were determined to make the case that the West was acting in defense of its values as well as its interests. Of course, this claim was easier to make in the south Balkans, where there were no economic interests, no oil, no pipelines, than it was in Central Asia, where strategic issues involving oil were not irrelevant. But as in Kosovo, the moral problem in Afghanistan was that defending one's values when no casualties could be accepted all but guaranteed that civilian casualties would be higher than they otherwise would have been and the damage to the enemy's forces lower, since it is virtually impossible to distinguish an army truck from a civilian bus at fifteen thousand feet.

The high moralizing rhetoric of the Bush administration, as it set out to destroy those the president called the "evildoers," included no such admission. From the beginning, the administration prepared the U.S. public for a long war, for the involvement of U.S. ground troops, and for U.S. soldiers coming home dead. Before the air campaign started, five thousand body bags were sent to an air base in Uzbekistan, where American forces were deployed. But the humanitarian rhetoric of the U.S. and British governments about Afghanistan descended almost directly from Bernard Kouchner's rhetoric about Kosovo. When he became UN proconsul in the province, Kouchner stated flatly that this represented the logical conclusion of thirty years of humanitarian activism. By this, he meant politics, first and foremost. Not for him the notion of humanitarian neutrality, or the need to keep humanitarian action and politics apart—the issue that had precipitated his break with MSF. They were the same cause. "Have I ever done anything except politics?" he asked in his book, *What I Believe*. "When I was named [a cabinet minister], I was not entering politics [for the first time]. I had been in it for thirty years, first opposing the war in Algeria, then at the Union of Student Communists (though never in the Party), fighting against Stalinism, and then in Biafra and in the humanitarian combat."

One may certainly doubt whether Andrew Natsios or any other member of the humanitarian apparatus of the Bush administration (or, for that matter, its Democratic predecessor) had such a checkered political past. But the shared conviction that humanitarian action is inevitably political helps to account for the ease with which the humanitarian enterprise in Western Europe, at the UN, and in the United States was assimilated into the war effort. Indeed, it was during the Clinton administration that many of the institutional battles in which the military was eventually persuaded of the need to join in humanitarian and peacekeeping operations were fought—battles over "operations other than war."

As Eric Schwartz, former senior director for humanitarian affairs at the National Security Council, has written, "We can only provide effective and efficient humanitarian leadership if we are also prepared to address the political and security issues that are so often the proximate causes of humanitarian suffering. If we are not, we simply end up spending many millions of dollars to address suffering that does not end."

By Schwartz's reasoning, a war in Afghanistan to unseat the Taliban, who were indeed much of the proximate cause for the suffering of the Afghan people, surely made more practical sense than simply pouring money, as the United States had done for so many years, into programs run by UN specialized agencies and private relief groups. Schwartz was not arguing that a war should be started for that purpose. For that, one has to turn to Mario Bettati, the legal scholar who pioneered the idea of the right of intervention. Bettati wrote of the war in Afghanistan as a "missed opportunity." The Americans, he said, had acted to force the Taliban to deliver Osama bin Laden instead of to "punish the Kabul government for the crimes committed against the people of Afghanistan." That, he said, was a great pity, for "overthrowing a government that massively violates human rights [should be] the ultimate goal of the right of interference."

Bettati's position is extreme, even by the standards of this kind of militant (and militarized) humanitarianism. In effect, he was elaborating a position that had been suggested by Kofi Annan's more utopian speculations on rights, state sovereignty, and the duty to act, but which Annan himself had been careful not to endorse explicitly. The prospect Bettati offers as an improvement over the current situation in the world is one of endless humanitarian war. In the case of Afghanistan, Bettati insists that, rather than authorize the United States to act out of its self-interested concern, the UN should have acted in the interests of humanity. It might, he writes, have invoked "the massacres committed [by the Taliban] in the north of the country in 1997; the terror exercised by the Ministry for Virtue and for the Elimination of Vice; the forced marriage of very young girls; the oppression of minority groups." These crimes are not unique to Afghanistan, and if the UN had acted as Bettati wanted, it is hard to see how it could defend a subsequent refusal to act in a dozen other crises from Somalia (again) to Indonesia and still retain its moral authority.

Bettati goes further. The Taliban, he insists, are guilty of "the ruin of their own country." Here is where humanitarian need and the priorities of relief agencies all but offer themselves up as a rationale for this new twenty-first-century interventionism that in many ways recapitulates the "new imperialism" of the 1870s, when Europeans justified their takeover of Africa on humanitarian and antislavery grounds. Bettati, Kouchner, and even, at times, Annan are comfortable with a new interventionist world order, so long as the interventions would be grounded, as Bettati put it, in "the necessity of assuring the respect for the principle of unfettered access to the victims on the part of humanitarian organizations."

Bettati does not seem troubled by the prospect of endless wars, nor does he say how these wars would be fought. In declining to do so, he avoids having to grapple with the moral challenge posed by the Western theory of just war going back to Aquinas, which demands not only that a war be fought for a just cause but that it be fought justly as well, and prohibits the employment of incommensurate means. He focuses on how many lives militarized humanitarianism has saved in places like Somalia, Bosnia, and Kosovo, and might have saved in Rwanda. He does not focus on how many lives it has cost, starting, precisely, in Somalia, where for the first time in the history of modern humanitarianism soldiers killed people in the name of getting humanitarian agencies the "unfettered access" to victims of which Bettati speaks. It is all so virtuous . . . and so abstract. Bettati's dominant feeling is one of exhilaration over what elsewhere he has called a "new humanitarian international order." His only regret, it seems, is that Afghanistan has proven to be a missed opportunity for the furtherance of this nascent order.

It is easy to mock Bettati. As MSF's Françoise Bouchet-Saulnier once remarked caustically, "Reference to law is always strongest at precisely those moments when respect for the rules disappears." And yet there is much about Bettati's position that makes intuitive sense. What *is* the point of trying endlessly to help when, as an aid worker, one is at the mercy of regimes, and warlords, and local commanders who care nothing for the welfare of their own people and sometimes—as was the case with the Taliban, above all with regard to the treatment of women and the denial of education to girls— seem bent on insuring that things get worse for ordinary people? Compared to such situations, the everyday difficulties of humanitarian work, such as theft, or the creation of a culture of dependency among beneficiaries, seem trivial. Surely the only way out of this dilemma is to institute a new humanitarian order, one in which these contradictions, constant in humanitarian relief work, might finally have a chance of being resolved.

An autonomous humanitarian space? It sounds good when groups such as MSF argue for it, but in the field might it mean condemning aid workers to remain at the mercy of warlords? An Andrew Natsios or a Bernard Kouchner would surely argue that political neutrality is all very well in theory, but in the field, relief workers may have to compromise that neutrality if they are to contribute to the greater good of the victims they are pledged to serve. In this sense, Bettati's vision of humanitarianism as the bedrock of a new and more moral order in international affairs cannot be dismissed out of hand, however risky some of its implications. What, after all, were the MSFs and the ACFs offering as an alternative? To many observers, it seemed as if they were simply upholding a principle that had little relevance and less moral force when applied to what was happening on the ground in Afghanistan.

By the time the bombing began, the humanitarian crisis in the country had far outstripped the abilities of relief organizations to cope with it. This is not to denigrate their efforts. Aid workers in Afghanistan had always been working both at the edge of their capabilities and at great personal risk. But the reality was that by the summer of 2001, they were losing, not gaining, ground. After twenty years of war, a drought in 1998, and then a second and more severe drought in 2000, Afghans were at the end of their capacity to cope. Afghanistan is an overwhelmingly rural society, and by 2001 there had been massive crop failures for three years in a row. Aid agencies were recording huge increases in malnutrition, and famine loomed. Austen Davis, the head of MSF-Holland, was understating the case when he commented that, even before the bombing, aid agencies had found it "increasingly difficult to meet Afghanistan's vast medical and nutritional needs," which, he took pains to point out, were much less the product of natural conditions than of the seemingly endless war.

That said, even before the war, as Norah Niland of the UN mission for Afghanistan put it, "The country was desperately poor and under-developed." She added, "The socio-economic situation is so poor that the country lacks even the resources to document and understand the desperate state of the economy." What was known was that Afghans had one of the highest maternal mortality rates in the world, that one-quarter of all children died before they reached the age of five, and that, in Taliban-controlled areas—95 percent of the country before the U.S. attacks began—women were barred both from all employment outside the health sector and from all access to education. Six million land mines were said to lie buried underneath the soil of Afghanistan, while the drought alone had created at least a million internally displaced people.

To make matters worse, the Taliban were increasingly uncooperative. To read the press releases for 2000 and the first part of 2001 by UN agencies such as the WFP is to enter a world in which constraints on humanitarian work grow steadily harsher. The Taliban's leader, Mullah Omar, had apparently developed a particular dislike for the WFP's executive director, Catherine Bertini. At the same time, in part because of pressure from feminist groups in the West, there was increasing reluctance to fully fund relief programs in Taliban-controlled Afghanistan. In principle, the developing integration of human rights norms into humanitarian work may have seemed like an unqualified good to most relief organizations and to the UN agencies. Norah Niland referred to a human rights deficit in Afghanistan. In practice, however, what Afghanistan under Taliban rule seemed to demonstrate was the degree to which upholding human rights norms got in the way of humanitarian work, and vice versa.

Clearly, by the summer of 2001 the situation of the Afghan

people was spiraling toward disaster. At the same time, contradictions within the aid effort were also becoming harder and harder to sort out. What did the agencies hope to accomplish? Did they see their presence as furthering human rights, or were those commitments hampering their work in the field? There was no consensus. As an Organization for Economic Cooperation and Development (OECD) evaluation report had put it two years earlier, "As a matter of principle, the aid community wants the Taliban . . . to respect international norms while at the same time it wants to respect Afghan culture and tradition. As a matter of principle [also], the aid community wants its aid to be only humanitarian, yet conditional in respecting human rights, while also upholding the right to humanitarian assistance."

The conclusions of the report were grim. "Aid providers," the report stated, "should be more modest about the influence they can hope to exercise on a conflict through aid." In any case, it pointed out, not only had "insufficient aid [been] on offer, relative to the ambition of the changes [relief groups] would like to secure," but "the Taliban authorities perceive Western donor governments as essentially hostile."

The Taliban were correct about the West's hostility, however morally justified that hostility was. Donor governments made no secret of it. In 1997, Emma Bonino, the Italian politician who was then head of the European Commission Humanitarian Aid Office (ECHO), the biggest single humanitarian funder in the world, flew to Kabul and denounced her Taliban hosts for their oppression of women. She was entirely correct to do so. The question, though, as many relief workers in Afghanistan asked at the time, was what purpose Bonino's gesture served. It would be one thing had she then recommended that ECHO withdraw its funding from all NGO operations in Afghanistan. But she had no such intention in mind.

Indeed, when Oxfam decided that there was no point in continuing its operations in Kabul because Taliban restrictions on Afghan women working for NGOs meant that Kabuli women were being denied access to humanitarian relief—since given the realities of Afghan society only women staff could carry out the surveys necessary to see what the real needs of the women of the Afghan capital were—the major donors were unsympathetic. They believed that being able to offer even *some* help was preferable to withdrawal. Most aid agencies agreed. They might withdraw for a time, as both NGOs and UN agencies did at various moments during the six years the Taliban ruled most of Afghanistan, but invariably they returned, even as the conditions under which they worked moved further away from established minimum humanitarian standards.

Under these circumstances, it was hard at the time to fathom why Bonino behaved as she did. She certainly knew the Taliban were firmly in control, and she must also have known that there was no will in the West to cut off relief assistance. She must have been briefed, and, for that matter, have seen for herself the reality on the ground. But though she had not a clue as to what to do about it, she opted for an empty gesture. It was as if Bonino did not understand, or at least no longer believed, that even in her official capacity as head of ECHO she had to take into account the operational and moral imperatives of a humanitarianism that did not construe itself as a force for social transformation.

Françoise Bouchet-Saulnier has described this attitude in the following way: "This tendency . . . to group humanitarian action together with peacekeeping, the restoration of democracy, and human rights . . . is comforting, because it obscures the relatively modest impact of humanitarian action in situations of conflict or crisis, by integrating it within a grander design of conflict resolution and the restoration of peace."

Throughout the period of Taliban rule, aid workers lived with the paradox that, as a private report for CARE put it, the values they held "were constantly undermined and challenged" yet they felt morally obliged to remain. Some relief workers rationalized the decision to remain by claiming far more for their actions than the reality warranted. An ACF nutritionist, Charlotte Dufour, wrote in ACF's internal journal, "Beyond all [questions of] material assistance, our action also allows us to give a reason for hope to all these women [working for or aided by foreign NGOs], a reason to get up in the morning, because they will be able to go to work or get care for their child."

But most aid workers in Afghanistan did not have such a comforting perspective on their actions. To the contrary, as the UNHCR's Soren Jessen-Petersen had said about the problem of staying or withdrawing from the eastern Congo refugee camps in 1994, most tended to see their situation as one of "lose if you stay, lose more if you go." Yet unlike in eastern Congo, where aid workers had not yet fully taken in the bad news, working in Afghanistan under the Taliban cruelly highlighted the hollowness of the NGOs' claims to be committed to new principles based as much on human rights as on charity. CARE's "Principles of Humanitarian Assistance for Afghanistan," issued in March 1997, had included the assertion that the organization was "guided by internationally defined standards of human rights and [used] them as a basis to determine its decisions and actions within the realm of local communities and the nation of Afghanistan." It talked of access of vulnerable groups to aid being "a fundamental human right." And it declared that it would not "work in an environment where authorities and/or communities attempt to force CARE to break its core values or program principles."

But of course the history of CARE's efforts in Taliban-ruled Afghanistan involved systematically contravening these principles.

The mission statement, like that of many other relief agencies, was pure rhetoric, designed, it seemed, to make aid workers, their donors, and the general public feel better. In fact, in Afghanistan a serious commitment to humanitarian relief and a serious commitment to human rights, as long as the Taliban remained in power, were irreconcilable, and every relief worker knew it. The norms had outstripped the realities to a grotesque degree. As the CARE report pointed out acidly, "An accurate Taliban notion is that many international agencies will not leave Afghanistan for a host of reasons, and will inevitably move their 'bottom line' lower each time a new demand is made."

The only way to square the circle—to allow the humanitarian agencies to work according to the broad new norms they had pledged themselves to—was for an outside event to change the conditions under which the agencies worked. That deus ex machina was the American attack on Afghanistan. And since so many agencies were no longer content to be what Sergio Vieira de Mello, the UN undersecretary-general for humanitarian affairs, had contemptuously referred to as "an international welfare system of last resort," and were inspired by what he had called the "promising precedent" of East Timor, where an international humanitarian intervention had provided "an international security framework for human rights and humanitarian concerns," what is surprising is not how many relief agencies welcomed the U.S. strike but how many continued to harbor reservations about it.

The Taliban were prey to no such confusion. After the bombing began, it almost immediately became clear to what degree they associated the NGOs with the great Western powers that financed them. It is not simply that foreign workers from groups like the IRC, Oxfam, MSF, and the others were expelled. Their offices, and those of the UN agencies, were targeted by Taliban fighters in Afghanistan and pro-Taliban mobs in Pakistan. For them, there was no distinction between the Western relief agencies and the U.S.–led coalition that was bombing Afghanistan. Unfortunately, given the incoherence of the relief groups' position, and their increasing participation in the developing international military-humanitarian *system*, it is difficult to argue that the Taliban's supporters were mistaken. At the same time that attacks on UN and NGO installations were taking place, the U.S. government was reiterating that humanitarian relief was an integral part of its war effort. Meanwhile, although many of the humanitarian agencies themselves privately harbored grave doubts about the wisdom of the U.S. campaign, most were unable to establish any distance from this official embrace.

With the exception of MSF and ACF, which had remained faithful in Kosovo to the idea of an autonomous humanitarianism that refused to be part of a broader effort and were therefore somewhat inoculated against this tendency, most humanitarian agencies had been moving steadily toward Kouchner's vision of humanitarian military intervention, and had already cooperated eagerly with NATO in the Balkans. This was true not only of the U.S. agencies, with their history of ideological and financial dependence on their government, but even of groups such as Oxfam that still prided themselves on their left-wing commitments. The reason for this was clear enough: The dream of a new humanitarian order was particularly powerful in the context of an Afghanistan, where humanitarian action alone would never do enough to ease the sufferings of the people.

Humanitarians, in any case, did not need to get the moral warrant for this view from the U.S. government. They could look to the United Nations. Indeed, the decision of Kofi Annan, who was viewed almost as a secular saint among the liberal elite in the West, to make humanitarian intervention one of the elements he consistently chose to emphasize in his speeches as he endeavored to focus the work of the world organization more and more on human rights, certainly made cooperating with NATO more palatable to such groups. For Annan, as for many relief workers and Western government officials who shared the view that humanitarian aid was one important element in the attempt to cope with poverty, war, and disaster, its importance was largely instrumental. In the UN's new Office for the Coordination of Humanitarian Affairs (OCHA), emphasis was placed on the Executive Committee for Humanitarian Affairs, whose mission was to help adjudicate and coordinate the sometimes competing, sometimes complementary imperatives of relief, human rights, UN peacekeeping, and political action.

On one level, Annan was only streamlining a process already in place. From a purely bureaucratic standpoint, after becoming secretary-general he had actually downgraded humanitarianism's importance by replacing a full-fledged UN department, the Department for Humanitarian Affairs (DHA), with the lower-ranking OCHA. For many humanitarian officials, both inside and outside the UN, this suggested that Annan was actually less interested in humanitarianism per se than his predecessor, Boutros Boutros-Ghali, had been.

But what importance Annan did attach to the humanitarian idea accurately reflected the preoccupations of mainstream humanitarian and human rights groups. As Hugo Slim, a British relief expert who was also a great admirer of the secretary-general, wrote, "The first driver to be actively shaping a form of rights-based humanitarianism is the United Nations." He added that Annan had made it a priority to "put human rights at the center of all UN agencies and their activities, albeit with limited success."

In the view of an increasing number of aid workers, this change, which Slim described as a move from the philanthropic perspective of needs to the political principle of rights, was long overdue. An-nan's critique of sovereignty—his conviction that, in the post–Cold War world, states must not be allowed to act with extreme cruelty toward their citizens simply because that was the way international relations had been structured since the Peace of Westphalia in 1648—dovetailed perfectly with the revised moral expectations of many relief workers. Convinced that there were no humanitarian solutions to humanitarian problems, they welcomed the secretary-general's suggestion that, in extreme cases, force would have to be used, in effect, to save the victims from their own governments.

Some relief workers went further. For many (and it is important to acknowledge that they would be vindicated by events), the paradox of the U.S. bombing campaign was that it might accomplish what endless negotiations with the Taliban had been unable to secure: a better future for the people of Afghanistan. Theirs would no longer be an "orphan" conflict. Instead, these (mostly American) relief work-ers pointed out, the unintended consequence of the U.S. decision to go after Osama bin Laden and the Taliban leadership was that the humanitarian needs of Afghanistan would finally be addressed. In-stead of tens of millions of dollars for aid, there would be hundreds of millions, if not several billion. Instead of an international com-munity that, as Salvatore Lombardo of UNHCR put it, had "forgot-ten about Afghanistan for many years," great powers that were committed to proving their commitment to the Afghan people would not evaporate from the scene the moment Al Qaeda and the Taliban were destroyed.

These aid workers accepted that the United States and its allies were acting in this way because, at least in part, they needed to mol-lify those, particularly in the Islamic world, who had bitterly opposed the war. For them, if humanitarianism was being exploited, it was being exploited for a good cause. But more than that, they believed that what mattered most was that, at long last, the people of Afghanistan would be relieved of the oppressive rule under which they had suffered and finally given the kind of help that was required if Afghanistan was ever to recover either economically or socially from its twenty-year-long catastrophe. Just as important, Afghanistan, like Kosovo before it, seemed to demonstrate that, to be effective, aid must always be political, and that, if it was indeed true that there were no humanitarian solutions to humanitarian problems, the destruction of the Milosevic regime in Serbia or of the Taliban–Al Qaeda nexus in Afghanistan were examples of what was needed.

"Do you know the story of Alexander the Great and the Gordian knot?" an American aid worker who very much supported the Afghanistan campaign asked me shortly after the bombing began. "For all of time, the legend went, people had tried to untie it. Then Alexander came along, drew his sword, and cut the knot apart. That's what the bombing campaign has done. We tried and tried to deal with the Taliban, even though we all knew it was a law of diminishing returns. At the same time, we tried to get our own governments to fully fund the programs that were so desperately needed in Afghanistan. It was only a matter of time before the whole thing fell apart. Then suddenly, the U.S. needs to justify what it has done and for the first time in three decades the future of Afghanistan might actually be brighter than its past."

John Fawcett, who had been watching events in Afghanistan closely, put it this way: "Due to the drought and the general idiocy of the Taliban, the at-risk population, as defined by the pre–September 11 UN appeal, was to rise to 5.6 million people inside Afghanistan. Which meant doubling the amount of food that the aid agencies had to deliver before and over the winter. Then the bombing started and everyone began panicking that now they had no chance." But the collateral effect, Fawcett said, was that widespread starvation might be avoided because of both the imminent change of regime and U.S. pressure on neighboring states to open their borders to allow relief shipments through. Paradoxically, after years of diminishing returns from even the strictest depoliticized humanitarian perspective, it looked to Fawcett as if it would be the bombing, for all its costs in human suffering—suffering about which he was anything but indifferent or dismissive—that would finally open up Afghanistan to an effective program of humanitarian assistance.

At the time, most non-American UN and NGO officials took a more pessimistic view. In October, when the bombing campaign seemed to be having little result, the private consensus within the UN's humanitarian leadership in Pakistan appeared to be that the bombing would push Afghanistan over the precipice into full-scale famine. As Stephanie Bunker, the spokeswoman for the UN's Afghan programs, put it, "The Afghans simply can't cope. With WFP unable to bring in food, with foreign relief workers forced out and programs curtailed, we could be looking at something unimaginable in the next few months. And winter is coming. The question is, 'How are the people in Afghanistan going to survive this?' We're all well aware that so much more could be done. But what we are doing is saving lives, every day, in Afghanistan, and that's what is at risk now."

Bunker had vast experience in Afghanistan. When I repeated to her the claims of some American aid workers that in the end the war would be seen as a blessing in disguise for the people of Afghanistan, she simply shook her head. "What if a hundred thousand people die this winter?" she asked. "Will it matter to those who died if you finally get to do postconflict reconstruction? How do you do the algebra? Please tell me. In Afghanistan now, people are literally surviving from day to day. So you tell me: Morally, how do you make that calculation?"

As things turned out, the calculation never had to be made. The American bombing campaign proved to be singularly effective, particularly in the colder northern half of Afghanistan, whose population had been of particular concern to aid workers. Before long, aid convoys were getting through, foreign NGO workers were back at their posts, and the worst fears of the UN staffers were shown to have been misplaced. But none of this invalidates Bunker's concerns. The Afghanistan that the United States attacked was a country at the brink of humanitarian disaster, and the bombing did increase the possibility of famine. Military experts in Europe and America were skeptical about the American air campaign when it began. Why should the aid workers have been more sanguine?

Apocalyptic forebodings are the aid worker's stock-in-trade. The entire history of modern humanitarianism is a demonstration of this. Think of what Rony Brauman called "the salutary mistake of Biafra," the founding moment of the new movement in which aid workers such as Bernard Kouchner mistakenly believed that the goal of the Nigerian army was to destroy the Biafran civilian population. It now appears clear that, for all the horrors of that conflict, there was no genocide in Biafra. Or think of Sarajevo, in 1992, when the UN confidently predicted that tens of thousands would die of cold. For all the heroism of the UN airlift, and the good it did, there is in retrospect no question but that the Bosnian people were simply more resilient and resourceful than aid workers and UN officials had thought. Similar mistakes were made in Rwanda and Kosovo. In short, aid workers are as often wrong in their fears as they are right. They were, in the event, wrong in Afghanistan, too. But what if they had not been? Despite what critics of aid say, surely it is better to predict the worst and be pleasantly surprised if it does not come to pass than to be too sanguine and then discover, as people begin to die, that one was wrong.

And things are more complicated still. One does not have to be a skeptic about aid to recognize that it is in aid workers' institutional interests to put themselves at the center of crises such as the one in Afghanistan. Oxfam, Children's Aid, and a number of other relief groups appeared to have taken humanitarianism's centrality so much for granted that, shortly after the crisis began, they demanded a month's pause in the bombing so that aid could be gotten in. Even assuming the United States and the Taliban had agreed, much more time than a month would have been needed for a proper humanitarian operation to be mounted. Some speculated at the time that this was precisely what Oxfam and the other groups really had in mind— an end to the war using the humanitarian imperative as a pretext. But the more interesting question is why this humanitarian imperative should have been assumed to take precedence over all others.

After all, all wars have disastrous humanitarian consequences. On strictly humanitarian grounds, the war against the Nazis should have been halted. The same could be said of the American Civil War. Think of the humanitarian catastrophe that General Sherman's forces caused as they burned their way through Georgia, killing comparatively few, but intentionally destroying the economy and creating tens of thousands of what relief workers now would call internally displaced people (IDPs). If the humanitarian yardstick is to be employed, then even these two just wars should have been halted.

It is a problem without an easy solution unless one is a pacifist. I supported the war in Afghanistan. The horror that anyone who has seen war must feel did nothing to modify my judgment that war was the only option—that the threat from an Afghanistan that had become the private fiefdom of the Al Qaeda network was simply too grave. I still believe it, though I have no faith that the successor regime to the Taliban will be such a vast improvement. And yet one day in Peshawar in October 2001, at a school for Afghan refugee girls, I met a small child in one of the classes who had lost her father three weeks earlier to an American bomb. She was composed, dignified, and appeared quite numb as she told the story of his death. As I listened, it was as if my opinions were in one universe and her experience in another.

Listening to her did not turn me against the war, though I shall go to my own grave wondering whether it should have. What the time I spent with that child did persuade me of was that a humanitarianism that supports the idea of war carried out in its name is unworthy of that name. This is not to say that individual relief workers should not have the right to support a war—whether undertaken by their own government or another—or any other just cause, even one whose imperatives undermine or contradict those of humanitarianism. They should not lose their civil rights simply by joining the IRC, or MSF, or Oxfam. But the idea that, in the new world order of human rights and humanitarian intervention—as imagined, in their very different ways, by Mario Bettati, Andrew Natsios, Bernard Kouchner, and Kofi Annan—one can call "humanitarian" these actions in which children like the girl I met will *predictably* lose their fathers exemplifies a moral newspeak that is indeed worthy of Orwell. Humanitarian war should be seen as a contradiction in terms, not an increasingly sought-after "solution" to the ills of the world.

To be sure, the rationale for such interventions was never military necessity in the brutal sense employed by the American soldier who said, during an engagement in Vietnam, "We had to burn the village in order to save it." But if the humanitarian rationalization was not on the same level of moral obtuseness, it was still dangerous. From the intervention in Somalia forward, humanitarians all but insisted that the soldiers guarding them had to shoot the looters so they could get the supplies through to the beneficiaries. Whereas taking lives in order to save lives had once been anathema to relief workers, it was increasingly understood as something that might be necessary, at least in the most extreme situations. In Afghanistan, this reasoning was extended still further. The humanitarian requirements of the Afghan people, it was claimed routinely, could be secured only by war.

Perhaps that was indeed the case. But, as Rony Brauman observed, "modern humanitarianism had come into being by emancipating itself from its thralldom to the political." Brauman added that to subordinate it to reasons of state—even good and justifiable reasons—was nothing other than "a dangerous regression."

For Brauman, to call the aid the U.S. Air Force was providing to Afghanistan—let alone the war itself—the new, and presumably improved, twenty-first-century version of humanitarianism was an obscenity. Call it politics, call it reason of state, call it nation building; but don't call it humanitarianism. Yet for the most part, that is just what the relief organizations did. Increasingly, they seemed resigned to or actually in accord with the militarization of their vocation. Examples of this abounded in the internal debates of mainline NGOs, even some of those that had had qualms about the war when it first began. Before too long, some NGOs were expressing publicly the belief that they could not do their work without some sort of armed force to protect them.

On November 20, 2001, a consortium of American relief groups demanded that an international security force be deployed. Huge areas of Afghanistan might have been purged of the Taliban, but the country remained lawless. Again, Ken Bacon took the lead. The war, he said, affords "a real opportunity for the world to reverse twenty years of war . . . [But] the sooner these areas are made secure, the better the relief effort will be." Others echoed his view. Mary Diaz, of the Women's Commission for Refugee Women and Children of the International Rescue Committee, put forward the feminist argument for this international security force. The events of the past months, she said, "have finally opened doors for the restoration of women's rights." And she insisted that Afghan women's groups were interested in an international force as well.

Perhaps they were. The question was, what business did relief organizations have making such demands? And the answer was simple. For many humanitarian practitioners, humanitarianism was no longer enough. Denis Dragovic, a former field coordinator for the International Rescue Committee, was speaking for many of his colleagues, and about all the humanitarian action in war, when he wrote: "Never has there been a war without human rights violations and humanitarian disasters. Without recognizing this and acknowledging that, first and foremost, peace needs to be brought to Sudan, all other interventions are mere red herrings, distracting attention from the reality on the ground."

The growing consensus among aid workers was that they did not want simply to give relief to people in need; they wanted to build new societies. And for that, force would be necessary. Françoise Bouchet-Saulnier's injunction that humanitarian action must not be used "as a bargaining chip to secure . . . respect for human rights" was almost like a message from the long-forgotten past of humanitarianism—a past in which relief workers "settled" for doing what they could and had no ambitions to build peace, or redeem whole societies, or resolve conflicts. And yet it is hardly surprising that the more political version of humanitarianism had prevailed by the time the war in Afghanistan was coming to its close. It, and it alone, claimed to offer real hope for the future. In contrast, MSF and the few other aid groups that rejected these messianic promises about what aid could achieve, and continued to insist that modest parameters had to be drawn around what the humanitarian enterprise could accomplish, seemed to offer a more dispiriting vision of the future.

A few French NGOs might respond to the military-humanitarian compact proposed by the U.S. government in the first days of the bombing campaign by insisting that humanitarianism could have nothing to do with war, even just war. Their refusal to become part of a humanitarian coalition standing side by side with the military coalition had little impact. Other NGOs had already signed up for the coalition. Luminaries of the aid world, notably Sadako Ogata, the former head of UNHCR, had been enlisted. So had Mark Malloch Brown, the head of the United Nations Development Programme, who, having started his career as a UNHCR official, was being asked to cap it as the man charged with rebuilding Afghanistan.

There was little public opposition to the confusion of those roles. The notion that an independent humanitarian space was necessary in a country like Afghanistan, where humanitarianism on its own had made little headway, seemed counterintuitive and fruitless. And the concern that aid workers would be confused with soldiers seemed too parochial—assuming, of course, that the soldiers were serving a decent cause. Finally, a successful humanitarian aftermath to the war in Afghanistan would serve to make the horrors of the campaign more bearable. The guilty would have been hunted down, the innocent succored. What was there to object to about that? And, in fairness, there is plenty of evidence that state humanitarianism can get things done that independent humanitarianism cannot.

Both before the conflict, and then again immediately after the fall of Kabul, NGOs and UN agencies warned of an impending famine unless much more food could be gotten to the north of Afghanistan. The most efficient way to do this was by truck and rail over the so-called friendship bridge that linked Uzbekistan with the northern Afghan city of Mazar-e Sharif. The Uzbek government had long rebuffed efforts by the UN and the NGOs to reopen the bridge, which had been closed since the Taliban took Mazar in 1998. But when

U.S. Secretary of State Colin Powell visited Tashkent, the Uzbek capital, in early December 2001, he quickly secured a commitment from the Uzbeks to reopen the bridge.

It was a perfect emblem of the power of state humanitarianism. And in its aftermath, aid officials went from predicting disaster for the Afghan people over the course of the upcoming winter to reassuring both donors and the media that, relatively speaking at least, things would probably be all right. "We [had been] trying to reach six million people," said Mike Huggins, a spokesman for the World Food Programme. With the opening of the bridge, he added, "We believe we are getting ever closer to that goal."

The humanitarians were either reaping the benefits or paying the price for the expansion of the mandate that they themselves had sought. After all, what had the intertwining of democratic activism, human rights, and humanitarianism—a trend that had been welcomed by most decent people in the West—been if not the confusing of roles for a higher end? And the concrete benefits of this approach were real, as Secretary Powell's visit to Tashkent had demonstrated. As the fighting ebbed, the French and British governments' boast that their principal military contribution would be to help make the humanitarian operation more secure was proving to be more than rhetoric. Clare Short, the British secretary of state for international development, even reproached the Americans at one point for not putting troops on the ground sooner to aid the humanitarian effort in Afghanistan. And of Jacques Chirac's two announcements about France's participation in the campaign—his promises to deploy combat aircraft and to put in place "a humanitarian air bridge"—the latter was far more credible than the former.

That the NGOs on the ground would welcome these developments is understandable. One of the evangelical Christian aid workers who had been imprisoned by the Taliban for proselytizing—they were guilty as charged—spoke for many relief workers, including those that did not share her faith, when she said that finally there was a chance to rebuild Afghanistan. In such a context, the pitfalls of collaboration with states appear a minor drawback. For the most part, relief agencies were indifferent to the fact that, assuming the effort succeeded, they would also have made the aid workers, many of whom came from the same countries as the soldiers about to be deployed, all but indistinguishable from the foreign soldiers and international bureaucrats to ordinary Afghans.

That was probably not the plan, though it would be the effect. And in any case, if so many NGOs had shown themselves eager for forces to be deployed, it would have been unrealistic to expect Western governments to hold back. In any case, most agencies had become so dependent on these governments for funds that it was often difficult to say where the interests of an NGO ended and that of a European Commission Humanitarian Aid Office or a United States Agency for International Development began. When Secretary of State Powell said, "The United States and its coalition partners, the United Nations and others, all of us in the international community, are moving quickly to provide lifesaving humanitarian supplies," he was speaking for most Western governments in that he took the collaboration between humanitarian workers, soldiers, and government officials for granted. Each, as many American officials liked to say, had a job to do.

This view was forcefully expressed by former senator and presidential candidate George McGovern, who, after his retirement, had become an activist in the international campaign against world hunger. Writing in *The Wall Street Journal* on February 5, 2002, McGovern said that the "seemingly impossible" Afghan crisis had been resolved by the collaboration of the UN's World Food Programme, what he called "a marvelous assortment of religious and philanthropic organizations," Andrew Natsios's USAID, and a "make-shift fleet of Afghan truck drivers." If there had been no starvation in Afghanistan, as relief agencies had feared, it was because the relief effort had "quietly gone forward day and night even as bombs fell from the sky." It was, McGovern added, "a modern-day miracle with no apparent downside."

The views of McGovern were, at their best, what all U.S. officials thought, and, for that matter, could be reasonably expected to think. But in the aid world, where the implications of these transformations are so much greater, it would have been reasonable to expect more controversy, more debate, more anxiety. No apparent downside? Not for the humanitarian NGOs. Afghanistan had proved to be a watershed. Looking back over the more than thirty years of humanitarian action since Biafra, it was in Afghanistan that the vision of aid long championed by Bernard Kouchner won its decisive victory, and where, in practical terms, the triumph of state humanitarianism became well-nigh complete. Poor humanitarianism. Who would have imagined the price of success would have been that high? MSF might continue to insist, as in a provocative piece by Fabrice Weissman, called "When Good Bombs Happen to Bad People," that the agency had to remain "in the service of victims, not regimes." Most aid workers, overwhelmed with relief that their worst fears were not being realized, and that they would be able to alleviate what they had feared would be a famine in Afghanistan, did not even seem to take in what they were yielding in terms of the autonomy of their future operations in whatever crises succeeded Afghanistan, let alone protest its passing. And yet the transformation, which had been well in motion long before the Afghan crisis, was epochal. In short order, aid workers had surrendered autonomy in the name of effectiveness, impartiality in the name of politics (the fact that NGOs still distributed aid to victims regardless of whether they were Taliban or anti-Taliban did little to mitigate the implications of the collaboration with and dependency on the United States), and an autonomous humanitarian space in the name of the imperative of access and the increased efficiencies of "coordination."

Of course, to the general public in the West, humanitarian action had become inextricably linked with the use of force, and, paradoxically, with the furtherance of human rights goals. The revolution of moral concern, it appeared, would be armed to the teeth. Perhaps that, too, was inevitable. The point is not to challenge the need to go to war; the point is to challenge the humanitarian justification for such wars. And yet when, in the wake of the Taliban withdrawal from Kabul, the European Union enjoined the Afghan capital's new rulers to respect "human rights and international humanitarian law," and warned that responsible behavior on their part would be "a key factor in determining the aid that the European Union is ready to make available to rebuild the country," none of the aid agencies protested, even though this kind of muscular liberalism, which subordinated the immediate needs of victims to the imperatives of human rights, made a mockery of humanitarian principles by in effect holding aid to victims hostage to the good behavior of states.

They did not protest for a simple reason. By the time the Afghan conflict drew to its conclusion, the marriage of war and mercy, and of humanitarian assistance and human rights conditionalities, was all but complete. The idea that even when an intervention was undertaken for humane and decent reasons, it might still not be humanitarian was seen as little more than Jesuitical hair-splitting. Médecins Sans Frontières might continue to insist that military interventions could be right but could not be humanitarian, but it was increasingly isolated. For most NGOs, as for the Western public at large, what Afghanistan demonstrated was that humanitarianism was too important a matter to be left to humanitarians alone.

CHAPTER 8

Endgame or Rebirth?

S OME WORDS ARE INCANTATORY, and none more so, by the end of the millennium, than "humanitarianism." Only "human rights" comes close to having the same quality of seeming morally impeccable. To be sure, in the poor world and among some radical Western humanitarian activists these concepts often had another resonance, and seemed, to some at least, to be code names for new forms of Western hegemony. Some mocked the humanitarian "adventure" (as Jean-Christophe Rufin once dubbed it), claiming that it was not only linguistically but intellectually and morally compromised, that the echoes of Kipling, Saint-Exupéry, and all those other colonial adventurers resonated too powerfully. Others compared humanitarianism to the good works that wives of nineteenth-century factory owners pursued among the "deserving poor," even as their husbands made sure they remained poor. Even those who did not go that far found it hard to reconcile the support of Western governments for the International Monetary Fund's economic policies, which seemed to increase economic misery in the poor world, and those same governments' support for humanitarian relief in the very countries that were net losers in globalization. At the very least, an ethos of compassion, as Jean-François Vidal of Action Against Hunger put it, had left "everything in place" then and would leave everything in place now. What he meant above all was that, on its own, humanitarianism could do little to alter economic exploitation or the denial of human rights.

Many Third World intellectuals went even further. In Delhi, Amman, or Mexico City, the reality that nineteenth-century imperialism had had a "humanitarian" justification seemed to render the contemporary humanitarian enterprise, no matter how much good it might do, politically suspect if not morally repugnant. "It is not as if the 'right of interference' cuts both ways," a friend in South Africa once said to me. "I cannot even imagine the U.S. or France letting medical teams from this country or any other African country in because one of those teams had identified some humanitarian need. And I certainly can't imagine the West conceding that they too should be subject to these new norms of humanitarian military intervention on human rights grounds."

The dominant Western liberal response, of course, has been that human rights are universal and that, in any case, the last thing the Western powers want or need is new colonies, let alone new imperial responsibilities. Those who have concluded that nineteenth- and early twentieth-century European and American imperialism's altruistic side outweighed or at least balanced its cruelty and injustice find the prospect of a humanitarian "recolonization" of the world in some extreme cases like Sierra Leone something to be welcomed. To them, these "human rights protection operations"—the name, meant to replace the more controversial "humanitarian intervention," was put forward in the 2001 Canadian government–sponsored report, "The Responsibility to Protect"—were an obligation for "the broader community of states" when sovereign states no longer can protect "their own citizens from avoidable catastrophe—from mass murder and rape, from starvation."

But both those who welcome and those who only reluctantly endorse the principle of humanitarian military interventions, and the subsequent establishment of temporary international protectorates, agree that it is unlikely to become the principal response to the problems of war, poverty, and humanitarian disaster. After all, imperialism had been first and foremost a profitable venture, while this effort to occupy and rebuild failed states is going to cost the West money, not make it more prosperous. For this reason alone, it is not likely to be used very often.

Of course, it is possible to make the argument that if nothing is done about the problems of failed states, these problems will eventually affect the rich world as well. Indeed, such claims are commonplace in international studies of peacekeeping and humanitarian intervention. But while this argument may be compelling to policy intellectuals and aid workers, it does not resonate with a Western public that sees little evidence of any such spillover. Even the most important historical event of the post–Cold War period, the rapid rise of mass immigration from the poor world to the rich world, is only marginally related to the kinds of wars and civil conflicts humanitarian interventions are meant to address. For every Afghan or Sierra Leonean trying to start a new life and get away from the killing, there are twenty Mexicans or Moroccans simply trying to escape the poverty in which they are mired.

And immigration is not a context in which anyone acts altruistically. If the West has accepted this mass migration, this is due far more to low birthrates at home and the unwillingness of Europeans and North Americans to do the dirty jobs that immigrants accept than to any disinterested concern. In contrast, disinterestedness is

exactly what humanitarian intervention requires. Under the circumstances, it is not surprising that UN officials, at least once Kofi Annan became secretary-general in 1996, seemed more perturbed by
the *unwillingness* of Western states to intervene in the poor world on
humanitarian or human rights grounds than they were troubled by
the idea of humanitarianism and human rights serving as a moral
warrant for a new colonial era.

Shashi Tharoor, the former UN Department of Peacekeeping Operations desk officer for the former Yugoslavia and an Annan loyal-
ist who became the acting head of the UN's Department of Public
Information in 2000, wrote that American unilateralism made him
want to cry out: "Humanity is a strategic national interest."

But the widespread doubt that many humanitarian interventions
will actually take place sits oddly with the conviction, widely shared
at the UN, among many Western government officials, and, of course,
among human rights activists and many relief workers, that, from a
normative point of view anyway, the matter is settled and no longer
subject to debate—the ethical equivalent of what judges call black-
letter law. Reasonable people may differ in their evaluation of the
way a particular humanitarian intervention, or human rights campaign, or relief effort is carried out, but not over the desirability or
the moral imperative of such undertakings. To say anything else is to
lay oneself open to the charge of being against humanitarianism and
human rights. It is like saying one is against a better world.

Even those like Tharoor and his colleagues at the UN who take
the objections of the poor world seriously believe that this only
obliges the proponents of humanitarian intervention to join Annan
in promoting "a political and human rights environment in the
world that will make it more difficult for states to abuse the rights of
their citizens, judging that the world will stand idly by." Intervention
is caring. Intervention, if done for the right reasons, under the right

circumstances, and with proper safeguards, is, as Annan has put it, "testimony to a humanity that cares more."

Who could be against humanity? How could such good intentions be controversial to anyone of goodwill? The secretary-general, a man who was once described to me by one of his close advisors as "someone who simply does not believe in irreconcilable differences," seemed genuinely puzzled by such criticisms when he was confronted by them. And most activists, not to mention most Western governments, appeared to agree with him. Small wonder, then, that by the end of the 1990s in Western Europe—where, unlike the United States, politicians did not often claim the moral warrant for their action came from their Christian faith—humanitarianism and human rights really did seem like the established churches of the establishment. The French political scientist and Central Asia expert Olivier Roy has remarked that where, twenty years before, states had opened cultural offices, now they funded humanitarian operations. And it was hard not to feel—to hearken back to the words the French had used to justify their colonial empire—that Europeans and North Americans saw humanitarian and human rights activism as their new "civilizing mission."

This is not to say that the major powers want to recolonize, as figures on the hard left like Noam Chomsky or the Indian writer Arundhati Roy often choose to imagine. In reality, no policy could be farther from the one they would prefer to implement. There was no desire to intervene in Bosnia, Rwanda, Kosovo, or Afghanistan. To the contrary, the Western powers did everything they could to avoid intervention, even if it meant watching Afghanistan destroy itself or coming to understandings with Slobodan Milosevic. Interventions took place only when it was either comparatively safe to deploy troops, as in the case of the French intervention in Rwanda and the end of the genocide or the UN peacekeeping deployment in its immediate aftermath, or when other interests were at stake, as in the case of Kosovo and Afghanistan.

But like elite military forces always at the ready, by the beginning of the new millennium the language of human rights and of the humanitarian imperative had become both so familiar and so unassailable it could be deployed at a moment's notice. Everything, both problems and solutions, was being called humanitarian. And in this world of humanitarian disasters and humanitarian interventions, this world of malign warlords and peace-loving victims, in which moral and political complexities and ambiguities were minimized, what mattered was less understanding than action. Paradoxically, the more influential the humanitarian ideal has grown the more incoherent it has become. By now, it is virtually the linguistic equivalent of the second law of thermodynamics. For when humanitarianism can mean anything and everything—relief, human rights, refugee protection, charity, conflict prevention, conflict resolution, nation building—what does it exemplify if not the principle of entropy?

Those most worried by all of this were the humanitarians themselves, who had realized for some time that their ideas were being put to uses and stretched in ways they had never intended or imagined. What was unclear at first was how relief workers would react to this appropriation and instrumentalization of humanitarianism. Would they resist, and remain faithful to the "disobedient" humanitarianism of a Rony Brauman or a Françoise Bouchet-Saulnier? Or would they succeed in fashioning a historic compromise with the state humanitarianism and the humanitarianism of international organizations, the humanitarianism of Bernard Kouchner, Kofi Annan, the U.S. State Department, and the European Union?

From the mid-1990s almost all relief agencies were agreed that much in their practice had to change. At least at the outset, the problem was that there was little consensus among them either about what that change would consist of, or how in practical terms it could be realized. Countless studies were done. A World Wide Web search for NGO-sponsored reports produced in the second half of the 1990s on such subjects as ameliorating agencies' own standards; improving coordination among agencies, with the UN, and with donors; becoming more responsive to beneficiaries; and incorporating human rights norms would produce literally thousands of matches. And it is by no means clear even today, when the debate has largely been settled in favor of state humanitarianism, that all the dilemmas were resolved. Perhaps that was an impossible expectation. Certainly, what Afghanistan proved, as if after Kosovo yet one more shattering disappointment were necessary, was that the dilemmas of humanitarianism remained as agonizing and intractable and the paradoxes as acute at the end of this process of self-questioning as they had been at the beginning.

Why did this come as a surprise? Part of the answer, I think, is that, despite the reality of its financial dependence on states, humanitarianism had always been something a bit like Communism, even in the minds of those of its defenders who were alive to its flaws. For Communist fellow travelers, there had always been a clear distinction between what they were pleased to call "actually existing Communism"—that is, regimes such as the Soviet Union, China, Vietnam, and Cuba—and the Communist ideal. And no horror—not the Gulag, not the famine that was unleashed in the late 1950s in the wake of Mao Tse-Tung's so-called Great Leap Forward, nor any of the other disasters of the seventy-one-year reign of the dogma—was able to unseat this ideal. What the German Marxist Ernst Bloch, who was by no means immune to it, had called "the spirit of utopia" reigned supreme; it was just that allegiances—or were they hopes?—kept shifting from one state to the next, until all that was left was a China that was no longer Communist in anything but name, a Cuba ruined by Fidel Castro's consummate vanity, and, worst of all, totalitarian, famine-stricken North Korea.

A similar dualism afflicted adherents of what Alex de Waal, in a caustic allusion to the Communist movement, called "the Humanitarianism International." For them, there was the actually existing humanitarianism pertaining to needs too vast ever to meet, challenges too daunting to fully address, and the reality of a world too sad, murderous, and wicked to transcend. This world of confused and often contradictory motives and often ill-conceived and unfulfillable mandates was the one that relief workers both incarnated and in which they spent their working lives.

In a world made up largely of volunteers who, in the words of the IRC's emergency response coordinator, Gerry Martone, were too often either "mystics or misfits," it has always been easy to see the fault lines—human, moral, and operational. As an MSF official once put it, "Joining a humanitarian organization [and going into the field] always represents a break—whether it is with the consumer society at home, or the breakup of a relationship." He did not need to add that such breaks are usually possible only for the young, or that relief work has always been something of a children's crusade. At least for anyone over thirty-five, it is the youth of most aid workers in the field that is immediately striking.

That humanitarians had become, by the time of the Bosnian crisis at least, an instrument and emblem of the reach and power of Western governments was equally obvious. In Africa, it already had been clear for a long time. There, like the missionaries whose charitable functions they had largely supplanted, aid workers seemed to represent the soft side of Europeans' power—white people in white four-wheel-drive vehicles with African drivers running around the countryside giving orders, organizing, taking charge. That humanitarian workers usually had an entirely different conception of what they were up to changed little. Yes, they thought of their presence as an expression of solidarity, not a continuation of colonial roles. But for all the talk that began to permeate aid circles in the 1990s about the need to be responsible to beneficiaries as well as to donors, and all the moves undertaken to make that laudable goal a reality, anyone who has been on the ground in a relief operation anywhere in sub-Saharan Africa knows perfectly well that the African reading of the power relationships is often closer to the truth.

When one goes to a poor country where the humanitarian role is vital, the colonial atmosphere is unmistakable. Humanitarians live in houses previously occupied by cabinet ministers, or at least by the richest person in the village. Their user-friendly democratic attitudes can do nothing to disguise their power. Whether they are in sandals and old jeans or not, the reality is the same. And the youthquake clothing only makes them masters in mufti. They are there to help; they are not there to share power in any serious sense.

It is hard to imagine how it could have been otherwise. The idea that relief workers should not only have made sacrifices by the standards of their classmates back home in North America, or Western Europe, or Australia, but should also live as meagerly as the people they were aiding is unrealistic. If those had been the requirements, then *only* misfits and mystics would have applied. The point, after all, is to bring relief, not to don a hair shirt. But the situation is complicated. It is the aura of sanctity around aid workers—a reputation that had much to do with the image, repeated ad nauseam in the Western media, of the pietà-like image of the Western nurse cradling a black child in her arms—that did so much to enthrone them in the imagination of the Western public. That public included government officials, who proved as susceptible to humanitarianism's

allure as anyone else in the West. President George W. Bush expressed this view in a speech at Tsinghua University in Beijing, during his February 2002 visit to China, when he spoke of "America's
compassion [stretching] way beyond our borders." America, the
president said, is "the number one provider of humanitarian aid."

Obviously, most major donors have always seen and continue to
see humanitarianism instrumentally. But the degree to which Western politicians such as Bush or British Prime Minister Tony Blair,
and Western political institutions more generally, are seduced by its
moral prestige is important, though not perhaps in the way humanitarians themselves would have liked. One of the most important
purposes contemporary humanitarianism has served has been to allow government officials to see their support for it as an expression
of their best selves. That, at least as much as any desire to assuage
the anger and sense of injustice with which much of the Islamic
world reacted to the U.S.–led coalition's bombing of Afghanistan,
accounts for why President Jacques Chirac of France and Prime
Minister Blair kept speaking of their commitment to using troops to
pursue Osama bin Laden and the Taliban and to provide humanitarian relief as if the two enterprises were indistinguishable.

Humanitarians and their supporters know this better than anyone. They experience during almost every day of their working lives
the gap between the lip service Western governments pay the humanitarian ideal and the hardheaded calculations that go into decisions
about which relief efforts to fund and under what circumstances.
And yet, somehow, humanitarianism as humanitarians have imagined it has continued to transcend these realities. Many if not most
relief workers have retained their faith in an "essential" humanitarianism that no failure in the field, and, indeed, no ethical contradiction or unintended negative consequence, can ever impugn. The UN
has a similarly Church-like quality. People at the UN often turn to

the language of religion, saying, when other justifications fail, that they still "believe" in the world body.

Writing about a similar conceit in the world of development assistance, the French social critic Serge Latouche observed that it was long overdue that, after fifty years of failure, the development world admit that it would not, in fact, get it right with just one more "tweak," one more improvement in methodology, some reform in governance across the poor world, or some new commitment by the rich donor countries. Actually existing development, he wrote, was what development was. Even at its apogee in the late 1960s and early 1970s, development never enjoyed the prestige that humanitarianism had come to enjoy by the 1990s among a far wider general public, except possibly in Scandinavia. But this only made it harder for aid workers to admit that "actually existing" humanitarianism might be all there is. They had made such extraordinary claims for and to themselves that admitting theirs was an inherently limited activity—believing, *really* believing, as opposed to saying, and then incorporating into their practice in the field the dictum that there are no humanitarian solutions to humanitarian problems—must have seemed like an unbearable fall into defeatism.

Whatever claims they had made for themselves had been amplified by the media. Television, in particular, had provided humanitarianism with an outlet and sometimes egged the agencies on. But the claims that the NGOs had made for themselves were, at least in retrospect, hubristic. MSF's famous ad campaign in France asserted, "We have two billion people in our waiting room." The implication was clear. If given the resources, they could save them all. They must have known this was nonsense. The gap between the way aid workers describe what they do among themselves and how they describe it in fund-raising materials is one of the great tensions in the day-to-day practice of contemporary humanitarianism. But it certainly captured the imagination—first theirs, then the general public's. And it was a self-confirming rhetoric, an approach that fed on itself. It was ads such as that which brought volunteers to MSF. In the field, of course, they would be disenchanted, but by then, like young conscripts to Western militaries lured by slick publicity campaigns, they would have already become part of the system.

MSF was hardly alone in indulging itself in this kind of ecstatic overstretch. ACF, whose technical capabilities in the field of famine relief were as exceptional as MSF's were in that of emergency medicine, was similarly tempted. ACF, which had been founded in 1979 by a group of French intellectuals including the writers Bernard-Henri Levy and Marek Halter and the politician and futurist Jacques Attali, had originally set as a goal nothing less than mobilizing French public opinion against what they termed the "scandal" of world hunger. By 1989 they were going still further, running ads and paying for billboards all over France that said simply, "We shall conquer hunger." They did not say, "We can." "Can" was crossed out and "shall" written in red letters above it.

Such ads were typical, above all in Western Europe. Indeed, they were a demonstration of the fact that, for all the supposed self-examination, in some important ways little had changed. Many aid workers appear to be nostalgic for the days when it was possible to believe and employ such rhetoric, among them Sylvie Brunel, the former president of ACF. She has written bitterly that, in contrast to our own time, the period of the organization's founding was one in which "no one was afraid of verbal excess," as if in the service of the right cause that was invariably a virtue. Before her astonishing change of heart in March 2002, when she resigned from ACF and excoriated the NGOs as inefficient and often unworthy of the trust placed in them by both the public and the donors, Brunel had taken something of a hard line within the humanitarian movement. She had insisted over and over again in speeches and articles that the attacks upon it have little or no merit. "It is," she has written, "because the humanitarian movement has applied to itself the same moral rigor and firmness that it has used to denounce the ills of the world that it today finds itself in the hot seat." Humanitarianism is anything but dead, she concludes defiantly. Rather, "It has entered into a stage of responsible maturity."

Brunel is only expressing in an extreme way (in the same article, she launches a bitter attack on Rony Brauman, who had been her mentor at MSF) what many senior NGO officials and many if not most relief workers in the field believe. Indeed, it is this oscillation between defiance and self-flagellation that has marked much of the internal debate within NGOs since at least the Goma refugee crisis. This is much less true within UNHCR, still less true within the WFP and other UN agencies, and almost impossible to discern within the UN Secretariat, which remains by and large resistant to such self-interrogation, preferring to shift the blame to the world body's member states, a hostile or uncomprehending press, or the indifference of the Western elites. But among relief workers from groups as varied as MSF, IRC, and Oxfam, it has become a commonplace since the mid-1990s to hear defeatist language in private almost as often as one hears self-justification, self-praise, and confidence about the future in public.

It is understandable. In Somalia in 1991, the NGOs had seen for the first time soldiers, whose presence they had called for, killing in their name—the name of the international social mission that was humanitarian action at its best. They had been horrified, but most did not know whether to repudiate humanitarian military intervention or just call for it to be done better; in other words, for a technical more than a moral fix. In Sarajevo in 1992, they had watched with anger and grief as the humanitarian ideal they had pledged themselves to was used as a justification for the world's inaction. Over and over again, both publicly and privately, they had said that such a perversion of aid was intolerable. But they did not know whether to withdraw, or call for military intervention.

In eastern Congo in 1994, in the aftermath of the Rwandan genocide, they had come face to face with the real harm they could do. They discovered that solidarity with victims, political impartiality, and aid deployed simply on the basis of need could restore an army of genocidal killers to health and threaten to plunge Rwanda further into a nightmare of blood and fire. Some had withdrawn, but most had not. In Kosovo in 1999, many had felt their control over humanitarian action slipping away. NATO, they discovered, did not just want to call the military shots; it wanted to make the crucial humanitarian aid decisions as well. But again, most went along. Later, Afghanistan would appear to combine the worst features of all these crises.

But already by the late 1990s, it was as if the NGOs were drowning. Accountable at once to everyone and to no one, lacking either the constitutional legitimacy of state agencies or the legal legitimacy, grounded in international conventions of the ICRC, and torn between the imperatives of bringing aid to victims and preventing the humanitarian enterprise from being hijacked by donor governments, they were verging on cognitive and moral meltdown.

It was not that they saw no way out. They saw too many ways out. They had come up with all sorts of solutions to the problems of relations between humanitarians and NATO military forces; between the imperatives of human rights, conflict prevention, and humanitarianism; and with the best way to coordinate humanitarian action. But the solutions were either contradictory or else appeared, when one considered seriously how they might be put into practice, to be

little more than hollow slogans in which the NGOs presented prescriptions for reform that were, in reality, fantasies about what humanitarianism would be like in a world in which justice reigned.

In such a world, the commitments of powerful states to the Universal Declaration of Human Rights and to international humanitarian law would be substantive rather than formal, and the general
public in these countries would not just see the sufferings of faraway
peoples as wrong but would make the remedying of that wrong a political priority for their leaders. But in such a world, where laws
would be binding, and the moral consensus deeply rooted, the need
for an independent humanitarianism would be minimal. And in any
case, as MSF's Eric Dachy warned, the evolution of human societies
toward a state of law will not be reached "through the actions of humanitarian or human rights activists." "On the contrary," he wrote,
"genuine compassion and generosity are not on the same register
as . . . political and structural solutions."

But leaving the utopianism of this vision of the likely effects of a
new rights-based humanitarianism to one side, even the practical
reforms in which relief agencies increasingly put their faith were
more debatable than they appeared at first glance. Take the idea of
coordination. In theory, it sounds unobjectionable. The term "international community" may be a fiction, but there is, unquestionably,
an international humanitarian system, whether independence-
minded NGOs are comfortable with the fact or not. It therefore
seems only commonsensical that UN specialized agencies, private
relief groups, and donors would consult one another more scrupu-
lously than in the past and with more forethought and agreed-upon
presuppositions, as well as try to devise a common approach in each
crisis so as to avoid duplication, make the relief effort more efficient,
and use what funds were available to best effect. As the then presi-

dent of the ICRC, Cornelio Sommaruga, put it in a speech at the United Nations, "The strengthening of humanitarian coordination is of paramount importance, both in order to better respond to the needs of the victims and to render the deployment of humanitarian action safer."

But what in practice did coordination actually mean? The official UN view of coordination, expressed on the UN Office for the Coordination of Humanitarian Affairs (OCHA) website, has been that "humanitarian emergencies are both multidimensional and complex, and many actors—such as governments, nongovernmental organizations (NGOs), UN agencies and individuals—seek to respond simultaneously. OCHA works with them to ensure that there is a coherent framework within which each actor can contribute effectively and promptly to the overall effort."

This "coherent framework" had a cost. It effectively ruled out, or at least marginalized, the independent humanitarianism MSF had pioneered. Kofi Annan made this plain in his 1998 report to the UN's Economic and Social Committee. He wrote: "There is growing recognition of the essential linkages between all aspects of external support for countries afflicted by conflict, whether political, humanitarian, developmental or human rights. The challenge is to establish joint planning and coordination mechanisms in the field and at Headquarters that reflect this understanding. The participation of donor governments, host governments and non-governmental organizations in this effort is essential to its success."

The answer to this, of course, is that it all depends on what you mean by success. For Annan, as for everyone who has been deeply influenced by the essentially legalistic framework of the Western human rights movement, the major moral and intellectual questions about human rights have been settled. There are adjustments that need to be made, and, importantly, there is also the moral imperative to extend and expand existing rights to cover new categories of people. The comparatively recent idea that antidiscrimination statutes should apply to gays and lesbians as well as racial and religious minorities is a good example of this. But the principal task at hand— grave, daunting, and at times obviously not yet possible as it is— involves turning the agreed-upon norms into realities. As Human Rights Watch's *World Report 2001* put it, "Enforcement is needed." The contours of that enforcement regime remain to be decided. But that is where human rights activists believe they need to focus their efforts.

For those who share this vision of the world, coordination of humanitarian efforts will seem like an unmixed blessing. But Annan's vision implies that all goods are complementary. Truth and justice, peace and justice, and, of course, human rights and humanitarianism: these are simply aspects of the quest for a better world—the radiant legal future already imagined in the 1950s by the World Federalist Movement, of which Annan is in many ways the ideological inheritor.

But such visions are fantasies, and self-indulgent ones at that. Annan's speeches are replete with references to the sorrows and miseries of the world. But one searches them in vain for an acknowledgment of tragedy in the Hegelian sense of the conflict of two rights. By the same token, his prescription for mitigating the unintended negative consequences of good actions has usually been to appeal for sounder planning, or more serious thought, or better coordination. Reading his writings and public declarations, it seems as if, for Annan, all competing claims can be reconciled—the interests of a multinational corporation and a human rights NGO, of sovereignty and humanitarian intervention. And yet it is a truism to say that, in the world as it is, good ends are often in opposition.

Kofi Annan must know this. He is a man of vast experience of the horror of the world. Surely he is aware that neither peace and justice, nor truth and justice, always go hand in hand. And yet, as UN secretary-general, Annan has insisted again and again that, with enough effort, goodwill, and commitment, what are now little more than hopeful fictions about a new international order based on peace, justice, and truth can be transformed into reality.

In the case of humanitarian intervention, Annan's optimistic account of what "the international community" could achieve if only it would muster the will and the commitment to do so is even more likely to engender false hope. He has rightly insisted that just wars are sometimes necessary. But by emphasizing the need to protect civilians, in extreme cases even from their own governments, he gives the impression that what he is talking about is sending a few humane policemen, when what he is really talking about is sending warriors—men whose business it is to kill, within the limits of the laws of war, anyone who gets in the way of the mission they have been assigned.

To speak, as Annan has done, of the "developing international norm in favor of intervention to protect civilians from wholesale slaughter," without emphasizing the horror of what such an intervention will involve, *assuming* it is justified, is the gravest mystification. It is not that what Annan is saying is necessarily false. But no less serious is his failure to emphasize sufficiently the reality that, even at their most just and most defensible, wars involve, *centrally*, the slaughter of innocents, no matter how hard scrupulous soldiers, or their political masters, try to minimize such killing. This is not true only when armies violate the laws of war; it is true when armies obey the laws of war *to the letter*.

It is also not only true of wars fought in the name of nation-states; it has been true of the few wars fought in the name of the United Nations, as Somalia in 1992 should have demonstrated. Annan has talked eloquently about protecting civilians from slaughter, famine, and the worst forms of oppression. Would that he had been candid enough to acknowledge that, if this is to be achieved, we will often have to commit slaughter ourselves—as the UN peacekeeping force, sent to protect aid convoys, did during its campaign against Mohammed Farah Aidid's militia in Mogadishu. In fact, that particular operation was misconceived from the start. But the point about humanitarian war is that invariably it is the logic of war, not the logic of humanitarianism, that prevails. Time and time again, from Somalia to Afghanistan, the soldiers have called the tune. It will never be otherwise, no matter how many coordination meetings are held, studies done, and contacts established, because it is part of the irreducible essence of war.

Whether or not he intended his words to be understood in this way, Annan's speeches on the need to consider humanitarian military interventions have let slip the specter of endless wars of altruism. His defenders insist that this was not what he had in mind at all, and that, in any case, he knows there is no chance of such an outcome since the Western nations that would have to undertake such operations have little or no appetite for them. And yet even if this political estimate is correct, a new crusading era undertaken in the name of humanitarianism and human rights remains the *logical* conclusion of the secretary-general's reflections.

Evidence of this can be found in "The Responsibility to Protect," the Canadian-sponsored report of an international commission headed up by the former Australian foreign minister Gareth Evans and the former UN special representative for Somalia Mohammed Sahnoun. The report was explicitly an attempt to put Annan's idea of sovereignty as responsibility into a practical framework. "The very term 'international community' will become irrelevant unless the community of states can act when large groups of peoples are being massacred or subject to ethnic cleansing," Evans said in a December 19, 2001, press conference at the UN called to present the report to the public. And yet if one is to take Evans at his word, even leaving out interventions in the affairs of powerful states (in Tibet, say, or Chechnya), which the report rightly ruled out on prudential grounds, this still would involve "the international community" in dozens of interventions around the globe, since large groups of people are being massacred or "ethnically cleansed" in dozens of comparatively powerless countries from Sudan to Indonesia.

The affinity of the human rights movement for such views is understandable. Because it is law-based, the human rights movement must be absolutist or it is nothing. By definition, its demands are maximalist, its standards inflexible. In the case of humanitarianism, however, things are more complicated. The daily experience of humanitarian workers in a war zone involves either cooperating with murderous thugs, as, say, in Burundi, or calling for foreign soldiers to protect them, as, say, in Somalia. Moral grayness is the aid worker's stock-in-trade. The issue is not whether a responsible relief worker should reject Annan's vision of a world in which civilians would be protected from wholesale slaughter. Who would not desire such a wondrous thing? Rather, it is that every aid worker knows that the imperatives of human rights and humanitarianism often are at odds. But once the Rubicon has been crossed, and humanitarianism is enlisted as part of the army of peace—as it was in Kosovo, and again in Afghanistan—its autonomous interests will count for less than those of the "mission."

Examples are legion of the UN's interpretation of "coordination" signifying that humanitarians must put themselves at the disposal of the world body's political goal. In Sierra Leone in 1998, the UN wanted to pressure the guerrillas of the Revolutionary United Front (RUF) in the region around the city of Bo in the south. To do this, it decided that relief workers needed to withdraw for a time. This is not an uncomplicated story ethically; it is one that, as is so often the case, involves the clash of two rights. Few more horrible groups of guerrillas have ever disgraced the earth than the RUF, even if it was also much more a political movement than the criminal band that it was represented to be in the Western press. The UN had good reasons to want to do whatever it could do to dilute the RUF's power. MSF, which refused to obey the UN's order to suspend temporarily its operations and pull out, was also right to want to remain faithful to its imperative of remaining with the victims, whether or not this somehow benefited the RUF—*as it may well have done.*

In Sierra Leone at that particular moment, it is false to say that coordination was an unalloyed improvement over the previous humanitarian chaos, just as it is false to claim, as the architects of the NGO program for common and improved technical standards known as SPHERE routinely did, that SPHERE helped to reestablish "the legitimacy of the humanitarian system." Instead, what it actually accomplished was to throw the power, prestige, and influence of many of the best-respected NGOs in the world (although many of the mainline French relief organizations maintained their distance from the project) behind the holistic, human rights–centered conception of humanitarian action that groups such as Oxfam had long favored and that had found its most influential advocate in the person of Kofi Annan.

It is hard to see how it could have been otherwise. The power of the humanitarian ideal combined with the evident failure of humanitarianism to provide "solutions" in the crises of the 1990s in which the most humanitarian resources were committed—Somalia, Bosnia, Rwanda, Kosovo—had turned out to be the humanitarian movement's Achilles' heel. The general public expected more of it than the providing of what a young American UNICEF official in

Burundi named Susannah Campbell once described to me derisively as "mere charity." And Bernard Kouchner's view, which was that, when aid was deployed in tandem with (well-intended) military power, political will, and public commitment, there *were* humanitarian solutions to humanitarian problems, had struck a chord not just with the general public but also with relief workers, UN officials, and liberal Western government bureaucracies. "Classic humanitarianism," Kouchner repeated time and time again, "protects the victims and accepts [massacres] as a reality. Modern humanitarianism accepts no such thing. Its ambition is to prevent the massacres."

The MSF view was eloquently expressed by Nicholas de Torrente, the head of the association's U.S. branch, who adamantly upheld the idea that relief workers "should not see [themselves] as part of the global response to crisis." It was far less compelling than Annan's, Kouchner's, and Bettati's vision of a humanitarianism that "could." Had not this sense of possibility been incarnated even in MSF's name—translated as "Doctors Without Borders"? And had not the point of this insurgent humanitarianism been to reject limits and the sense of failure? Historically, no social movement has ever succeeded for very long in retaining sole custody of the ideas it has championed or the values it has tried to stand for. Cooptation has been the historic destiny of most if not all large moral ideas. An obvious example is the Christian religion itself. What began as an emancipatory creed in the mystical sense, and, arguably, in the political sense as well, derided by educated Romans as the religion of women and slaves, was transformed almost beyond recognition after it had been adopted as the state religion of the Roman empire. This is not to say that none of early Christianity's values survived, but it is to acknowledge that the faith's encounter with state power and its institutionalization altered much about it, including the nature of many of its ideals. The same could probably be said about Marxism, although whether Communism was ever worth rescuing is more than doubtful.

Humanitarianism's amalgamation with state power and the UN's peace-and-alleviation agenda has something of the same quality of an epochal break. In fairness, the ground had been set by all the movements that followed MSF—organizations that were grouped together, in Europe at least, under the name Sans-Frontièrisme, which translated clumsily into English is "Without-Bordersism." As well as Pharmacists Without Borders, an organization that at least preserved MSF's medical character, there were also Reporters Without Borders and Lawyers Without Borders, organizations whose inspiration was MSF but whose practice was largely in defense of human rights. The line had been blurred long before Kofi Annan gave the revised credo of a rights-based humanitarianism his nihil obstat, or when Bernard Kouchner was installed as the first (humanitarian) viceroy of Kosovo.

As for humanitarianism itself, the fact that it had come to be understood as including the right of military intervention, or that by the year 2000 it had become part of the official ideology of the West as well as of the UN, should have come as no surprise to anyone. In true postmodern fashion, it could still present itself as an antiestablishment voice. But then, in a world in which advertising agencies have successfully appropriated the language of May 1968 (in Europe) and of the American counterculture (in the United States), and now present buying a particular model of car or acquiring a certain computer as a revolutionary gesture only slightly less radical than the storming of the Bastille or running away from home to become a hippie in Haight-Ashbury, this should hardly come as a shock.

The new humanitarian consensus has posed a daunting chal-

lenge to groups such as MSF that remain unreconciled on principle
to this new turning in humanitarianism. Pascal Meeus of MSF-
Belgium spoke for many within the association when he wrote that
the right of intervention amounted, in humanitarian terms, to
"abuse." Eric Dachy could write, bitterly, "The ability of the Western
powers to impose their principles and policies within their sphere of
influence is based on an approach allegedly reflecting a spirit of generosity (humanitarian), justice (international courts) and fairness
(human rights)." But when Françoise Bouchet-Saulnier wrote of the
need to strengthen the traditions of a "rebellious" humanitarianism,
her call rang hollow, given the circumstances her MSF colleagues
had anatomized so precisely.

For there was something disingenuous as well as moving about
MSF's demurrers. At headquarters and, of course, in those dreaded
coordination meetings, MSF might remain the determined naysayer,
a thorn in the UN's side and a constant irritant to other NGOs. Gerry
Martone of the IRC probably voiced a common grievance when he
called MSF's uncooperativeness a kind of "horizontal violence"
against other NGOs. But in the field, MSF had long since become
largely part and parcel of the humanitarian system as it was re-
created over the course of the 1990s. Not only has it usually been
willing to take responsibility for certain (medical) parts of an aid effort, but it has assumed that other NGOs, most of which can be depended upon to have very different perspectives, will assume other
parts. In other words, to a disturbing extent, MSF could stick to its
own principles because it knew other humanitarian NGOs were not
so purist. In any case, the Western governments that funded MSF
tended to be unimpressed. They tended to see the group as an integral part of a generalized response to humanitarian crises.

A typical example of this was the French Ministry of Foreign
Relations account of its humanitarian programs in Kosovo in

1999. These, it declared, included "two components: the aid of civil society"—that is, NGOs such as MSF, which was mentioned by name—and bilateral government-to-government aid. In these new conditions in which the division of humanitarian labor was assumed, any particularity of understanding, no matter how divergent, was largely irrelevant, at least as long as groups such as MSF continued to participate in the system. At their most radical, and in spite of their best efforts, they had become little more than the loyal opposition within the humanitarian movement.

It was not only an astonishing journey, but an astonishing transformation—and not just for MSF. The humanitarianism that was created in the 1960s to challenge governments' refusal to act at least to alleviate the most terrible consequences of wars, famines, and mass movements of refugees had become, by the end of the 1990s, the humanitarian component of the official response that governments often deployed to respond to those crises. And most relief agencies welcomed the change. Unlike the leadership at MSF, they did not rue the fact that things had moved as far as they had, but rather that they had not moved further. David Bryer, the director of Oxfam, asked in a 1998 speech to the International Peace Academy in Vienna: "Globally, would we be more likely to get coherent policies to internal conflicts, weaving humanitarian aid, diplomacy, if necessary peace-keeping into a single mission, if the Security Council, the body with the highest responsibility to uphold civilians' rights in conflicts—including internal conflicts, most people would now accept—had a structure which presented to it the humanitarian as part of the whole?" To this, he answered triumphantly in the affirmative.

In Bryer's account, humanitarianism simply could not be effective were it to be orphaned from the wider international response to a given crisis. Such a view was certainly one of the tendencies within humanitarianism in the 1970s and 1980s, but by no means the only one. To understand why it came to dominate, it is necessary to remember just how defeated and thwarted many humanitarians felt in the aftermath of the catastrophes in the Balkans and the Great Lakes region of Africa. Jean-Christophe Rufin, the former MSF official who went on to become both a novelist and an advisor to the French Ministry of Defense, summed this up well when he wrote in the spring of 1999, "A malaise is gripping the humanitarian world, a languor, a [sense of] sadness, a strange sentiment of failure. The colloquia multiply, each taking as its theme this word failure."

Rufin's prescription was less satisfactory than his diagnosis. He went on to insist that relief workers have no reason to feel demoralized in this way, that in fact they had been far more successful than they realized. And yet one of the three major elements of his definition of their "success" was the need to recognize the limits of what humanitarian action could actually accomplish. This was hardly the triumphalist tone that the aid world had grown accustomed to. And in fact, many aid workers were not content to take Rufin's advice and view their vocation more modestly. Even Rufin himself, who in 1994 had criticized Kouchner's doctrine of the "right of intervention" as "an infantile disorder" (the phrase is borrowed from a pamphlet of Lenin's), had written that "there is no real humanitarianism except where liberty exists. Anything else is a caricature."

This sweeping, and almost certainly false, assumption (most humanitarian action is called for precisely because there is no liberty) is emblematic of the triumphalist attitude that has always been deeply engrained in the collective psyche of the humanitarian world. It is difficult to imagine a humanitarianism shorn of it. Such a humanitarianism would mean a return to the norms of the ICRC. And this would lead to limitations that most members of MSF, let alone

those belonging to the British or American tradition of humanitarianism, would find unacceptable. Small wonder, then, that instead of
cutting back on their ambitions, what many relief groups did was to
expand them to include the moral and operational mandates of peace
building, conflict resolution, refugee protection, human rights, and,
at times, humanitarian military intervention.

Psychologically, the decision to make a larger rather than a
smaller claim seems understandable. To have been placed on a
plinth that high for so long—even if the NGOs had climbed up on it
themselves and not simply been hoisted on it by the adoring media—had to have been a heady and even a disorienting experience.
Certainly, it was not a place that they could climb down from easily.
To be sure, many aid workers routinely complained about such media attention, insisting that it got in the way of their doing their job
properly. But one claim did not exclude the other. And in fact, by the
early 1990s, not only had all the big NGOs set up sophisticated press
operations both at headquarters and in those crisis zones where the
stakes for the donors and the NGOs were high, but they were cooperating with almost hagiographical television programs and providing the material for (and sometimes publishing themselves) admiring
books about their organizations, or personnel, with titles such as
"The Human Orchestrators of Humanitarianism" and "Touched by
Fire: Doctors Without Borders in a Third World Crisis." Certainly, it
was the experience of many journalists that the willingness that
many aid workers evinced to talk to them at length was not solely
due to their need to get the stories of the victims out to a broader
public back home.

There is nothing wrong with this, and I would not even mention
it were it not for the somewhat sanctimonious tone, reminiscent of
Captain Reynault, played by Claude Rains in the film *Casablanca*.

Many aid officials have a stake in the fiction of being "shocked, shocked" to find aid workers who love the press attention in their "selfless relief outfit."

The reality is, in relations between relief workers and the media it has never been entirely clear who was exploiting whom. Nonetheless, the sense of disappointment, if not betrayal, that many relief groups felt when the press began to run critical as well as admiring articles about them was one more symbol of the malaise Rufin had identified. That said, giving in to such a sense of loss and impotence could not be the option for humanitarian institutions that it was for individual aid workers. It was too demoralizing to remain mired in doubt and a sense of failure. And yet, for most aid workers, Sylvie Brunel's brand of humanitarian stonewalling, in which she could write that "today, to cultivate hopelessness, even hatred for humanitarianism seems to have become fashionable among those who had been its advocates," was going too far in the opposite direction. What, then, was to be done?

Nicholas Stockton, a senior official of Oxfam, provided part of the answer. He began a talk at the British government's Overseas Development Institute by telling his listeners, "I want to persuade you that the non-governmental humanitarian community has embarked upon a radical journey from being a rather selective and ad hoc conduit of charitable giving, accountable only to donors, as we have traditionally behaved, towards being the champion and monitor of universal human rights and sometimes fulfiller of humanitarian claims, as we are gradually becoming."

This was much closer to a vision of humanitarianism that would break the defeatist logjam than simple defensiveness or angry rejoinders in specialized journals and on NGO websites. In conflating humanitarianism with human rights to both the media and the educated public, Stockton managed, in more measured tones than

Rufin's, to make humanitarianism "part of the solution," thus rescuing it from its own sense of futility and from the public's disenchantment. And it was important in practical terms as well. Stockton
seemed to say as much later in the same address. "In the current environment where resources for all 'universalist' and 'international-
ist' projects are under growing financial pressure, the contemporary
debate about humanitarianism (most importantly the charge that it
fuels conflict and only treats symptoms) is being conducted within
an increasingly desperate search for legitimacy on the part of all sections of the aid system."

In other words, saying you were just bringing relief to people, but
could do little more for them, was not enough to galvanize the
donors. To do that, it was important to be efficient and conscientious. In turn, this entailed higher standards of performance, which
was where the minimum standards for disaster relief spelled out in
the SPHERE project came in. But implicit in Stockton's argument
was the conviction that, whatever its advantages or disadvantages, a
humanitarianism bound up in charity was just not going to succeed
in the competitive post–Cold War world.

Oxfam and Stockton were hardly alone in believing this. In 2000,
CARE International received a multimillion-dollar grant from the
Ford Foundation to study how human rights could be assimilated
into its field operations. And even the ICRC, recognizing that it had
lost its virtual humanitarian monopoly and now had to compete for
funds with other NGOs, began to broaden its human rights "port-
folio." It appeared that the allure of human rights was both balm
for the frustration relief workers felt about their own effectiveness,
and one more instance of humanitarianism remaining, as Stockton
might claim, almost completely driven by the wishes of the major
donors.

Stockton was right about the desperation. The budgets of the mainline humanitarian NGOs grew so enormously between the 1980s and 2001 that many agencies found themselves unable to reduce their overheads without, at least in their view, losing their administrative effectiveness and ending good programs. Believing this, they saw no reason to cut back. If there were a need for any change, they reasoned, it was for them to secure the funds to do more, not less, and to grow, not shrink. In the IRC, this was announced explicitly to senior staff. The president, Reynold Levy, and the financial officer, Rick La Roche, were reported by colleagues to emphasize that the organization needed to "grow or die." But for all the breadth of the ideological divide that separated an Oxfam from an IRC, Stockton was not really saying anything that different. He was just dressing it up better.

The economics of relief work were an invitation to a dependence on growth. The structure of grants given by donors to NGOs usually included money that went toward overheads. Thus, getting more donor funds became an institutional imperative. For relief officials, this was justified because increasing their capabilities involved, in their eyes, an obvious moral good—helping more victims. The perfect neoliberal marriage of virtue and the bottom line had been consummated—the virtue assured by the identification of humanitarianism not with the ethical limitations of charity but with the millenarian promise of human rights.

In any case, the bigger and better publicized the crisis, the better the chances were that major donors would contribute. Afghanistan is a good example. Before September 11, 2001, the annual humanitarian aid budget for Afghanistan provided by Western donors either through NGOs or through UN agencies was approximately $180 million. By the time the bombing began, $800 million had been pledged. Agencies that were running $9 million programs were being deluged with money. And 5 to 7 percent of those funds went to the particular agency's organizational expenses, not just in the field, but at headquarters in the European or North American city in which it was based. This is not to suggest that the agencies were soliciting funds simply to insure their institutional survival, as some of the more inflamed critics of humanitarianism have charged. That is factually unsustainable and much too deterministic. Doubtless there are instances of such corruption, but no more than there are in hospitals or civil rights organizations, let alone the worlds of the media, business, or government.

The problem is both more structural and more innocent. Convinced, with good reason, that they were doing the right thing, and that without them the people whom they were helping in dozens of the world's most hellish places would be infinitely worse off, if, indeed, they survived, aid workers had become increasingly unable to distinguish their interests from those of the people they were pledged to help. And they have always been desperate to help. That determination to help is the relief worker's abiding glory and the reason why, for all my criticisms, I shall always admire them more than any other group of people I have ever met. Where I am skeptical is in whether, in their new confidence born out of the triumph of state humanitarian ideas, they can do it. They say that if only they can wrest the chance from Western donors, feral warlords, and a fickle public back home, not only can they save people, but they can contribute to a more profound and welcome change. I hope they are right. But I don't believe it. Rather, I think the more humanitarian NGOs meld their efforts with the campaigns for human rights and global good governance, the less their own enterprise will be able to preserve its specific moral gravity.

Where I agree with them, of course, is that once the decision has been made to deploy in a crisis zone, the dilemma for relief workers over how to get the necessary funds is a cruel one. To help, aid officials know that their track record, or the quality of their assistance, or their commitment may not be enough. In a media-drenched world where the public's attention span is measured in seconds, and in the atmosphere of fierce competition between NGOs, and, for that matter, between UN agencies, aid officials need to be *seen* as helping.

Examples of this dilemma are legion, and anyone who spends more than a day in the company of an aid worker will have heard endless variations. One example that I witnessed occurred in the winter of 1995 in a refugee camp deep in the bush along the Sudan-Uganda border. There were two field-workers from ACF in the camp, one a feeding expert and the other a water specialist. They had been there for months and were desperate to move on. The ground was hard and the water expert was unable to dig deep wells without equipment, for which there was no budget. And the feeding expert had nothing to do because there was no famine in the area that required her competencies. There had indeed been a famine, some years earlier, which had triggered the massive UN-run humanitarian effort in the region that became known as Operation Lifeline Sudan (OLS). But in 1995, that part of Sudan had enjoyed an excellent harvest, the best in some years.

The ACF field-workers busied themselves with projects they made up as best they could, and they helped their colleagues from the IRC and Catholic Relief Services, whose activities were better suited to the actual conditions in the area, which was near an active frontline between the forces of the government of Sudan and the Christian and animist rebels of the Sudan People's Liberation Army.

But though they bore their situation with grace and style (one mystery I have never resolved is how the French manage to live so much better than all other foreigners in such austere and punishing places, where supply planes land once a week at best), they were obviously at the end of their patience. A week or so later, I left the two ACF workers and returned to the Operation Lifeline Sudan staging base in the village of Lokichokkio, in northern Kenya. There I ran into ACF's regional coordinator. I told her about the unhappiness of her staff. "Yes, I know," she said regretfully, "and they're right to be impatient. The problem is that while there is little for them to do up there at the moment, the guerrillas want us to keep a presence in the area, and for our own reasons we need to do so."

I asked her why. "There are other parts of southern Sudan," she said wearily, "from which the NGOs have been barred. We don't know when it will be safe to return to them, but obviously without the goodwill of the SPLA, we will obviously never have a chance there."

She was certainly right both in the sense that ACF's presence in the camp was doing no harm (indeed, the presence of foreign relief workers in southern Sudan probably served to make the life of the population there slightly more secure, if only because the northern government in Khartoum had usually shown itself reluctant to bomb quite so wantonly when Westerners were known to be in the area), and that if ACF managed to get into one of those closed areas to the north and west, it would be able to do a considerable amount of good. Nonetheless, I remained puzzled by her answer. I asked her, "But why, in the final analysis, is it necessary for you to be in southern Sudan at all? The ACF is doing wonderful work all over the world, and if you 'miss' Sudan, does that change all that much?"

She looked at me almost pityingly, as if she were suddenly trapped in conversation with the village idiot. "You don't get it, do you?" she said. "Humanitarianism is a business now. It's not the spontaneous gesture that it was after May '68, at the beginning. My job is to assure ACF's survival. If we are out of Sudan, and MSF is here, or the Anglo-Saxons are here, then the hard truth is, we are less likely to get funding from ECHO. That's the reality. An NGO simply must be in certain areas that the donors are paying attention to. If they are not, there is the sense that they are doing something wrong, that perhaps their projects are after all really not so worthwhile. I hate it that it has come to this, but there is nothing that I can do."

When I told this story a month later to Philippe Biberson, then the head of MSF-France, he laughed and said, "That's it, I'm closing MSF in the morning." And yet the situation was more complicated than that then, and is, if anything, more complicated today. Many funders view MSF's holier-than-thou attitude with disdain because, they insist, the group routinely engages in such calculations. And despite MSF's remarkable ability to raise money from individuals, it often competes just as fiercely for donors' monies as any other NGO. In my own experience, it has been MSF's sense of its own competence, combined with a particular sense that they know how to analyze both humanitarian need and the political dimensions of crises better than any other NGO, that caused it to believe that it, rather than some other NGO, needed to be in the field in order for beneficiaries to be properly served (an exception would be when the issue was famine, when MSF tended to defer to ACF).

That had been Eric Dachy's point about the decision to rush into Kosovo at the end of the war there, rather than wait for the UN to co-ordinate what each NGO would do. And such an attitude is hardly peculiar either to Dachy or to his Belgian section of MSF. If anything, the opposite is true. What makes relief organizations believe they can take on what are, objectively, virtually impossible challenges in the field also leads them to think that *only* their group can do the job as it needs to be done.

They are not completely wrong. MSF's slogan is *Soignez et témoignez,* "Care for and bear witness." They have thought about both these activities for more than thirty years, refining both their medical procedures and their methodologies for testifying to the horrors they see (sometimes the group goes public, but often it does not), to the point that they are far better at these particular activities than an NGO that has just instituted a human rights component to its programming or gotten the funding for a medical unit.

Other groups have developed their own strengths. The ACF official I met in northern Kenya was either too disengaged from our conversation or too dispirited to add, as she could have done, that her organization had particular technical and analytic competencies in fighting famine that no other NGO came close to approaching. In that context, the rather trivial "sacrifice" the two aid workers I had met had been called upon to make might have seemed well worth it in the long run, given the number of lives ACF, and probably ACF alone, would be in a position to save.

The marriage between humanitarianism and human rights has only strengthened this conviction that aid workers need to be everywhere, all the time. In 2002, the aid world is infinitely more professional than it was when MSF was launched. Programs like SPHERE that mandate minimum standards for relief work, for all their overreliance on technical criteria, and the do-no-harm concept associated with the American Quaker humanitarian relief specialist Mary B. Anderson, indicate how conscious relief workers have become of how much technical expertise, moral scruple, and, yes, coordination are necessary to do this impossible job creditably.

"Compassion is one thing," a UN official, Suadesh Rada, once said to me, "but the institutionalization of compassion is another." And yet in coming to view its commitments as going beyond providing relief, in allying itself with the human rights movement, and in committing itself to an interpretation of international law in which aid must be allowed in because, according to the UN's Uni-

versal Declaration of Human Rights and other subsequent instruments, people have a legal right to food (ACF), medical care (MSF),
and protection, whether they are refugees or are internally displaced
(the IRC), the question must be, "Has the humanitarian international gone too far?" Obviously, this book has been an attempt to
make the case that, even for the best of reasons, it has done precisely
that, and that this decision is one from which it may never recover.

Humanitarianism has not come to its end at the beginning of the
new millennium. Given the tragedy and horror of the world, there
will always be victims and appalling need. And given that there is
good in this sad world as well as evil, there will always be relief workers as well, committed both to the practical business of relief and the
moral imperative of solidarity. The problem for aid workers all
along, to use the American aid official H. Roy Williams's fine formulation, is how to "match our material means to our moral and
emotional aspirations." It would be wrong to say that none of those
aspirations have been fulfilled. Aid accomplishes a great deal—far
more, in some important ways, than it did thirty years ago. There is
no reason to think that it won't go on to accomplish even more. It is
independent humanitarianism—the humanitarianism that felt itself diminished as it became a "pillar" of the postwar UN protectorate in Kosovo, or the justification for an international "protection"
force in Afghanistan—that I have in mind when I speak of the death
of a good idea. But surely that is loss enough.

HUMANITARIAN ACTION WAS NEVER the appropriate response to the boundless sufferings of the poor world, or, for that matter, even to the Balkan wars in the European backlands during the 1990s. That much, at least, should be clear by now. But whether or not that bitter lesson has really sunk in, and, more to the point, what the implications of this Promethean knowledge are for humanitarianism, is another matter.

The humanitarian world emerged saddened and chastened from the 1990s. H. Roy Williams, the former overseas operations director of the IRC, summed it up well when he declared flatly: "Humanitarian organizations are not capable of dealing with the crises we see around us." This did not mean that they were giving up. To the contrary, the 1990s were a period in which relief NGOs and UN agencies multiplied their efforts to refine their operations in light of the lessons of Somalia, Rwanda, Bosnia, and Kosovo. They were painfully aware that time and time again they had been overwhelmed by the magnitude of many of the particular crises—as when two million people crossed from Rwanda into Zaire in 1994, or when eight hundred thousand Kosovar Albanians were forcibly deported from the

province by Serb forces in the spring of 1999. Even more anguish-
ing was their sense that, in many cases despite their own best efforts, the moral dilemmas attendant on their action had only grown
more acute over the course of the decade. As a result, in stark contrast to the early 1990s, by the beginning of the twenty-first century
every experienced relief worker needs no reminder of the new conventional wisdom that there are no humanitarian solutions to humanitarian problems.

But diametrically opposing conclusions about what humanitarian action should be, or needs to become, can be drawn from this
simple truth. Indeed, it has become almost as much of an impediment to critical thinking about both current practice and the future
of aid as the relief cliché of earlier years that humanitarians, who
mean to do good, do good, and therefore should not be subjected to
criticism that is not wholly "constructive." In fairness, understanding what has taken place, let alone coming up with a new humanitarian paradigm, has been particularly difficult. Here, another
inescapable fact about humanitarianism has to be faced—that, even
at its best, humanitarian action is always an emblem of failure. Since
there has been only failure to study, it should come as no surprise
that the dilemmas of aid have seemed unresolvable and, to make
matters worse, relief workers increasingly find themselves under
threat in the field as they try to do their jobs—a reality that makes reflection even more difficult.

What ought humanitarian action to be in what Bruce Jones, one
of the UN's ablest humanitarian officials, rightly has called these
new "mean times"? For many, this view was simply far too bleak and
pessimistic. Kofi Annan, Bernard Kouchner, and most human rights
activists and their supporters in the West were hardly blind to the
harsh experiences of the post–Cold War era, and yet the lesson they
drew from them was one of hope rather than despair. For them, hu-

manitarianism is best seen as one of a number of "pillars" supporting the promising new liberal world order that they seem to believe
can be created in the vacuum left by the undermining of the idea of
state sovereignty by globalization, as well as the rise of the human
rights movement and the increasing incorporation of its key assumptions into international laws and treaties. There is simply no
basis for Jones's gloom at a time when the consensus in the theory
(if not yet the practice) of international relations is that individuals
have rights that neither their communities nor their governments
can abrogate. Or, as the authors of the report on "The Responsibility
to Protect" put it, "What has gradually been emerging [since 1945] is
a parallel transition from a culture of sovereign impunity to a culture
of national and international accountability."

This account too often goes unchallenged. True or not, the old
cliché that if one is not part of the solution, then one is part of the
problem makes obvious intuitive sense. And what could be less
"constructive" than insisting that this new culture of accountability
is a chimera? But even leaving aside the question of whether the assumptions that underpin "The Responsibility to Protect" are true, or
if, instead, the fine new norms of the past half century will do little
to mitigate the reality of the mean times Jones anatomizes, the question for humanitarians remains what role they can or should play. In
other words, even if there is progress and evolution in international
affairs, is humanitarianism the appropriate instrument to further
those developments?

A few dissenting figures, notably in certain French humanitarian
circles, have argued that humanitarianism as a vocation needs to
separate itself from this project, no matter how worthy the larger
goals of human rights, conflict resolution, and the creation of the
conditions for peace and development in the poor world may seem
to aid workers, and no matter how fervently, as citizens, they hope

for the success of such efforts. Where other NGOs, particularly those issuing from the British and American aid traditions, often assume aid groups could play a useful role if only they could develop further their human rights and peace-building "capacities," many of the most influential figures within MSF and like-minded agencies such as ACF continue to insist that such projects take humanitarianism far beyond any role it is suited for.

To take such a stance, or, for that matter, even to consider an alternative vision of humanitarianism that entails turning one's back on such hopes, no matter how reluctantly, usually seems both mystifying and utterly counterintuitive to people outside the humanitarian world. Yes, relief work traditionally has been understood by most of its practitioners as being inseparable from impartiality and neutrality. Why should not this paradigm, whose limitations and shortcomings were tragically revealed in the major humanitarian operations of the 1990s, be altered? For someone like James Orbinski, the former president of MSF-International, to insist to the UN officials and NGO colleagues with whom he otherwise shared so many core assumptions that for its own moral coherence humanitarianism needed to remain independent, seems almost perverse. Orbinski once told me that the response he usually received from these colleagues often reflected this incomprehension. His stance was all well and good, they told him, but after all, the NGOs, liberal Western governments, and the UN were "all in this together." And, he said, they tended to look at him with disbelief when he told them that he did not believe this was always true.

Of course, Orbinski understood perfectly well that a majority of aid workers had, over the course of the 1990s, come to share a belief in the need for holistic answers to the world's problems—one in which humanitarianism would play only a part. This, too, was understandable. Indeed, given the fact that however hard they worked at improving the quality of aid through new normative structures such as the SPHERE program and the Red Cross Code of Conduct, most relief workers were aware that the only way they would ever begin even to approach the Hippocratic ideal of "First, do no harm" would be if a way could be found to address the root causes of the disasters.

Even those who felt that human rights and humanitarian action were distinct and in some ways irreconcilable imperatives shared the Western public's sense that something more had to be done. To settle for alleviation was to turn oneself and one's action into the humanitarian equivalent of Sisyphus. Instead of pushing a rock up the hill only to see it roll back down just before one got it to the summit, the relief worker would be condemned endlessly to deploy expertise, resources, and commitment, only to be left with the realization that the crisis, and the need, just went on and on and on, with little or no likelihood of any hopeful long-term outcome, and the risk that the humanitarian effort might actually fuel or help conceal from the outside world the true horror of the conflict.

This fear was what lay at the heart of the growing consensus that disaster relief had to become more self-conscious and more political if it was to do more than, as one aid worker I met in Kosovo phrased it, "put Band-Aids on malignant tumors."

But it was less that the NGOs had desired such an outcome; instead, most felt that the realities of the field and the new agendas of donor governments had made such a transformation inescapable. Whether they liked it or not, states were involved as actors in humanitarian operations as well as funders of them; aid had political consequences, and therefore could not restrict itself to—in John Fawcett's disdainful phrase—the provision of "beds and blankets"; and grave human rights abuses, let alone a genocide, could not be remedied by humanitarian action.

By 2001, the conviction that aid had to become more political, and that it could not remain bound by its original principles if it was to be effective and morally coherent, united most people within the humanitarian movement outside the ICRC, even within MSF. What Hugo Slim called "the philanthropic paradigm" was increasingly discredited, replaced by a humanitarianism grounded in human rights. Somewhat unexpectedly, this ideological shift was made easier by the increasing role of logisticians, many of whom had formerly served in similar capacities in NATO armies. It was not that these ex-soldiers had some special commitment to human rights or refugee protection. But their presence in effect meant that NGOs were being "militarized" from within, as the ex-soldiers played an increasingly essential role in the field. This helped make cooperation with Western armies seem much more normal to NGOs whose staffs, a generation earlier, would have found such collaborations quite alien both culturally and politically.

Of course, the underlying reasons for the shift had little to do with staffing changes. Rather, they were the result of the humanitarian movement's new operational imperatives, as well as its increasing professionalization. By the mid-1990s, degrees in humanitarian assistance were being offered at important American, British, and Swiss universities. Rony Brauman, who had conceded in 1991 that a lack of "general training" was one of MSF's prime weaknesses, by 1999 had taken to observing ironically that he might not be accepted by MSF were he to be evaluated according to the agency's contemporary standards. And the changes within MSF, for so long a humanitarian country apart, ran deeper. In 2001, it was wracked by an internal debate about whether to remove the commitment to neutrality from its charter. Aid, advocates of this change argued, had always been political. Why not admit the fact? Neutrality remained, but many MSF staffers remained convinced that sooner or later it would have to be abandoned.

Others insisted that, whatever the organization's charter did or did not say, MSF's actions had never been neutral. When the group won the Nobel Peace Prize in 1999 (an event that may well prove to have been the high-water mark of the humanitarian movement), Bernard Kouchner insisted to an interviewer that "MSF's work was political from the start." He continued, "I hope that the prize marks the recognition of a type of humanitarian work which fights injustice and persecution."

Kouchner was in part seeking to claim that the prize had honored his version of humanitarian action, and not, by implication, those who had taken the organization in another direction after he split with it in 1979 and went off to found MDM. But his argument struck a responsive chord in a public conditioned, in part, by two decades of propaganda by humanitarian agencies that humanitarianism was more than charity, it was action—successful action. MSF's famous poster from the 1980s claiming it had "two billion patients in its waiting room" did not add that for most it could do little, even though that was probably the case. To the contrary, the implication was that the more money one gave to MSF the more people could be rescued.

In fact, it was the issue of sending a boat, grandiloquently called the *Island of Light,* to rescue and document the plight of Vietnamese boat people that had provoked the split between Kouchner and the other leaders of MSF. For Rony Brauman and Claude Malhuret, who led the humanitarian "autonomists," the boat project was pure symbolism. Few would be rescued, they argued, and, in any case, the most pressing need was not on the high seas but on land—first and foremost in Cambodia. For Kouchner, this was not the point. If the project received enough media coverage, Western states would be forced to act, and to do something for all Southeast Asian refugees.

In retrospect, the quarrel over whether or not to send what Kouchner called his "sea-borne ambulance" served as a pretext for the long-overdue debate within MSF over what had become a conflict of visions about whether humanitarianism should ally itself with states or try to be independent. But though Kouchner lost the battle within MSF, and resigned angrily, he was successful in ensuring that the image of the relief worker as rescuer became the iconic one in the Western popular imagination and, to a large extent, in the minds of aid workers themselves.

That, too, was probably inevitable. By itself, relief work seemed too austere, too ICRC-like despite the addition of "testimony," but also too paternalistic, and too reminiscent of the humanitarianism of nineteenth-century colonialists and missionaries. And this was where the insights and practices of the human rights movement, and the placing of humanitarianism within the context of international humanitarian law, seemed to offer the humanitarian movement a moral revalidation. As ACF's Jean-François Vidal put it, "The problem with the traditional idea of humanitarianism is that it demands access for [NGO] workers to reach victims who then become the object of 'our' compassion. What I support is the victims' access to their rights—that is, a construction that makes them subjects, not objects."

This question, not just of access but of what the demand for humanitarian access implied for both relief workers and the people they were trying to assist, was crucial. By the mid-1990s, humanitarian aid workers did not need outside critics to tell them they were unable to effect meaningful change on their own. And they were particularly frustrated by the increasing difficulty they had in reaching those zones where the needs were most acute, and, even when

they succeeded in doing so, in operating independently. When warlords or repressive governments did not want relief workers around,
the solution was simple: they targeted them. In practice, this meant
that NGOs often were unable to send people into the field where
they were needed most.

In this context, too, the language of rights has proven command-
ing. In the minds of many aid workers, the right of victims under international humanitarian law and the Universal Declaration of
Human Rights to receive assistance restored their human dignity
and made them more than passive recipients of the charity of others.
This shift did not take place in a vacuum. Rather, in the minds of
many of its most intelligent and scrupulous practitioners, the transformation of humanitarianism was part of a broader shift in the
post–Cold War era toward a rights-based universalism. But there
were also antecedents within the humanitarian movement for the
identification of humanitarianism with human rights. For example,
Eglantyne Jebb, who had founded the Save the Children Fund in
1919, would go on four years later to draft a document called "The
Rights of the Child" that seventy years later formed the basis for the
UN's Convention on the Rights of the Child.

For humanitarian agencies, many of which had always had other
commitments—to development, to a socialist or a Christian social
agenda, to international humanitarian law—the argument for the
confluence of interest between the humanitarian enterprise and the
human rights movement was simple and seemingly morally im-
pregnable. How could individuals not deserve protection from their
rulers, just as they deserve help when they are overwhelmed by natural disasters? And how could humanitarian aid workers not want to
be part of that struggle or not feel bound by that duty? To do anything else would be to condemn everyone who had had the bad luck
not to be born rich, or at least not to be born in or able to emigrate to

a rich country, to a life of misery and oppression, to a future of intolerable vulnerability. The moral language of humanitarianism might have failed, or at least been partly impeached by the "lose-lose" ambiguities of Sarajevo and Goma. But the language of human rights had not failed.

As Michael Ignatieff put it, "The language of human rights is the only available moral vernacular that validates the claims of women and children against the oppression they experience in patriarchal and tribal societies; it is the only vernacular that enables dependent persons to perceive themselves as moral agents and act against practices—arranged marriages, purdah, civic disenfranchisement, genital mutilation, domestic slavery, and so on—that are ratified by the weight and authority of their cultures. These agents seek out human rights protection precisely because it legitimizes their protests against oppression."

From both a historical and a philosophical point of view, there are reasons to find this an oversimplification. Ignatieff does present an accurate account of the role of individual political and cultural rights—what Isaiah Berlin called "negative freedoms," that is, the freedom not to be tortured, killed, or deprived of the vote or of the freedom to practice one's religion. But Ignatieff ignores the legal reality that the second part of the UN's Universal Declaration of Human Rights specifies a whole series of "positive liberties," such as the right to work, the right to education, and, most tellingly, in Article 28, the specification that "everyone is entitled to a social [i.e., internal] and international order in which the rights and freedoms set forth in this Declaration can be fully realized," that have very different social and moral implications. Article 28, if it is to be taken seriously, is as much a new world social charter as it is a shared vocabulary. After one of the bloodiest centuries in human history, it certainly cannot be reduced to being described as the starting point for what Ignatieff calls the claim that "all human beings belong at the table in the essential conversation about how we should treat each other."

But while Ignatieff's argument fails to take into account fully the genuine radicalism of the Universal Declaration of Human Rights, neither Bernard Kouchner and the humanitarian tradition he pioneered, nor the contemporary human rights movement, at least as it has intersected with Kofi Annan's UN, have made the same mistake. Annan's acceptance speech upon receiving the Nobel Peace Prize jointly with the UN in 2001 was a comprehensive restatement of this position. Emblematically, it simply took for granted that humanitarian assistance and human rights were part of the same struggle for a more peaceful, fairer world. "Today's real borders," Annan said, "are not between nations, but between powerful and powerless, free and fettered, privileged and humiliated. Today, no walls can separate humanitarian or human rights crises in one part of the world from national security crises in the other." It is clear that for Annan there is no break in the rights continuum between "fundamental freedoms," by which he means political rights, and the economic and social rights such as the "fundamental right to education, food, and security" that he enumerated in his Nobel lecture. Both kinds of crises are affronts to human dignity, and both need to be remedied in the interests of individuals.

Although Annan served as an official of UNHCR for a time, during his tenure as secretary-general his deepest engagements have been with human rights, not humanitarian action. But his vision resonates with that of a mainstream humanitarianism haunted by its failures to do more than alleviate, and unreconciled to the idea that the ICRC's brand of self-limitation is a condition to which the private voluntary agencies could or should resign themselves. This understanding gathered momentum over the latter part of the

1990s. By the end of the century, its ascendancy was almost complete. As a British relief specialist, Fiona Fox, put it in early 2001, "There is a new humanitarianism for a new millennium. It is principled, ethical, [and] human rights–based. It will not stand neutral in the face of genocide or human rights abuses. It will assess the long-term impact of each humanitarian intervention on development and peace. It will withhold aid if to deliver it could prolong conflict and undermine human rights. [And] it rejects the traditional humanitarian principle of neutrality as on the one hand morally repugnant and on the other hand unachievable in the complex political emergencies of the post–Cold War period."

What is particularly striking about Fox's approach is that it seems to assume the commonality of interest (not merely the inevitability of some collaboration) between governments and NGOs. When Fox referred to "prominent humanitarian actors," she made no distinction between governments and NGOs. The European Commission Humanitarian Aid Office and the private British relief group ActionAid had both, she insisted, begun to sign on to this new humanitarianism. Interestingly, Fox compared the new humanitarianism to Tony Blair's New Labour Party, an analogy that must have made at least a few of the old leftists who remained in the emergency departments of some mainline British NGOs wince. "Like New Labour," she argued, "[the new humanitarianism] is a clear, conscious attempt to break from the past, from traditional humanitarian principles that guided us for more than a century but which for many are now discredited."

According to Fox, the main aspects of this new humanitarianism are human rights and development relief. The rights-based approach insists that "all humanitarian aid be judged on how it contributes to the protection and promotion of human rights." But as Fox acknowledged, this represents a drastic move away from the traditional bedrock principles of humanitarian relief. It is not simply a question of a retreat from neutrality, but still more importantly of re-treat from the universal right to relief based on human need. In the future, humanitarian action would be based at least in part on how much it furthered the cause of human rights. Obviously, many hu-manitarian agencies were more comfortable in theory than in prac-tice with this changed perspective. Nonetheless, Fox was correct in pointing out how far along the process of self-transformation among the NGOs and donors had gotten.

Fox quoted a Catholic Relief Services discussion paper whose conclusion was that, "when considered through the justice/human rights lens, the mere provision of foodstuffs or medical support is an insufficient response to a humanitarian crisis." In fact, the document was quite typical of the direction of the thinking of a majority of NGOs at the millennium. Not all went as far as CRS, but many were drifting that way. The conclusions of a 1998 Ford Foundation–funded CARE study of its operations in the Rwandan refugee camps between 1994 and 1996 had among its recommen-dations that CARE "integrate the two domains" of humanitarianism and human rights and consider making "protecting basic human rights" part of its core activity in any field operation. "If donors now view human rights monitoring as a costly 'extra,'" the report's au-thor, James Ron, wrote, "CARE can work to change that perception, turning monitoring into an integral part of all refugee camp con-tracts."

CARE was hardly alone. The International Rescue Committee not only had signed its memoranda of understanding with Human Rights Watch and the Lawyers Committee for Human Rights (LCHR), but it began to undertake the responsibility of prescreening refugees to judge whether or not their claim to need resettlement in a third country had merit. In other words, by 2001 at least some IRC field staff had become subcontractors to the UNHCR protection effort. In any case, many donors needed no prodding from the mainline NGOs and were eager to embrace the new dispensation. Fox quotes an ECHO discussion paper that made the radical claim that "From a rights perspective, access to victims of [a] humanitarian crisis is not an end in itself, and will therefore not be pursued at any cost. Access will be sought if it is the most effective way to contribute to the human rights situation."

This was going much further than Bernard Kouchner would suggest or agree to. Whatever can be said about the politicized core of his views, or his ideas on the symbiotic relationship between disasters and the way they were covered in the media, withdrawal based on the grotesque notion that one was being "cruel to be kind"—in the words of the old pop song—was not in Kouchner's moral lexicon. Indeed, what Fox had uncovered was chilling. Although couched in the language of human rights, Fox's "new humanitarianism" was reminiscent of the idea of the so-called deserving poor that had been one of the dominant ideas of charity in Victorian England. Far from having escaped, as Hugo Slim had claimed, the paternalistic limitations of philanthropy, rights-based humanitarianism seemed to carry with it the risk of recapitulating some of its worst excesses.

Here, Fox's comparison of the "new humanitarianism" with Blair's New Labour may have been apter than she intended. In mid-nineteenth-century Britain, many of the organizations and philanthropists who provided what we now call relief restricted it to those among the destitute willing to stop drinking, cease beating their wives, go to church, and, above all, work. They were the deserving poor. The rest, no matter how deep their need and how pathetic their situation, were considered undeserving and consigned to prison, the workhouse, or the gutter. Victorian worthies justified this triage on moral grounds, much as Tony Blair does today. If the undeserving poor are not aided, it is for their own long-term good. They have only to mend their ways, and a helping hand will swiftly be extended to them.

What is surprising is to see what is, in effect, the analogous argument, made by aid groups whose original purpose was to alleviate suffering. It is almost as if both relief agencies and donors were intent on replacing the supposedly overly paternalistic model of depoliticized charity with this new model of moral triage based on human rights and good governance. They are, of course, influenced by the fact that development aid to corrupt or oppressive regimes was shown, after four decades of wasted effort, to do little good. As the Norwegian development aid minister, Hilde Frafjord Johnson, put it in March 2002, "We have to evaluate the tendencies of young democracies over time. But if a country systematically . . . moves in the wrong direction, without showing the will to change, we won't want to be a partner."

For Norway, which for decades has been, per capita, one of the leading aid donors, to take such a stance represented a radical break with the way aid had been conceived of in the West. Emergency relief had always been about saving lives—that is, until the "new humanitarianism" came along. If anything, the Norwegian argument was crueler than even the Victorian conception of the deserving poor had been. After all, the claim that the drunkard or the wife-beater bore the responsibility for his conduct was just. But in the case of the misuse of aid, it was not the people but their governments that were responsible for the abuses. An ordinary Zimbabwean or Angolan could do little to prevent despots like Robert Mugabe or José Eduardo dos Santos from misusing the aid they received from the West. Norwegian officials were certainly correct in claiming that by withholding aid from countries that were, as they put it, "moving in the wrong direction," they would avoid becoming accomplices in bad governance or human rights abuses. But did this really benefit the masses of people the aid was meant to assist? The assumption of many "new humanitarians" was that it did. For them, such withholding of aid, however cruel it might seem at first glance, was at times actually done to help those in direst need. As a New Labour parliamentarian, Tess Kingham, put it, "Surely, taking a view of the wider good—for the long-term interest of the people—to actually achieve real stability and development it may be better to withdraw aid."

Obviously, the proponents of the "new humanitarianism" drew the line at applying such criteria to the most pressing emergency situations. No one was arguing for doing nothing to stop a cholera epidemic such as the one that had ravaged the eastern Congo refugee camps in the summer of 1994. But though the aid agencies accepted that aid would sometimes have to be given even if it contributed nothing to human rights improvements, or even where its delivery risked making the rights situation worse, the idea that there was now to be, as Nicholas Stockton of Oxfam angrily observed, a new class of "undeserving victims" suggested that the question that most urgently needed to be asked about this "new humanitarianism" was whether there was still anything humanitarian about it.

After all, what was being proposed was not simply the right of withdrawal as the IRC and MSF had employed it in eastern Congo in the aftermath of the Rwandan genocide, where they concluded they were doing more harm than good. Nor was it a case of an NGO deciding that, whether it was because of the obduracy of a warlord or a government in letting supplies through or permitting them to be fairly distributed to those most in need of them, or because of security concerns, it was impossible to help victims. Instead, the "new humanitarianism" insisted that humanitarianism's traditional focus on trying to help could at times be trumped by the moral imperatives of the human rights movement and might therefore sometimes need to be sacrificed.

In 2002, Zimbabwe epitomized both this dilemma and the decision of many international donors to withdraw or scale back on human rights grounds. A number of major Western funders argued that it was morally unacceptable to cooperate with Robert Mugabe's tyranny. By withdrawing, they certainly demonstrated fidelity to the principles of an aid regime linked to human rights and the rule of law. They also showed the Zimbabwean government and people the extent of Western displeasure. But just as surely, the withdrawal of aid worsened an already deteriorating humanitarian situation. This was true not only in Zimbabwe itself, but in neighboring Malawi, where famine began to appear in the late winter of 2002.

If this had been presented as a great defeat for humanitarianism, it would have been troubling enough, but the idea that many, though certainly not a majority of humanitarians, were willing to reconsider their own first principles in the name of human rights and considered this a step forward—a new "moral banner" under which to march, as Hugo Slim put it—was one of the most disturbing effects of the crisis the humanitarian movement had undergone in the latter part of the 1990s. For a trustee of Oxfam and a former Save the Children official, Slim was strangely unperturbed by the change. Humanitarian organizations, he wrote in an essay called "The Humanitarian Endeavor," can be "considered to be as much like organisms as they are the embodiment of a moral idea and may be analyzed in the essentially survivalist, non-teleological and amoral terms of Darwin's evolutionary theory."

Perhaps Slim is right to put things so cynically. Certainly a human rights–based triage has the advantage for donors of allowing them to cut aid budgets in the name of a higher moral purpose. And

if humanitarian agencies were, as Slim contended, merely survivalist, then resisting the human rights tsunami, when it had the backing of all the major Western governments, the United Nations, and
the major charitable foundations, would indeed have been suicidal.
An agency could hardly grow its market share—to use the term that
so obsessed Reynold Levy, IRC's president in the late 1990s—while
bucking the major intellectual and political fashion of the age. And
as Slim pointed out, agencies had come under considerable pressure to "engage either in 'peace-building' or, at the least, to ensure
that their humanitarian interventions 'do no harm' and do not esca-
late violence." He added tartly that "this new policy climate rains
money to encourage such adaptation."

Slim was even tempted by Isaiah Berlin's idea that in intellectual
history ideas had often turned into their opposites. Whether he
hoped humanitarianism would so transform itself as to become un-
recognizable he did not make clear. What he treats lucidly is the degree to which humanitarianism came to be associated with the use
of outside military force during the 1990s. "Can the humanitarian
idea," Slim asks correctly, "which may be said to be paradoxical
enough already in its relationship to war, allow war to become a
means to its own ends?"

The question lies at the heart of the debate over the future of humanitarianism. For the reality is that no version of the intermingling
of humanitarianism and human rights makes sense except in the
context of a world order in which humanitarian military intervention, or at least its credible threat, is one standard response (it need
not, however, be frequent) to a so-called humanitarian crisis. Again,
it is possible to be cynical and say that the major donors have imposed this human rights agenda on the aid agencies in order to reduce the number of cases in which they will have any involvement,
let alone a military one. I do not believe this to be true. But even if I

am wrong (and as an explanation it is at least preferable to the rav-
ings of a Noam Chomsky or a Regis Debray, both of whom seem to
have convinced themselves, against all evidence, that their governments wanted to intervene in Bosnia, Kosovo, and Afghanistan,
whereas in fact they did so only with the greatest reluctance), this
has not been the perspective from the NGO side.

It is Kouchner's and Bettati's "right of intervention," and Kofi Annan's doctrine of a state sovereignty linked to responsible behavior—in other words, the idea that states are accountable to "the
international community" for the way they treat their own people—
that fired the imagination of so many relief workers. How could it
have been otherwise? These were people who had observed at first
hand what happened when states and warlords were able to act
toward their own people with impunity.

In theory, of course, those agencies that believed it was appropriate for them to withdraw when the regimes they had to deal with
"descended" below a certain human rights standard were not necessarily endorsing the doctrine of humanitarian military intervention.
But in practice, they were increasingly unable to resist such calls,
whether these were voiced by the powerful governments that funded
them, private donors who had been persuaded by the idea of the
right of intervention, or field-workers from within their own organizations.

In an age of intervention, the role of the donors was particularly
important. Eric Dachy might have been correct when he wrote, "The
right of intervention, peace-keeping operations invoking the use of
force to guarantee the transport of relief aid and wars fought for so-
called humanitarian aims, these all constitute so many variations on
a misleading theme: to accompany, or mask, a deliberate political
choice with gestures of generosity and compassion." But the reality
is that by the time the war in Afghanistan began, it was increasingly

difficult to differentiate between the rhetoric or, in many cases, the policies, of humanitarian NGOs, the UN system, and Western governments. The problem was compounded by the fact that few agencies today either choose to or are in a position to refuse contracts from donors or UN agencies. And this trend toward seeing themselves as in effect subcontractors for major donors has increased rather than decreased since human rights considerations began to be incorporated more and more systematically into the plans and programs of the mainline NGOs.

That said, a majority of aid groups do not believe they should withdraw in the name of some radiant future. To the contrary, most are persuaded—usually rightly, despite what some critics of aid often claim—that if they are doing at least some good, they should remain. Afghanistan was a good example of this. Had the agencies withdrawn between 1996 and 2001 because of the cruel oppression of women by the Taliban, nothing would have changed for women except they would have lost what help they were getting from the IRC, Oxfam, or MSF. And however insufficient that help was, it was crucial to the survival of hundreds of thousands if not millions of Afghans. Taken to its logical conclusion, the so-called principled stance of a Tess Kingham, if applied to Afghanistan in 2000, when the Taliban were firmly in control, would have caused the deaths of thousands of people.

Aid workers have been drawn to the idea of human rights first and foremost because of their frustrations over the limitations of what humanitarianism can accomplish on its own, in a political vacuum. It is their grief and outrage over this, rather than some "neo-colonialist" hidden agenda that the Chomskys and Debrays claim to discern, that accounts for why so many of them have been mesmerized by the idea of humanitarian military intervention.

Those who take this view have become convinced that at least in the direst situations, either there must be force to ensure a minimal level of protection against human rights violations, or else relief programs will accomplish too little to be justifiable. A Slobodan Milosevic in Belgrade or a Mullah Omar in Kandahar are not going to permit NGOs to operate as anything but givers of charity. And while Serb fascism and the Taliban may seem like extreme examples, in fact the same constraints the NGOs experienced operating in Yugoslavia and Afghanistan apply in most countries where humanitarian agencies operate, above all in most of those places where the need is greatest, from southern Sudan to the Indonesian archipelago.

The claim that most humanitarian emergencies have their origins in human rights abuses is almost always correct and demonstrable. But the question that remains is whether this reliance by NGOs on the promise of a world order in which intervention would be a real possibility in any situation, not just one where one great power or another also had an interest, is wise or realistic. Unlike international humanitarian law, the laws of war are fundamentally modest and antiutopian. "We work in the context of war, and there will always be war," is the way one ICRC delegate in Rwanda described his work to me. Annan's vision of a world in which it behooves the powerful to undertake endless wars of altruism when states refuse to uphold their fundamental obligations toward their own citizens, hiding behind the doctrine of state sovereignty as they do so, is fundamentally utopian.

And crucially, that brand of utopianism consistently portrays the world as any decent person wishes it were—a world increasingly ruled by a humanist consensus and one in which the revolution of moral concern is increasingly the dominant moral and ideological current—rather than as it is. This is utopianism not as an expression of decency, but as wish-fulfillment. André Malraux said that utopianism is all well and good, if it proceeds from a courageous apprehension of the world as it actually exists. By this standard, human rights utopianism fails abysmally. It is advocacy, and eminently defensible as such, since advocacy involves making the best possible case even in situations where there is little likelihood of success. But it is bereft of critical thinking.

Reality is elsewhere. Take the case of Afghanistan. For seven of ten years during the 1990s, Afghanistan never received more than 50 percent of the monies requested of the major Western donors and the Japanese in the UN's annual consolidated humanitarian appeal. Aid agency representatives pleaded for more help, insisting that Afghanistan was one of the worst humanitarian disasters in the world, and one of the most forgotten. All that changed on September 11, 2001. Only in the aftermath of the attack did the financial commitments by the United States and its allies to relief and development become virtually unlimited. But even assuming they remain so for the foreseeable future, and that the presence of foreign troops and development and relief officials in the country ensures that the condition of middle-class women in the cities improves a great deal, and that of poor women and girls improves at least to the extent of their getting schooling, Afghanistan is a one-off, a special case, much as Kosovo and Bosnia were.

That Afghanistan will finally get some help is marvelous. And it would be immoral, in the name of a foolish consistency, to begrudge that country its widow's mite of good fortune just because equally deserving and victimized Africans are not being helped. For it is an obscene reality of our world that Africans are not going to be helped, unless there is a catastrophe of epochal proportions. The injustice is so profound, and so intractable, and the prejudice and indifference so ingrained, that in truth only a calamity of the magnitude of Somalia in 1992 or Goma in 1994 might actually galvanize "the international community." The world long ago grew inured to the sight of

Africans dying in anything but biblical numbers. Only then does the subcontinent again become the center of the West's attention long enough for public pressure to build, and for help—always insufficient, late, and transitory—to be marshaled.

To an outsider, it seems as if humanitarians have been persuaded or have persuaded themselves to "adapt" to the new centrality of human rights—to use Hugo Slim's image—under false pretenses and in the grip of devastating and destructive illusions made all the worse because, in the name of good intentions, political correctness, and, in all likelihood, harsh despair, they have become so pervasive and uncontested. And yet there is so much to contest.

To begin with, the language of rights is much more problematic than the NGOs have been willing to recognize. What can the "right to food" mean in the world we actually live in? It is one thing to talk about rights in societies that have the means to make them realities, and quite another to do so in the context of societies that are too poor, or too convulsed by ethnic war or political strife, to do so. Perhaps the Universal Declaration of Human Rights is binding in legal terms, but on the ground the consequences of this are minimal, and are likely to remain so. And yet it is as if, somehow, in the minds of NGOs, the law was somehow independent of state power, or could somehow be made to be. On MDM's website, for example, the section entitled "Our Commitments" declares that the agency has "reaffirmed its vocation to come to the aid of civilian victims of conflict." But then it goes on to remind its readers, "An international conference has recalled the necessity of protecting [these] populations during wartime."

The vagueness of the wording is enough to underscore the incoherence of the thought. An international conference did this? But it clearly had no way of enforcing its will, and it is not likely to acquire such means. And recalled to whom? Presumably MDM means the international community. But there is no international community. There are international institutions, but no community. But assume that the law is settled, and that, as Nicholas Stockton has said, there is "an implicit right to humanitarian assistance embodied within International Humanitarian Law." What has this meant in practice?

The reality is that in the absence of some radical reform of the global order—by which one can only mean global consciousness, in which the rich suddenly start caring about the poor to the extent of being willing not just to sympathize, as they watch a Goma or an East Timor unfold in all its epic horror, but to sacrifice some of their own comforts to help bring about Oxfam's "fairer world"—there is no one to enforce this right. The U.S. government could not even integrate southern schools in the 1950s without calling in the military. What on earth, in the absence of similar exercises of force, is the point of repeating the credo that victims of humanitarian emergencies have rights?

Who is being fooled by this? Perhaps the Western public? Certainly not the warlords. Who is being consoled by it? There, my answer is harsher still. We all are, every one of us who has ever dreamed of that fairer world. But it is the aid workers themselves, the people who have been willing to put their lives on the line time and time again, who are the greatest victims of this consoling fiction. One understands perfectly, given what relief workers do, and above all the terrible suffering and injustice that they witness, that many of the best among them would want to be more than just dispensers of aid. After all, the people they try to assist need protection at least as much as, if not more than, food, shelter, or medical attention. And yet protection is the one thing relief workers are rarely, if ever, able to provide.

Once, in a shell-torn town called Dolisi in central Congo-Brazzaville, in the aftermath of a civil war few well-informed people in my own country even knew had taken place, I accompanied an IRC team making an evaluation of what programs it could start up in a hurry. The fighting had finally ended, and the IRC's regional director at the time, John Keys, a man of vast experience and talent, was eager to get moving. One of Keys's staff had arranged for a car to take us around the town, or what remained of a car in what remained of a town. The driver was a local man and, though he had been a notable before, he did his job with great dignity. All went smoothly until we got to the last checkpoint. There, the soldiers were drunker than usual and the sight of our driver, a member of the losing ethnic group in the war, enraged them. While they left us alone, they accused him of all sorts of traitorous acts. Finally, Keys prevailed on them to let him go. As we were about to drive off, another soldier staggered out of the guardhouse. "No!" he shouted. "Make him stay here. I want to torture him."

He was not joking, and we were lucky that the other soldiers had lost interest and allowed us to drive off together. That story and other stories of murder, of rape, of everyday brutality that are far, far worse are taking place at almost every moment in every country where aid workers operate. How could a foreign military force that would, unlike UN peacekeepers in Bosnia or Rwanda, actually protect the local population not seem like a necessary alternative to the reality of aid as it now exists? Today, for all the talk of human rights, the imperative for most NGOs that want to remain operational is to cooperate with murderers and torturers. They have to do so to help the victims, and, quite rightly, they hate it. Of course, there can be MSF-style testimony, or Oxfam- or IRC-style lobbying in Washington, Brussels, Paris, or London. Sometimes those efforts do succeed in persuading powerful governments to pressure some regime in a failed state somewhere to behave slightly better. But the results are usually marginal. Small wonder that so many relief workers have taken to fantasizing about some international equivalent of John Wayne and the Seventh Cavalry coming to ensure that at least they can do their jobs and that those they are trying to help can regain their dignity.

But it is this, and not the reservations of humanitarian absolutists who hew to strict neutrality and the ideal at least of preserving an autonomous humanitarian space, that is the real retreat into wishful thinking. Soldiers who are competent enough to fight the Taliban, or the Yugoslav Federal Army, or the Somali warlords, are not going to do what relief workers want. Instead they are going to expect, in the case of any serious disagreement, that relief workers will do what they tell them to do. This is not speculation. For all the talk of improved coordination, the joint exercises, and the declarations of mutual respect, the history of humanitarian military interventions from Kurdistan in 1991 to Afghanistan in 2001 has demonstrated that.

Even assuming the U.S., British, or French armies are prepared to fight a war in the name of securing humanitarian access for aid workers, which they are not, they would still fight that war so as to win it. And to win it, as in Afghanistan, they would first make the humanitarian situation worse. As all wars do. That is why imagining that just wars can be joined with humanitarian imperatives is delusional and antihistorical. World War II made the humanitarian situation of noncombatant civilian "victims"—to use contemporary humanitarian language—far worse. On solely humanitarian grounds, that war should have been stopped, not prosecuted to the utmost.

When humanitarian NGOs talk about military intervention, they are evoking so-called police actions or robust UN peacekeeping missions, not war. The Confederate commander, Robert E. Lee, observed: "It is good that war is so terrible. Otherwise, we would come to love it too much." So far, in Bosnia, and Kosovo, and Afghanistan, by the standards of the wars of the past, the humanitarian and human rights–based interventions have not yet been terrible enough to give many of the humanitarians and human rights activists pause.

And without this necessary consciousness of the horror of war—even of just wars, wars that decent people are likely to choose to support—it is as if many humanitarians do not get much further than contrasting the military's wealth of resources and its logistical reach with their own perennially underfunded, underresourced condition.

As a result, instead of seeing warriors, relief workers too often see little more than armed humanitarian logisticians in the field. They even go so far as to deceive themselves and the public about the relationship between relief agencies and NATO militaries. Sadako Ogata, who was humiliated and marginalized by the great powers in Kosovo, could still write of her experiences that humanitarians should "not be frightened by new associations [with business or the military] even if prior experience tells us otherwise."

But why not? From a strictly humanitarian point of view, collaboration with the military has not been a success, nor should it have been expected to be. Obviously, in a postwar situation, where a military force is deployed not to go into combat but to intimidate belligerents who have signed a peace agreement and to police the territory (as in Bosnia after Dayton), soldiers and relief workers can work together successfully. But to imagine that war and humanitarian action go together in wartime is a fantasy. I am not saying that there should never be military interventions. I am certainly not arguing, nor have I meant this book to be an argument, against military force to stop genocide.

Like most humanitarians I have known, I am not a pacifist. Confronted by a Bosnia or a Rwanda, I have longed for Western military intervention, and argued for it often and unashamedly. And not just for intervention, for protectorates as well, whether under the auspices of the UN or of some great power. Given the choice between liberal imperialism and barbarism—while that is not the choice everywhere, it was the choice in Kosovo—I will take liberal imperialism. It may well be the best the people of a Sierra Leone or perhaps even a Bosnia can hope for at the moment, much as we might wish it otherwise.

But to argue for military intervention on political grounds—to believe that it would have been right for the United States to side with a Bosnian state based on citizenship and multiethnicity against a Serb nationalism based on blood, or to finish off Slobodan Milosevic in Kosovo once and for all—is not the same thing as arguing for military intervention on humanitarian grounds. For me, that will always be a contradiction in terms. It is a perversion of humanitarianism, which is neutral or it is nothing. This is not to argue that NATO, or the South African Defense Force, or the Japanese navy, if it is so inclined, cannot perform humanitarian missions. Relief agencies do not have a monopoly on aid the way the ICRC has a monopoly, elaborated in international law, on administering the application of the Geneva Conventions in the field.

The independence of the ICRC is itself hard-won. Indeed, it is the direct result of the Red Cross movement's having abandoned the neutrality that Dunant and Moynier had championed when they organized the movement and split it at the beginning of World War I along national lines, with each national Red Cross federation—British, French, German, Italian—in effect serving as part of the medical corps of its respective army. It was to restore the Red Cross's neutrality that, after 1918, the movement was split into these national federations, which were not expected to be neutral in any strict sense, and the rigidly neutral ICRC.

Eight decades later, what is now occurring within the humanitarian international is the same debate that occurred within the Red

Cross movement in 1918. The difference is that today "true" humanitarianism is identified with engagement rather than with neutrality. Indeed, there is an increasing questioning, and even repudiation, of neutrality by all the mainline organizations, from the UN specialized agencies to the principal NGOs. Only MSF still stands partly aloof. Within this organization that invented the terms of contemporary humanitarianism, there are those who agree with the trend, but others who believe their moral coherence depends on distancing themselves from the humanitarian mainstream. François Jean, who, along with Rony Brauman, did most to contribute to MSF's tradition of intellectual and moral rigor, told me shortly before his death that he felt closer and closer to the ICRC's approach. Those who had played Luther to the Red Cross's Rome were, it seemed, more and more ready to heal the schism.

MSF had never claimed a monopoly on the right to bring assistance. The agency was more than willing to stipulate that, in the contemporary context, it may be right and, for that matter, unavoidable that nations undertake humanitarian missions that will in no sense be either neutral or impartial. The objection of MSF, and, indeed, of Oxfam, MDM, and other mainline relief NGOs, to the American relief airdrops during the war in Afghanistan was never that the United States had no right to drop food packages. Rather, the relief agencies insisted that the Americans must not claim that this humanitarian activity was anything more than window dressing, or that somehow the humanitarian and military objectives could be talked about in the same breath.

In fact, these agencies took no position on the rightness of the war. Rather, they acted out of the conviction that independent humanitarianism, painfully created since Biafra in 1967, would emerge the poorer from serving as the moral warrant for wars, no matter how just. They would have agreed, I think, that humanitarianism could be most useful to warriors (as it was in the heyday of nineteenth-century imperialism). They would probably have felt more comfortable with its supposed compatibility with peacemaking efforts; and of course by 2001 they had come to share much of the legalistic mindset of the human rights movement. But MSF at least remained persuaded that for humanitarianism to do what it was pledged to do responsibly, it could only function independently.

So many inflated claims have been made for humanitarianism since the early 1970s that it is startling to realize that the reason is not that humanitarianism is too big an idea to be contaminated by these other political and moral constructs. If anything, the reverse is true. As Hugo Slim has argued, "Despite being founded on the broad base of a very big idea—the recognition of the fundamental dignity and value of an essential humanity common to all people—the humanitarian idea is in fact a very small idea . . . an interim ethic that seeks to preserve the value of essential human dignity within the very specific, extreme, and, thankfully, usually extraordinary situation of war and armed conflict." Slim is mistaken in imagining that war and armed conflict are somehow exceptional states. The reality is that for most of recorded history, war and not peace has been the norm, and in many parts of the world it is likely to continue to be, perhaps forever. But he is correct in emphasizing the modesty of the humanitarian idea.

And, he might have added, its precariousness. This is what many humanitarians, perhaps bedazzled by the prospect of becoming part of that far larger idea of justice incarnated by the human rights movement, seem to have forgotten. For despite all the efforts expended, studies done, speeches made, commitments affirmed and reaffirmed, it is anything but clear that the world is a fairer or a more peaceful place than it was at the beginning of the so-called human rights revolution. Indeed, there is plenty of evidence to the contrary—and if one looks only at sub-Saharan Africa, overwhelming evidence. George Orwell wrote, "If you want a picture of the future, imagine a boot stamping on a human face forever."

That describes much of Africa at the moment, and probably quite a bit more of the rest of the world than most of us are comfortable admitting. And lest this seem like nothing more than a case of one pessimistic writer quoting another pessimistic writer, here is the stony conclusion of Alberto Navarro, formerly the director of the European Commission Humanitarian Aid Office. In late 1999, Navarro said simply, "Mankind is slowly, but in a very determined way, going back to barbarism."

If Navarro's considered judgment, let alone Orwell's prediction, is even partly true, then surely what humanitarianism offers on its own terms is contribution enough. Let humanitarianism be humanitarianism. Let it save some lives, whatever the compromises it has to make along the way, and let it tend to the victims and remind that corner of the world that is lucky enough not to be in agony of the incalculable suffering, misery, and grief that literally billions of people feel every day of their lives. Is that really so little? Must humanitarians, whether out of despair, conformity to intellectual and moral fashion, or groundless hope—hope for hope's sake—insist on trying to be the Archimedean lever for perpetual peace, the universal rule of law, or even, in Oxfam's more modest formulation, a fairer world?

After ten years of following relief workers from post to post—Bosnia, Abkhazia, Sudan, Rwanda, Afghanistan, Angola, Tajikistan, and so many other coordinates of dystopia—I can only say that I hope not. To me, for all my reputation as a critic of aid, they are the last of the just, these humanitarians. There is nothing small or insufficient about what they do, except, that is, in the tragic human sense that all effort is insufficient, all glory transient, all solutions inadequate to the challenge, all aid insufficient to the need.

Can one do more? Always. Can one do all the things one would like to do? No, not with the best will in the world. The tragedy of humanitarianism may be that for all its failings and all the limitations of its viewpoint, it represents what is decent in an indecent world. Its core assumptions—solidarity, a fundamental sympathy for victims, and an antipathy for oppressors and exploiters—are what we are in those rare moments of grace when we are at our best. But there are limits. If one has a terrible disease, one may wish for a cure. But if there is no cure, then no doctor should say, "I know what to do for you." One is stuck in one's time, and with one's fate. Independent humanitarianism does many things well and some things badly, but the things it is now being called upon to do, such as helping to advance the cause of human rights, contributing to stopping wars, and furthering social justice, are beyond its competence, however much one might wish it otherwise.

I know how fatalistic this sounds. Once, in a debate on humanitarian aid when I had expressed these gloomy thoughts, Caroline Macaskie, then acting head of the UN's Office for the Coordination of Humanitarian Affairs (OCHA), replied, "I prefer to be optimistic." Well, I would prefer to be optimistic, too. The question is whether there is any reason to be optimistic. If I wanted, as so many writers of essentially grim books choose do these days, I suppose I could in effect go against everything I have written in this book and end on an optimistic note. The usual formula is to point to the arrest of a war criminal—a Pinochet or a Milosevic—or to one of the few examples of successful humanitarian military intervention as grounds for optimism. And there is always that great phrase of Galileo's, *E pur si muove*, "And yet it moves," to fall back on when all else fails. But when weighed against all the ways in which the world, as Navarro rightly said, grows more barbarous, such optimism is grotesque. It is a lie.

And if we are talking about humanitarianism, then it doesn't move, or else it is moving in the wrong direction. Instead, with the possible exception of MSF—and even MSF shares the reigning enthusiasm for international law as a way out of the humanitarian dilemma—most humanitarian NGOs seem more than willing to abandon their independence for seats at the big table with officials of the great powers and the United Nations.

But the change goes deeper than that. An ACF official once referred contemptuously to the "charity of despair." The notion that the world could not be transformed was, he wrote, "the myth of Sisyphus in all its horror." Instead, he proposed a "utopian" humanitarianism that "seeks to break with the vicious circle of misery and rescue, [and wants to move] from simple social solidarity to human fraternity."

He is not alone. So many people, including so many relief workers, talk these days about "mere" charity, "mere" humanitarianism. As if coping with a dishonorable world honorably, and a cruel world with kindness, were not honor enough. Instead, a serious, wonderful, and limited idea has become a catchall for the thwarted aspirations of our age. And few seem even to notice, and fewer still to care about what is being lost.

This book is the product not just of ten years of work in zones of war and calamity, but of ten years of conversation with humanitarian relief workers, debates with UN officials, and, of course, reading. One of the advantages of writing about the humanitarian world is how much intelligent debate there is within it. Some of these conversations—though not, unfortunately, among U.S. NGOs, which tend to frown upon open public exchanges among staff—can be found online at the websites of NGOs such as MSF and Oxfam. Over the years, I have drawn extensively on these resources, as well as upon the writings of the authors cited in these notes.

INTRODUCTION

"The international community" as rhetorical boilerplate: There are an almost infinite number of examples. These were drawn from a report by the Carnegie Commission on Preventing Deadly Conflict, *Preventing Deadly Conflict: Final Report* (Washington, D.C.: Carnegie Commission, 1997).

Kofi Annan is quoted in William Shawcross, *Deliver Us from Evil: Peacekeepers, Warlords, and a World of Endless Conflict* (New York: Simon & Schuster, 2000).

Michael Ignatieff is quoted from his book *The Warrior's Honor: Ethnic War and the Modern Conscience* (New York: Metropolitan Books, 1998).

Michael Edwards is quoted from his book *Future Positive: International Co-operation in the Twenty-first Century* (London: Earthscan, 1999).

Mary B. Anderson quotations are from her essay "'You Saved My Life Today, but for What Tomorrow?' Some Moral Dilemmas of Humanitarian Aid," in *Hard Choices,* edited by Jonathan Moore (Geneva: International Committee of the Red Cross, 1998).

H. Roy Williams on Rwanda refugee crisis: Interview by author.

*Prepared with Jeff Alexander.

Cornelio Sommaruga is quoted in Patricia Alliot's "Medias et Humanitaries: Les liaisons dangereuses," at http://www2.globetrotter.net/metamedia/Humanitaires.htm.

CHAPTER ONE: DESIGNATED CONSCIENCES

Philip Johnston's remarks, except where noted, are from his *Somalia Diary* (Atlanta: Longstreet Press, 1994).

Philip Johnston on military intervention in Somalia is quoted in Alex de Waal, *Famine Crimes: Politics and the Disaster Relief Industry in Africa* (London: African Rights and the International African Institute in association with James Curry, 1997).

Clinton on the Somalia mission: Scott Peterson, *Me Against My Brother: At War in Somalia, Sudan, and Rwanda: A Journalist Reports from the Battlefields of Africa* (New York: Routledge, 2000).

Gustave Moynier quote: See Rony Brauman and Réné Backman, *Les Medias et l'Humanitaire*.

Statistics of contemporary catastrophes are abundant. These are cited from Stockholm International Peace Research Institute, *SIPRI Yearbook 2000*, p. 15, and the UNDP *Human Development Report, 2001*.

Ignatieff on television images of disaster: Ignatieff, *The Warrior's Honor*.

Fabrizio Hochschild on giving aid to killers: Interview by author.

CHAPTER TWO: THE HAZARDS OF CHARITY

On the Congo, see Adam Hochschild, *King Leopold's Ghost: A Story of Greed, Terror, and Heroism in Colonial Africa* (Boston: Houghton Mifflin, 1998).

On the UN's current thinking on sovereignty, see Kofi Annan's lecture "Two Concepts of Sovereignty."

Marshal Lyautey's words are from Bernard Hours, *L'Idéologie Humanitaire ou le Spectacle de l'Atérité Perdue* (Paris: Éditions L'Harmattan, 1998).

Ignatieff on postwar human rights instruments: See Michael Ignatieff et al., *Human Rights as Politics and Idolatry*, edited by Amy Gutmann (Princeton: Princeton University Press, 2001).

Remarks by Rony Brauman, unless otherwise noted, are from his book *Humanitaire: Le Dilemme* (Paris: Les Éditions Textuel, 1996).

Vaux on the socialist roots of Oxfam: See Tony Vaux, *The Selfish Altruist: Relief Work in Famine and War* (London: Earthscan, 2001).

Secrecy in the ICRC: From Olivier Weber, *French Doctors* (Paris: Robert Laffont, 1995).

On Bernard Kouchner's break with the ICRC, see de Waal, *Famine Crimes.*

On the Biafra war, see Aengus Finucane, "The Changing Roles of Voluntary Organizations," in *A Framework for Survival: Health, Human Rights, and Humanitarian Assistance in Conflicts and Disasters,* edited by Kevin Cahill (New York: Basic Books, 1993).

Chapter Three: A Saving Idea

The interview with Bernard Kouchner on the humanitarian "adventure" appeared in *Paris Match,* 7 January 2002.

The critique of land reform by Anthony Low can be found in: D. A. [Donald Anthony] Low, *The Egalitarian Moment: Asia and Africa, 1950–1980* (Cambridge: Cambridge University Press, 1996).

Rony Brauman's remarks are drawn from his *L'Humanitaire.*

Hans Magnus Enzensberger's remarks on the idealization of the poor world are to be found in his book *Political Crumbs,* translated by Martin Chalmers (New York: Verso, 1990).

Alex de Waal's remarks can be found in his *Famine Crimes.*

On the UN's self-absorption, see Keith Doubt, *Sociology after Bosnia and Kosovo: Recovering Justice* (Lanham, Md.: Rowman & Littlefield, 2000).

Chapter Four: Bosnia

For Boutros Boutros-Ghali's view of the UN's future role, see his speech made on June 17, 1992, "An Agenda for Peace: Preventive Diplomacy, Peacemaking, and Peace-keeping," at www.un.org/Docs/SG/agpeace.html.

The best discussion of UNHCR is Gil Loescher's *UNHCR and World Politics: A Perilous Path* (Oxford and New York: Oxford University Press, 2001).

For the UN's own self-critical report on its conduct in Bosnia, see http://www.Haverford.edu/relg/sells/reports.

For Eric Dachy on the UN in Bosnia, see his "Médecins Sans Frontières and Military Humanitarianism," *Contact: [MSF/Belgium] Internal Newsletter,* Nov.–Dec. 2001 (special issue).

For David Owen's account of the interplay of political calculations and humanitarian imperatives, see David Owen, *Balkan Odyssey* (website) http://www.unhcr.ch/refworld/pub/wpapers/wpno8.htm.

For an inside view of UNHCR's role, see Nicholas Morris, "UNHCR and Kosovo: A Personal View from within UNHCR" (*FM Review* 5), at http://www.fmreview.org/fmr055.htm.

Mark Cutts's account of UNHCR's conduct is contained in his "The Humanitarian Operation in Bosnia, 1992–1995: The Dilemmas of Negotiating Humanitarian Access," *New Issues in Refugee Research,* published by UNHCR's Policy Research Unit. http://www.unhcr.ch/refworld/pub/papers/wpn08.htm.

Michael Barnett's account of the UN can be found in his book *Eyewitness to a Genocide: The United Nations and Rwanda* (Ithaca: Cornell University Press, 2001).

Claude Moncorge's appeal, "Stop the Lies," appeared in *Bosnia Report,* published by the Bosnian Institute, issue 11 (June–August 1995).

CHAPTER FIVE: RWANDA

For a fine discussion of the Western role in the Rwandan genocide, see Linda Melvern: *A People Betrayed* (London and New York: Zed Books, 2000), p. 126, as well as Michael Barnett's *Eyewitness to a Genocide.*

For Samantha Power's account of the U.S. government's internal debate, see "Bystanders to Genocide," *Atlantic,* September 2001.

Tim Schmaltz about working in Rwanda: Interview by author.

For Julia Taft's remarks on humanitarianism, see Hilton Foundation, "Conference Report on Humanitarian Challenges in the New Millennium."

CHAPTER SIX: KOSOVO

Clare Short's remarks are quoted at http://www.jha.ac/articles/a057.htm, p. 2.

Eric Dachy's analysis of Kosovo: See his "La Raison Humanitaire au Kosovo," *Les Temps Modernes,* no. 615–616 (October–November 2001).

For the Human Rights Watch Perspective, see its website and its annual reports. The introduction to its *World Report 2000* is salient here.

Solana letter: http://www.jha.ac/articles/a057.htm.

The off-the-record remark by a UNHCR official, overheard by a journalist, was quoted in *The Guardian,* 10 June 1999.

For the military's perpective on humanitarian-military relations, see R. K. Tomlinson, "Reversing the Downward Spiral: Exploring Cultural Dissonance between the Military and NGOs on Humanitarian Operations" (thesis, Royal Military College of Science).

General Shalikashvili's remarks can be found in David Hinson, *U.S. Military Interaction with Humanitarian Assistance Organizations.*

The remarks on humanitarianism by James Orbinski and John Fawcett were made in conversation with the author.

For an account of the new significance of humanitarianism, see http://www .radicalmiddle.com/x_intervention.htm.

Kofi Annan's speech at Ditchley Park can be found at: http://srch1.un.org:80/ plweb-cgi/fastweb?state_id=1014242147&view=unsearch&numhitsfound= 2&query=annan%20ditchley&&docid=893&docdb=pr1998&dbname= web&sorting=BYRELEVANCE&operator=adj&TemplateName=predoc .tmpl&setCookie=1.

For the debate within MSF-Greece, see http:www.mediologie.com/numero8/ art12.htm.

CHAPTER SEVEN: AFGHANISTAN

Paula Dobriansky's remarks can be found at http://www.usembassy.si/new/ PubAffairs/humasst.htm.

Andrew Natsios's view of aid can be found at http://www.usaid.gov/press/re-leases/2001/fs010515.html.

Eric Schwartz's view on the need for a politicized humanitarianism can be found in Eric P. Schwartz in *World Refugee Survey 2001*, U.S. Committee for Refugees.

Mario Bettati on Afghanistan as a "missed opportunity": http://www.lemonde .fr/article/0,5987,3210-6912-246545-,00.html.

For Sergio Vieira de Mello's remarks on humanitarianism, see *Humanitarian Action in the Twenty-first Century*, UN Inter-Agency Standing Committee.

Hugo Slim's evaluation of the UN's new role can be found in his paper "Not Philanthropy but Right: Rights-Based Humanitarianism and the Proper Politicization of Humanitarian Philosophy," Commonwealth Institute, London, 1 February 2001.

Stephanie Bunker's remarks were made in an interview with the author.

Secretary of State Powell on the U.S. humanitarian role in Afghanistan: http:// www.reliefweb.int/w/rwb.nsf/480fa.

For a critique of that policy, see Fabrice Weissman's "When Good Bombs Happen to Bad People," at http://www.Paris.msf.org/msf/Content/News.nsf/ 43a57aa5a73366e3d4125672.

CHAPTER EIGHT: ENDGAME OR REBIRTH?

Jean-François Vidal's remarks on the limits of humanitarianism as charity were made in conversation with the author.

For an influential critique of sovereignty, see the International Commission on Intervention and State Sovereignty report, "The Responsibility to Protect," International Development Research Center, Ottowa, 2001. idrc.ca.

For Tharoor and Annan remarks on humanitarian intervention, see Shashi Tharoor and Sam Daws, "Humanitarian Intervention," *World Policy Journal,* vol. 18, no. 2, p. 25. Further remarks by Kofi Annan can be found at http://www.un.org/documents/ga/docs/53/plenary/a53-139.htm.

The statements of Sylvie Brunel can be found in *The Geopolitics of Hunger, 2000–2001* (Boulder, Colo.: Lynne Rienner, 2001), the annual volume of Action against Hunger (ACF). Further remarks by Kofi Annan can be found at http://www.un.org/documents/ga/docs/53/plenary/a53-139.htm.

David Bryer's view of humanitarianism as part of a holistic solution to the world's problems: http://www.oxfam.org.uk/atwork/emerg/vienna.htm.

Jean-Christophe Rufin's account of the humanitarian malaise appeared in *Le Debat,* May–August 1999.

Nicholas Stockton's account of the transformation of humanitarianism can be found at http://www.odi.org.uk/speeches/stockton.htm.

Conclusion

The remarks by H. Roy Williams, James Orbinski, and Jean-François Vidal were made in conversation with the author.

For Ignatieff's remarks on the language of human rights as the only available moral vernacular, see Michael Ignatieff, "Are Human Rights Defensible?" *Foreign Affairs,* Nov.–Dec. 2001.

For the conclusions of a 1998 Ford Foundation–funded CARE study of its operations in the Rwandan refugee camps between 1994 and 1996, see James Ron, "Human Rights Case Study: CARE in the Rwandan Refugee Camps, 1994–1996," *CARE,* pp. 42–43.

For Slim on the nature of humanitarian organizations and the future of humanitarian action, see Hugo Slim, "The Humanitarian Endeavor," *Fletcher Forum,* vol. 24, no. 1.

MDM-USA's account of its mission: http://www.medecinsdumonde.org/3gcauses/gcauses_conflits.html.

Alberto Navarro's remark that "Mankind is slowly, but in a very determined way, going back to barbarism," can be found in Hilton Foundation, "Humanitarian Crises . . . Preventive Measures through Human Rights," Sept. 28, 1999.

Most of the major NGOs, though originating in one country, now have branches in several nations. Though in principle the various branches of an NGO share a common mandate, in practice the policies and approaches of different national branches can be quite different. I have added information and commentary on those organizations not discussed in the text.

ACF: Action Against Hunger (Action Contre la Faim). An international, non-governmental, non-religious organization created in Paris in 1979 by a group of French writers and intellectuals including Bernard-Henri Levy, Marek Halter, and Françoise Giroud. Its specific expertise is in famine relief and in the problems of global hunger. Today the ACF has headquarters in Paris, New York, London, and Madrid.
www.aah-usa.org
www.aahuk.org

ActionAid: A charity and development organization consisting of five independent European funding partners, located in Ireland, Spain, France, Italy, and Great Britain. These support ActionAid organizations in more than thirty countries in Africa, Asia, and Latin America.
www.actionaid.org

AFSC: American Friends Service Committee. The AFSC is a Quaker organization founded in 1917 to provide conscientious objectors with an opportunity to aid civilian victims during World War I. Today, increasingly left-leaning, the AFSC has programs the organization defines as being focused on issues related to what it calls "economic justice, peace-building and demilitarization, social justice, and youth, in the United States, and in Africa, Asia, Latin America, and the Middle East."
www.afsc.org

CARE: Cooperative for Assistance and Relief Everywhere. Originally known as the Cooperative for American Remittances in Europe, CARE is now one of

the world's largest private international relief and development organizations. CARE International is a confederation of 11 CARE organizations that sometimes work together, sometimes separately in both development and emergency relief projects. The member countries include Australia, Austria, Canada, Denmark, France, Germany, Japan, the Netherlands, Norway, the United Kingdom, and the United States.
www.care.org

Concern Worldwide: An Irish organization founded in 1968 to bring aid to Biafra during the Nigerian Civil War. Concern Worldwide is an international voluntary agency that describes its mandate as being devoted to relief assistance and development in the poor world.
www.concern.ie

CRS: Catholic Relief Services. Founded in 1943 by the Catholic Bishops of the United States to assist the poor in other countries. It is the official U.S. Catholic relief organization.
www.catholicrelief.org

ECHO: European Commission Humanitarian Aid Office. Established by the European Union in 1992 to provide emergency assistance and relief to the victims of natural disasters or armed conflict outside the European Union. It is now the largest single donor in the world.
europa.eu.int/comm/echo/en/index_en.html

ICRC: The International Committee of the Red Cross. Established in 1863, the ICRC remains the single most important humanitarian organization. Under international law, it is the custodian of the Geneva Conventions.
www.icrc.org

IFRC: International Federation of Red Cross and Red Crescent Societies. "Founded in 1919, the International Federation comprises 178 member Red Cross and Red Crescent societies, a Secretariat in Geneva and more than 60 delegations strategically located to support activities around the world. The Red Crescent is used in place of the Red Cross in many Islamic countries . . . The Federation, together with National Societies and the International Committee of the Red Cross, make up the International Red Cross and Red Crescent Movement."
www.ifrc.org

IRC: International Rescue Committee. Founded at the request of Albert Einstein to assist opponents of Hitler, and originally celebrated for helping get Jews out of occupied France during World War II, the IRC has become one of the largest American NGOs. It is different from other relief groups in that it is also a resettlement organization for refugees coming to the United States.
www.theIRC.org

MSF: Médecins Sans Frontières. MSF is the largest independent medical relief agency in the world. Founded in 1971 by a group of French doctors, and, interestingly, given the agency's skilled use of the media, by journalists, MSF sought to match the technical proficiency in emergency medical relief operations of the International Committee of the Red Cross while rejecting the ICRC's insistence on discretion even in the face of horror. MSF's slogan was *Soignez et témoignez*, "Care for and testify." More recently, MSF has tried to act and bring attention to the problem of access to drugs for populations with diseases like AIDS and tuberculosis as well as its more traditional focus on emergency operations.
www.msf.org

Oxfam: The acronym stands for Oxford Committee for Famine Relief. The group was founded in 1942 to get relief to civilians in Nazi-occupied Greece who were dying of starvation. After World War II, Oxfam became increasingly concerned with development in the poor world, and is today an organization that insists that it is equally committed to development, emergency relief, and advocacy. These agendas have led Oxfam to involve itself in campaigns for debt relief, reform of the terms of international trade, and human rights activism.
www.oxfam.org.uk

SCF: Save the Children Fund. SCF was founded in Britain in the immediate aftermath of World War I to try to help children in Austria and Germany who were at risk of dying of starvation or exposure. SCF has increasingly combined its work as an emergency relief organization with social activism. Now an international organization, SCF has been one of the most influential and effective lobbyists, urging the rich nations to provide more overseas development aid to the poor world. It has also taken an increasingly rights-based approach to its work, insisting on the legal rights of children as put forward in the United Nations Declaration on the Rights of the Child—including the right to be free of abject poverty—as providing the basis for the group's work.
www. savethechildren.org

UNDP: United Nations Development Programme. The UNDP is the UN's principal provider of development advice, advocacy, and grant support.
www.undp.org

UNHCR: Office of the United Nations High Commissioner for Refugees.
www.unhcr.ch

UNICEF: United Nations Children's Fund. Created by the United Nations General Assembly in 1946 to help children after World War II in Europe, UNICEF was first known as the United Nations International Children's Emergency Fund. In 1953, UNICEF became a permanent part of the United Nations system. Its missions are "to help children living in poverty in developing coun-

tries" and "to protect children in the midst of war and natural disaster." This second role involves it in humanitarian crises.
www.unicef.org

UNPROFOR: United Nations Protection Force: "Initially established in Croatia [ostensibly] to ensure demilitarization of designated areas. The mandate was later extended to Bosnia and Herzegovina to support [again ostensibly; there were other political motivations at play] the delivery of humanitarian relief, monitor 'no fly zones' and 'safe areas.' The mandate was later extended to the former Yugoslav Republic of Macedonia for preventive monitoring in border areas."
www.un.org/Depts/dpko/dpko/co_mission/unprofor.htm

USAID: U.S. Agency for International Development. The agency of the U.S. government principally responsible for funding both development aid and emergency relief. After ECHO, it is the second largest funder in the world.
www.usaid.gov

WFP: World Food Programme. Set up in 1963, WFP is the United Nations agency originally meant to lead the fight against global hunger. In 2000, WFP fed 83 million people in 83 countries, including most of the world's refugees and internally displaced people. But both in budgetary and operational terms, the agency is increasingly an emergency relief organization.
www.wfp.org

WHO: World Health Organization. A UN body whose mandate includes not just medical treatment, but a social and developmental mission based on a conception of health that, "as defined in the WHO Constitution, is a state of complete physical, mental and social well-being and not merely the absence of disease or infirmity."
www.who.int/inf

World Vision International: Begun in the United States in 1950 to help children orphaned in the Korean War, World Vision has become the largest Christian relief and development agency. The organization remains controversial among some secular humanitarian NGOs, who claim that World Vision is more like a classic Christian missionary group than a modern relief organization in that it mixes an evangelical and a humanitarian agenda. World Vision rejects these claims.
www.wvi.org

ACF: Action Against Hunger (Action Contre la Faim)

AFSC: American Friends Service Committee

CARE: Cooperative for Assistance and Relief Everywhere

CRS: Catholic Relief Services

ECHO: European Commission Humanitarian Aid Office

EU: European Union

ICRC: International Committee of the Red Cross

IFRC: International Federation of Red Cross and Red Crescent Societies

IRC: International Rescue Committee

NATO: North Atlantic Treaty Organization

MDM: Médecins du Monde

MSF: Médecins Sans Frontières

SCF: Save the Children Fund

UNAMIR: United Nations Assistance Mission for Rwanda

UNDP: United Nations Development Programme

UNDPKO: United Nations Department of Peacekeeping Operations

UNHCR: Office of the United Nations High Commissioner for Refugees

UNICEF: United Nations Children's Fund

UNPROFOR: United Nations Protection Force for Bosnia-Herzegovina

USAID: United States Agency for International Development

WFP: World Food Programme

WHO: World Health Organization

In writing this book, which was far too long in gestation, I incurred a raft of private debts—human, intellectual, and moral. So there are indeed a number of people inexpressibly dear to me whom I want to thank, and for whom I also give thanks. But I am averse to doing so in print and do not propose to. That said, I have a number of professional debts that I would very much like to acknowledge, while registering the conventional but necessary disclaimer that no one thanked in the paragraphs that follow is responsible in any way for anything I have written, or should be understood as endorsing it.

First debts first. This book would simply not have been possible without the help, both practical and intellectual, of a number of people at the International Rescue Committee, whose generosity, hospitality, good company, and wise counsel I have relied upon time and time again over the past ten years. I have been particularly harsh about U.S. NGOs, and often disagreed vehemently with the course charted by the IRC in particular, above all during the unfortunate presidency of Reynold Levy. But none of this detracts from the enormous admiration I feel for the vast majority of past and serving IRC officials I have known.

I realize that praise from me is not necessarily the best possible career booster for them, but I would above all like to thank Barbara

Smith, H. Roy Williams, Mark Bartolini, John Keys, Richard Jacquot, and the IRC's former president, Robert De Vecchi. They knew my views and yet not only were willing to talk to me, but accepted me as a consultant and "friend of the house" at the same time that I was increasingly arguing for a very different kind of humanitarianism from the one they felt bound to uphold.

I would also like to thank John Fawcett, formerly of the IRC and of the International Crisis Group, the smartest North American aid worker I have ever known. He will not agree with much of what is in this book, and will have good, perhaps even unanswerable reasons for his disagreements. But I have learned more about aid from him than from anyone else in the aid world. And I need to record my gratitude for the shards of time I got to spend with the late Fred Cuny, with whom John worked in Sarajevo.

As anyone reading this book will have realized, my own biases are closer to those of MSF than to any other understanding or practice of humanitarian action. Unsurprisingly, then, my deepest intellectual debt is to Rony Brauman, who, for me, remains the *maître-penseur* on all questions related to aid work. This book would have been impossible without his work and moral example.

At MSF, I am also intensely grateful for the chance to debate and learn from Fiona Terry, Eric Dachy, Jean-Herve Bradol, and Nicholas de Torrente. I also want to thank Jean-François Vidal of Action Contre la Faim (ACF) for conversations that time and time again over the past few years have challenged me and pushed me to rexamine my own views.

There is an American bumper sticker that reads, "Don't believe everything you think." At their best, disagreements with serious people push one in that salutary direction. This book, like its predecessor, *Slaughterhouse*, has been, among other things, a ringing indictment of the United Nations. If anything, my views are even more fervent on this matter than they were at the height of the siege of Sara-jevo. But, however paradoxical it may seem, that is why I am particu-larly grateful for what is now almost a decade of conversation with Shashi Tharoor, UN Under Secretary-General for Communications and Public Information. While never behaving toward me as anything less than a dear and loyal friend (a stance that must have been difficult at times, given my fierce disapproval of and unrelenting attacks upon Kofi Annan, who is not only his boss but someone he admires with all his heart), he remained a resolute and eloquent defender of a view di-ametrically opposed to my own. As he has consistently defended that view with such great scrupulousness, intelligence, and moral serious-ness, I have learned much, even if I have not been persuaded.

In contrast, having perhaps excessively admired the work of the agency in the Balkans in the early 1990s, I have grown increasingly critical of UNHCR over the years. Nonetheless, a number of serving and former officials of the agency are not only friends but people I continue to admire beyond words and measure for both the work they have done and the moral commitments to which they have ded-icated their lives. I think particularly of Fabrizio Hochschild. For him, my deepest respect is combined with the love that one might properly feel for a brother. But I would also like to mention and thank in particular Jose María Mendiluce, Soren Jessen-Petersen, Karen Abu Zayd, and Krystof Janowski.

Finally, I would like to acknowledge that whatever intelligence and moral scruple I have been able to bring to humanitarian issues is to a greater extent than any of them probably realize the result of the conversations I have had over the years with Aryeh Neier, Marie Spaak, John Ryle, Barnett Rubin, David Malone, Ken Anderson, Alex de Waal, Ed Vulliamy, Tom Keenan, and Anthony Richter.

—New York City, March 2002

concentration camps in, 2, 148–49
Dayton Agreement and (1995), 130,
    199–200, 329
European policy of containment in,
    126–27, 131, 134, 136, 138–44, 271
genocide in, 2, 7, 124, 130, 131–32,
    141–49, 174, 329
ICRC in, 132–33, 137, 148–49
internally displaced people in, 143–44
international law in, 141, 143–44, 149–51
IRC in, 146–47
Kosovo crisis compared with, 129, 144,
    154, 173, 197, 200, 213, 225
media coverage of, 2–3, 40–41, 127–28,
    129, 130, 137–38
"mission creep" in, 140–41
NATO military intervention in, 38, 39, 40,
    136, 251
NGOs in, 113, 129–30, 133, 134, 137, 138,
    139–40, 147, 150, 153
peace negotiations in, 130, 138–39,
    199–200, 329
as post–Cold War conflict, 123, 126, 128, 130
refugee crisis in, 126, 127, 130, 140–44, 153
Rwandan genocide compared with, 129,
    152, 156, 157, 165, 169, 173, 176, 177,
    207, 211, 212, 244
Serb attacks in, 7, 141–46
UNHCR in, 127–28, 132–46
UN peacekeeping mission in, 18–19, 39,
    116, 117, 127, 130, 131–32, 134, 135, 152,
    153, 157, 158, 177, 327
U.S. in, 37, 39, 125, 126, 130–31
Bouchet-Saulnier, Françoise, 150–51, 153,
    160, 244, 248, 260, 272, 290
Boudouris, Odysseus, 226–27
Boutros-Ghali, Boutros:
    Balkans policy of, 40
    Bosnian policy of, 131, 136–37
    media criticized by, 40–41
    peace agenda of, 123, 131
    Rwandan genocide and, 159, 163
    as UN secretary-general, 123, 124–25, 131,
        135, 159, 252
    see also "An Agenda for Peace"
Boyce, Michael, 72
Bradol, Jean-Herve, 163, 178
Brahimi, Lakdar, 19

Brauman, Rony:
    humanitarianism as viewed by, 25–26, 75,
        77, 86, 93, 110–11, 166, 175, 256, 258,
        272, 279
    as MSF president, 25, 98, 105–6, 107, 167–
        168, 170, 177–78, 186–87, 308, 309, 331
Brecht, Bertolt, xiii
Briquemont, Francis, 158
Brown, Mark Malloch, 261
Brunel, Sylvie, 278–79, 294
Bryer, David, 291
Bunche, Ralph, 217
Bunker, Stephanie, 255
Bush, George H. W.:
    Bosnian policy of, 125
    "New World Order" of, 123
    Somalian intervention approved by, 35
Bush, George W.:
    Afghanistan policy of, 9, 99, 235–36,
        240–41
    humanitarianism as viewed by, 276
    and war on terrorism, 49, 232–33
Byron, George Gordon, Lord, 65

Cambodia:
    famine in, 92–93
    genocide in, 41, 72, 92–93, 168
    humanitarian aid for, 112, 168, 309
    Khmer Rouge regime of, 92–93, 107, 168,
        174
    media coverage of, 38
Campbell, Susan, 287–88
Canadian International Development
    Agency (CIDA), 221–22
CARE (Cooperative for American Remit-
    tances in Europe/Cooperative for
    Assistance and Relief Everywhere), 79,
    80, 212, 221–22, 223, 227, 229, 249–
    250, 295, 315, 343–44
Castro, Fidel, 79, 274
Catholic Relief Services (CRS), 80, 298, 315, 344
Central Intelligence Agency (CIA), 79, 125
Chechnya, 2, 139, 215, 286
Cherne, Leo, 114
children:
    famine relief for, 80–81
    mortality rates of, 13–14
    relief organizations for, 26, 77–78, 257

international treaties rejected by, 68
in Kosovo crisis, 199, 200, 203, 205,
    206–8, 226, 240–41
NGOs in, 79, 81, 112–15, 176, 190–91,
    206–8, 209, 226, 228
racial discrimination in, 14, 326
Rwandan genocide and, 160–64, 167, 175,
    177, 179, 182–83, 184, 187, 190–93
Somalian intervention of, 35–37, 38, 54,
    65, 167, 210, 258, 279
Soviet relations with, 79, 103, 105, 111,
    124
see also September 11th attacks
United States Agency for International
    Development (USAID), 103, 113, 114–15,
    222, 237, 238–39, 263, 264, 346
Universal Declaration of Human Rights, 18,
    71, 149, 281, 301–2, 311, 312–13, 325
Urquhart, Brian, 9, 217
Uvin, Peter, 174
Uwilingiyimana, Agathe, 164

Vance, Cyrus, 134
Vaux, Tony, 81, 84, 104, 174–75
victims:
    access to, 244, 280, 310–11, 326–27, 333
    children as, 25–26, 55, 78, 128, 144
    "deserving" vs. "undeserving," 316–18
    empathy for, 6, 7–8, 47–48, 51–57, 268–69
    infantilizing of, 25–26
    legal protections for, 13–14
    oppressors as, 14, 25, 52–56, 180–81,
        316–18
    suffering of, 47–48, 51–57, 87, 93, 98,
        115–16, 154, 172, 178–79, 268–69,
        316–17
Vidal, Jean-François, 55, 267–68, 310
Vietnamese boat people, 107, 309–10
Vietnam War, 97, 99, 115, 239, 258
Vulliamy, Ed, 2, 148, 149

Wallace, Peter, 221
warfare:
    biological and chemical, 70, 77
    crime vs., 75, 218

global rate of, 46, 123–24, 128–29
humanitarian, see military intervention,
    humanitarian
infrastructure destroyed by, 11–12
just, 74–75, 198–201, 244, 257, 261, 328
laws of, 67–70, 149–50, 210, 284
as norm of human condition, 1–3, 5,
    71–72
and "operations other than war," 206–7,
    242
as "peace enforcement," 201, 217–18
total, 42, 49, 70–71
Weissman, Fabrice, 264
Westphalia, Peace of (1648), 71, 253
WFP, see World Food Programme
What I Believe (Kouchner), 241
WHO (World Health Organization), 21, 111,
    183, 346
Williams, H. Roy, 21–22, 302, 303
Wilson, Woodrow, 113, 123–24, 235
Winter, Roger, 238
women's rights, 244, 246, 247–48, 259–60,
    322, 324
World Bank, 9, 88
World Federalist Movement, 283
World Food Programme (WFP), 67, 85,
    118, 140, 169, 215, 239, 246, 255, 262,
    263–64, 279, 346
World Health Organization (WHO), 21, 111,
    183, 346
World Report 2000 (Human Rights Watch),
    201–2
World Report 2001 (Human Rights Watch),
    283
World Trade Center attacks, see September
    11th attacks
World Trade Organization (WTO), 9
World Vision International, 80, 237, 346
World War I, 49, 70, 77, 78, 79, 124, 330
World War II, 20, 46, 49, 50, 51–52, 71, 76–
    81, 99, 328

Yugoslavia, 124, 125–26, 197–98

Zinni, Anthony, 206

David Rieff is the author of five books, including the acclaimed *Slaughterhouse: Bosnia and the Failure of the West*. He continues to cover wars and humanitarian emergencies in many parts of the world. He lives in New York City.